PETER DONDERS

BLESSED PETER DONDERS

His Writings and Spirituality

Volume Seven (English Series)
Readings in Redemptorist Spirituality

TRANSLATED AND EDITED
BY J. ROBERT FENILI, C.SS.R.

Liguori
LIGUORI, MISSOURI

Imprimi Potest: Thomas D. Picton, C.Ss.R.
Provincial, Denver Province • The Redemptorists

Published by Liguori Publications • Liguori, Missouri • www.liguori.org

English translation and additional English text copyright 2007 by General Government of the Congregation of the Most Holy Redeemer

Originally published as *Espiritualidad Redentorista: La vida Espiritual del Beato Pedro Donders, Vol. 9*, by the Committee on Redemptorist Spirituality, Rome, 1996.

All rights reserved. No part of this publication may be reproduced, stored in a retrieval system, or transmitted in any form or by any means—electronic, mechanical, photocopy, recording, or any other—except for brief quotations in printed reviews, without the prior permission of the publisher.

Library of Congress Cataloging-in-Publication Data

Blessed Peter Donders : his writings and spirituality / translated and edited by J. Robert Fenili.
   p. cm.
   Includes bibliographical references.
   ISBN 978-0-7648-1478-5 (pbk.)
   Includes bibliographical references.
   1. Donders, Petrus, 1809–1887. 2. Catholic Church—Surinam—Clergy—Biography. 3. Donders, Petrus, 1809–1887—Correspondence. 4. Catholic Church—Surinam—Clergy—Correspondence. I. Fenili, J. Robert. II. Donders, Petrus, 1809–1887. Selections. English.
   BX4705.D585B54   2007
   266'.2092—dc22
                                              2006103435

Scripture citations are taken from the *New Revised Standard Version of the Bible*, copyright 1989 by the Division of Christian Education of the National Council of Churches of Christ in the USA. All rights reserved. Used with permission.

Liguori Publications, a nonprofit corporation, is an apostolate of the Redemptorists. To learn more about the Redemptorists, visit *Redemptorists.com*.

Printed in the United States of America
11 10 09 08 07 07   5 4 3 2 1
First English edition 2007

Contents

Introduction *ix*

Chronology of Donders' Life *xi*

Part I
Blessed Peter Donders: A Story of His Life 1
- I. Small Beginnings 3
- II. The Poor Young Weaver 10
- III. The Priest Who Could Not Be 15
- IV. Servant or Student? 21
- V. The Unwanted Religious 25
- VI. A Call from Over the Sea 28
- VII. Will He Ever Get There? 33
- VIII. Surinam, at Last 39
- IX. Two Hurricanes in Paramaribo 43
- X. Plantations of the Spirit 49
- XI. At Home in Batavia 53
- XII. The Late Vocation 59
- XIII. Back in Batavia 65
- XIV. Back to the Jungles 73
- XV. The Final Frontier: The Maroons 78
- XVI. The Way of the Cross to Paramaribo 81
- XVII. All Things Work Together 87
- XVIII. Rest in Peace? 93

Part II
Blessed Peter Donders: His Letters and Writings 99

    Chapter One: The Writings of Blessed Peter Donders *101*
        An Introduction by J. Robert Fenili, C.Ss.R.
    Chapter Two: Holland *103*
    Chapter Three: Paramaribo *106*
    Chapter Four: Batavia *142*
    Chapter Five: Paramaribo Again *195*
    Chapter Six: Coronie *199*
    Chapter Seven: Batavia Again *211*
    Chapter Eight: Autobiographical and Other Writings *217*

Part III
Blessed Peter Donders: His Spirituality 233

    Chapter One: The Missionary Spirit of Peter Donders *235*
        Fabriciano Ferrero, C.Ss.R.
    Chapter Two: The Spirituality of Father Peter Donders *260*
        Ignaz Dekkers, C.Ss.R.

Notes 277

Introduction

While there have been many great spiritual leaders of the Catholic Faith throughout all of history, only a relative few have been noted by the Church as "Saint" or "Blessed." These are the men and women who have witnessed to their faith in outstanding ways, some by their courageous deaths, others by miraculous interventions in peoples' lives, and some by being sure examples and models of what it means to be a disciple of Christ. Blessed Peter Donders is among these. He witnesses to the type of simple holiness that gives meaning to the saying of Saint Paul, "God chose what is foolish in the world to shame the wise; God chose what is weak in the world to shame the strong" (1 Corinthians 1:27).

This book is based on *La Vida espiritual del Beato Pedro Donders*, which constitutes Volume 9 of the series, *Espirtualidad Redentorista*. This series parallels the English series, *Readings in Redemptorist Spirituality*. Both of these series are publications of the Center for Redemptorist Spirituality, an organ of the Congregation of the Most Holy Redeemer (The Redemptorists). These series are meant to provide insight into the spirituality of the Congregation as well as that of its Founder, Saint Alphonsus Liguori, and its other great spiritual leaders.

Part 1 of this volume is a brief biography of its subject, Blessed Peter Donders. It has been written precisely for this volume and is based mainly on the classic biography written by John Baptist Kronenburg, C.Ss.R., in 1924 and translated into English by John Carr, C.Ss.R. (London: Sands and Co., 1930). It is no longer in print. References to this older work are only given when text is taken directly from it.

Part 2 consists of the first English translation of all Blessed

Donders' letters and other autobiographical writings. Donders wrote no books, essays, or spiritual works. Only fifty-three of his letters have come down to us, along with two short autobiographical sketches and two other brief writings. These are the privileged road we have into his life and spirit.

Part 3 contains two articles on Blessed Donders' spirituality written on the occasion of his beatification in 1982 by two Redemptorists and published in a collection of writings prepared for the event by the Historical Institute of the Congregation. Father Fabriciano Ferrero, a member of the Madrid Province, is a historian who has specialized in Redemptorist history. Father Ignaz Dekkers, a member of the Amsterdam Province, has served extensively in the General Government of the religious order. This is again the first English translation of these two works.

Since most people are not familiar with the small country of Surinam, we have included two maps: the first (page xii) shows Surinam's location in the north of South America; the second (page 98) is an enlargement of the area where the major locations of his ministry are indicated (see page 98).

The reader will find it difficult not to be impressed and inspired by the life of this great man and will certainly find in him a beguiling model and intercessor for anyone who seeks to trust in God.

J. ROBERT FENILI, C.SS.R.
DECEMBER 25, 2004
THE FEAST OF THE REDEEMER'S BIRTH

Chronology of Donders' Life

1809	October 27	Birth and baptism in Tilburg, Holland
1816	February 21	Death of his mother
1817	May 19	Father remarries
1821	April 8	First Communion
1823	November 14	Confirmation
1831		Enters minor seminary, first as a servant
1835		Jesuits, Redemptorists, Franciscans refuse him
1838		Offers to go to Surinam
1841	June 5	Ordained priest
1842	September 16	Arrives in Paramaribo, Surinam
1842	October 9	Offers first Mass at leprosarium in Batavia
1842 to 1856		Ministers in Paramaribo
1843		Begins pastoral journeys to plantations
1856	August	Begins full-time ministry in Batavia
1865	August 31	Surinam vicariate put under charge of
1866	February 20	First Redemptorists arrive in Surinam
1866	November 1	Begins Redemptorist novitiate in Paramaribo
1867	June 24	Professes vows as Redemptorist
1867	August 31	Returns to Batavia
1868		Begins ministry among Amerindians
1883	February 7	Returns to Paramaribo
1883	November 3	Moves to Coronie
1885	November 9	Returns to Batavia
1886	December 31	Becomes severely ill
1887	January 14	Dies a quiet and holy death in Batavia
1982	May 23	Pope John Paul II beatifies him and adds annual memorial in Church calendar on January 14

Part I

Blessed Peter Donders: A Story of His Life

I

SMALL BEGINNINGS

"It was a small house, just two rooms," recalled the elderly woman (she would soon be eighty-five). "Just a living room and a work room, with a little animal-stall attached at the rear....The living room was divided by a partition behind which were the two beds." There was also a little property along side the house to serve as a small garden.

Mary Mathijsen had come to live near the Donders' house in 1819 when she was about thirteen. Even though she had not seen Peter Donders for over half a century, she could still recall him and his family from those early years. She was, after all, his stepmother's niece.

The Donders were not the most fortunate family in Tilburg, a town in North Brabant (a misleading name for a district in the south of Holland). It was the northern part of the old duchy of Brabant, which after wars and treaties, had been split between Belgium on the south and Holland, making North Brabant southern Holland!

Arnold Donders was always struggling to make ends meet. The area was a rather barren place. The forests of the past had long ago been cut down for farming, which in turn eroded the land and turned much of it into heaths. It was not the healthiest place to live. Much of the flat land was given over to raising sheep, so it became a center for gathering wool and producing cloth.

Arnold was a weaver, as were most of the poor people of the area. That was the local cottage industry. Cloth merchants employed men and women to work for subsistence wages on their home looms. Arnold, and later his sons as well, daily labored over their loom. When wool was plentiful, they worked six days a week, practically around the clock, to earn their wages.

Arnold's greatest suffering, however, was not his poverty but one of its consequences, the frequency with which death visited his home. He had ventured away from his hometown of Tilburg to Loon op Zand and on September 13, 1789, when he was just about thirty-four (he was born October 9, 1755), he wed Jane Van Wanroy. Less than two years later, sickness took her from him on May 16, 1791, before they had any children. Within a few years, he married Jane Mary Van der Waarden. But his happiness was short lived as the two children she bore him did not survive their infancy, only to be followed in death by Jane Mary as well.

Arnold moved back to Tilburg around 1798, and married a neighbor, Petronella van den Brekel. She bore him a son on October 27, 1809. The same day, he was baptized Peter in her honor in a little barn of a church (literally, for the Catholics were using a former barn for their services) in the nearby village of De Goirke. Two years later she gave birth to another son, Martin. Both children were frail and sickly; Martin was also mildly handicapped.

Once again, Arnold had to face the suffering of loss, this time, of Petronilla who died on February 21, 1816. Peter was then not yet seven and his brother five.

Again a widower, but now with two young sons, a little over a year later on May 19, 1817, Arnold married Jane Mary Van de Pas. She proved to be a loving mother to her stepsons. Both parents were regarded highly by those who knew them. In the information gathered for the Church process to determine whether Peter Donders should be beatified (that is, approved as a model of heroic sanctity deserving honor as one of Christ's outstanding disciples), the references to his parents by people who remembered them were "honest folk," "plain and humble," "exceptionally virtuous."

It is very difficult to get a well-rounded picture of the early years of someone the Church declares "Blessed" or "Saint." This is because, in most cases, when the information is being gathered, a great many years have passed and everyone is relying on very old memories. Another reason is that the types of questions asked of "witnesses" are skewed toward the stereotype evidences of "sanctity." Did he or she pray a lot, speak piously, show exceptional gifts of virtue, spend a lot of time in church, and so on? Very little is asked about the everyday characteristics of the young person's life; instead, he or she gets treated as "a little saint."

In Peter Donders' case, we have nothing written by him before 1842 when he was thirty-three years old. We do have two brief "*curricula vitae*," short accounts of his "spiritual or vocational development." Again, a very limited source of information for the early years. We fortunately have another source in a diary kept by the teacher in the village school of De Heinant, Master Drabbe. Among his many remarks about his students, which did not limit themselves to when they were in school, we sometimes find little details of Peter's life. From Master Drabbe's notes, we can glean the picture of a close, loving family. One of these vignettes is particularly interesting:

> [Peter] was a great help to his father in the weaving. Many a time he would set to work on his own, and when he had prepared the warp, he would run his bare fingers up and down—whether it was warm or freezing—until he had it properly dried. Whenever there was a great deal of work to do (from the beginning of August to October), the weaving went on every day until ten o'clock at night. From then until the beginning of Lent, it would go until eleven o'clock and then it would go back to ten o'clock until Holy Thursday. It was not unusual when there was much work to do, for the labor to go on until midnight every day, including Saturday; it would then start up again on Sunday night at the same time. At these times, however, Peter would send his father and little Martin off to bed and worked on alone as hard as he could. To help his parents make ends meet, he would take on other odd jobs as well. "The poor little drudge," I was told by an

old man who knew him, "how hard he had to slave away for his daily bread! I would even see him cutting grass along the roadside and gathering up wood."[1]

Yet it is not as if this life of labor was imposed by inconsiderate or greedy parents. A grandson of Master Drabbe recalled this story from his grandfather:

> It was quite clear that what his father dreaded above all else for his dear boy was catching a cold. In rainy weather, he used to come to the school to bring Peter home. He would take him into a forge across the street from the school, have him stand on something as he held a bag open for him and have him step into it. Then he would wrap him up and carry him home on his shoulder.[2]

Peter's school days were not many. Besides the fact that he was frequently absent because of sickness or work, he only attended school from around the time he was seven until he was twelve. At this point, he had to give up schooling because he was needed to help with the weaving. We do not know when he made his first Communion, but it must have been before he left school. We have records to show he received confirmation on November 14, 1823 when he was fourteen.

Despite his application and good conduct, he did not seem to do well at study. Generally, Peter is considered to have been a rather slow student, not only during his five years of early schooling, but later as he did studies at the preparatory seminary. On the other hand, there are reasons to question whether his intellectual capacity was as limited as some say. First, there are remarks like that made by his brother, Martin, "Pete lived very piously...and spent his time working, reading, or praying. He read every good book he could lay his hands on from cover to cover."[3] Hardly the kind of remark we would expect about a slow learner!

There is also the well-attested fact that he excelled in learning anything that had to do with religion, faith, or doctrine. He was so capable in these fields that the parish priest asked him to catechize the young children of the parish. He remained at this task until he left for the seminary and seems to have done well, at least according to some of his charges who spoke of him in their old age. For example, one of his pupils, Peter Spijkers, recounted, "He began by giving out the answers in the catechism, which he afterwards made us repeat. He then explained them in his own way and urged us to live up to the lessons we had learned. The children I knew best—as well as I—went to his classes eagerly." Another woman remarks how "the children used to listen with attention and in perfect silence to their young teacher. To gain this hearing, he would sometime produce a few pieces of candy from his pocket to hand out."[4]

An avid reader who could learn the intricacies of religion well enough to teach youngsters only a few years younger than he hardly seems to merit being tagged stupid. He had great difficulties later in classical studies, but much of this can be attributed to his poor early schooling. Who can ask a person with only a fifth-grade formal education to do well in Latin and Greek among well-to-do students with years of schooling? Who can expect a child of frail health who spent many hours at home working to help his family not to have difficulties learning lessons? In any case, in the fields that mattered most to him, Peter showed a good bit of intellectual competence.

Those who remembered him as their catechist held him in high regard. Their accounts are full of little stories about how well Peter could keep his charges in line without growing angry at their restlessness. ("All right, now! One, two, three, Quiet!" seems to have been a constant refrain of his.) They could remember how he visited their houses and gave them a little holy picture if they could recall their lessons. Sometimes, at the end of the lesson, young Peter would get up on his mother's washtub, give his companions a little homily, and lead them into the church for a closing prayer.

This frailty, intellectual effort, and piety did not leave Peter untouched by the criticisms of others. Any quiet youngster, especially if he or she exhibits a reluctance to get into mischief or a penchant for prayer, knows how easy it is to become the object of teasing or downright maliciousness of other youngsters with a more rambunctious disposition. Peter's usual response was to walk away. "Whenever unpleasant things were said to him, he just went outside for a while; and when he came in again, he looked as if nothing amiss had happened," a former schoolmate reported.[5]

Even his brother Martin found him a little hard to take at times. He resented the attention others paid his brother because of his dedication and piety. All these kids flocking around Pete struck him as silly and he told his brother so. Later in life, especially after his brother had gone to Surinam, he appreciated him more and came to admit that Pete "will certainly have a very high place in heaven."

Martin's remarks also remind us about an interesting fact, namely, that hardly anyone who knew him ever called him Peter ("Petrus" in Dutch). He seems always, except on the most formal occasions, to be known as "Peerke," "Little Peter," or as we might say today, "Pete." And when he was ordained, he became "Father Pete." There was always this air of simplicity about him that needed no "proper" name. And so too, from now on, we shall call him "Pete."

Pete showed great love for his family. An old family friend, James Paulussen, reported in his old age of the memories he had of Pete. "How wonderfully good he was to his parents. He would have given them everything, done anything for them....Anything he got, he handed over to them at once."

Pete's dedication to teaching others of God, Jesus, Mary, and all the elements of Catholic faith, eventually led to his being accepted as the volunteer catechist and "youth minister" in his home parish when he became a teenager. The parish priest was happy to have him spend his free time working with the youngsters. One of them later recalls: "He did not work for pay but out of sheer devotion. He taught catechism two or three times a day at meal times. His parents never minded because they knew he would not give a moment to it when he was supposed to be working." Years later, an elderly widow, Mrs. Van de Wouwer, tells us, "One day—he was probably sixteen at the time—he was commissioned by the parish priest to give an instruction to the children in the church itself and both the parish priest and the curate, who had listened from the sanctuary, agreed they had never heard the catechism better taught."

It is strange that, years later, when Father Pete wrote his two brief autobiographical reports, he does not mention a word about his work as a catechist that occupied so much of his early years. It can hardly be believed that he had completely forgotten it. Was it modesty on his part that left this great involvement in evangelization, so often noticed by others, unmentioned? Or was it more likely that there was some other matter in these early years, something that so occupied his awareness that even this role of teacher seemed not to matter? We will take that question up in a moment. But first a few words on the surroundings of Pete's early life to give us a better perspective on this young man.

II

THE POOR YOUNG WEAVER

The community into which Pete was born had a centuries-old history of habitation. What had started as a grouping of settlements for farmers gradually grew together into the town of Tilburg. As time went on, the poor land began to be more favorable for sheepherding than agriculture. The poor dirt farmers began to see that they could earn more from their wool if they stopped selling it directly to others, but began to weave it themselves. Rooms were added to the one-room dwellings and these extra workshops held the family loom(s). By the beginning of the eighteenth century there were over three hundred home looms in operation and by the late 1700s these had spawned a sizable textile industry, the first in the Netherlands. The Premonstratention (Norbertine) Abbey in Tilburg seems to have been at the center of much of the early development.

Since this industry was not based in factories or concentrated work centers, it came to need some organization. Entrepreneurs began to make arrangements with individual families, provided them with wool, and in turn paid them for the cloth produced from it. These producers, most of whom did not live in Tilburg, had local agents who organized the operation. This availability of cheap labor and nearby flocks of sheep allowed for the production of rough, common wool cloth for sale at a much lower cost than what was available from other areas. Tilburg also became a center for the production of finer cloths for export and quality clothing, but the production of basic woolen cloth was a mainstay during Donders' lifetime.

This was the commercial context of Pete's early life. It was soon to change with the introduction of machine-made cloth in factories and the growth of the cotton industry. Tilburg became known as the "Wool City" of Holland and kept this status until the Second World War.

This gives us an insight into the context of Pete's life. He lived in one of the clusters of poor homes surrounding the main town center. The low, damp lands surrounding the city were an unhealthy place. It did not avoid the high mortality rate of the time, as we see from Arnold Donders' own family: two children lost in infancy; three wives dying at a very early age; Pete's and Martin's poor health. It is hard to believe the Pete lived almost to the age of eighty, especially considering the strenuous life he was to live for the last half of his life.

Pete's health did not improve as he grew into early adulthood. He tells us himself about the situation when he turned eighteen and became eligible for military service. The draft of the period was done on a lottery system, each young man being assigned a random number. "When I was eighteen, I had to submit to the military service lottery, and I drew a low number. [He drew 57 out of 106.] Even here the Good God helped me. How? Since at the time I did not seem to possess a strong constitution and I appeared outwardly unhealthy, I was given a year's postponement by a doctor's advice. This was stretched out for five years until I was declared exempt from military service by the special Providence of God."[1] Pete's thankfulness is not based on fear of military service or lack of patriotism, but on a deep-seated conviction that God had other plans for him, as we shall see.

Even though his health exempted him from military service, he was not exempted from work. Pete himself wrote, "My profession was first as a thread-spinner and then I learned to weave textiles, which I did right up to the day I left for the minor seminary at S. Michiels-Gestel...."[2] That would have been when he was twenty-two. While weaving could not be considered heavy labor, it was strenuous, repetitive, and slow. Wool is not light, so bolts of finished cloth were heavy. Sending a thread through the warp with a heavy wooden block, shifting a warp and doing it again, hour after hour. The assembly line of today with all the physical problems it causes is certainly no worse. The boredom of the task can be imagined.

Pete, however, made the work a prayer. Early on, he began to treat the loom like a rosary, with a prayer woven into each passing of the weir. Mary Mathijsen tells us, "Anyone who entered the workroom was sure to find him busy, working and praying diligently."[3] Prayer alone, however, does not seem to create master weavers. His employer, Jansenns Van Buren, found his work at times below par. "Oh well," he said, "the poor fellow does what he can. I suppose we can give him some breathing-room since he spends half the time with God."[4]

The other children of his time must have had to labor as hard as Pete. Poverty was general among these people who owned only their home and a small garden, and who depended on this constant labor to pay for their daily bread. The fact that Arnold could only allow his son five years of schooling before calling him to work is clear evidence of their poverty.

The later accounts of Pete's life given in the process of his beatification do not tell us much of Pete's early life: games with other children, childish indiscretions, his friendships. These only appear in the accounts if they suggest "holiness." We are thus presented with the picture of an angel come down to earth instead of a human being blessed by God with a great sensitivity to the divine presence in his life and a tender friendship with Christ. For example, we are told that when he was five or six, he would get Martin, go into the yard and build a little altar out of mud, and then mimic the priest saying Mass. It is presented to us as a practice of deep piety instead of the simple case of a child playing in the dirt and following his flights of imagination. Granted it shows his great interest in matters liturgical, it is not out of step with children playing house, or doctor, or cowboy. Each is expressing what interests the child at the moment. Should a child of pious parents not show an interest in religion? This simple play-acting just manifests Pete's special awareness of God; it does not make him some heavenly alien in human form.

Indeed, a few little glimmers of Pete's human weaknesses have snuck through to us. In the process of beatification, someone is appointed "Promoter of the Faith," a sort of prosecuting attorney who is to ferret out any discrepancies or objections in the evidence of the person's sanctity. In Pete's case, it can be as picayune as saying he didn't follow all the rubrics (God help us if we are barred from sanctity because we forgot to bow). There are a few examples, however, that are no less finicky but do prove to reveal something of Pete's reality as a human being. Here is one such case:

In the testimony, we read, "I once heard someone mention that while [Pete] lived in Tilburg, before he went to the seminary, one day he was being teased and got so angry that he threw his wooden shoe at the person teasing him." The defender of Pete's cause responded wisely, probably with tongue in cheek, "Well, you become a saint, you're not born one!"[5] Pete's anger appeared several other times in people's comments on his life, never as a common thing, but as an occasional, uncharacteristic slip. "One day," a man who knew him as a priest in Surinam recounts, "…I saw him get very angry at the people he had asked to clean out the church when they were dilly-dallying. I said to myself, 'I guess even saints get angry.'"[6]

But this rare anger was certainly out of character. We rather hear tales of his phenomenal patience. Physical weakness and notable piety in a child almost invariably bring with them openness to the ridicule and teasing of children. A friend of Pete's youth, Matthias Broeckx, recalled, "We went to Master Drabbe's school together for six months. As he was a delicate looking boy and very quiet, he had to put up with a great deal from others, but he never minded and just let it pass.…We were both around twelve at the time. We all regarded him as an extraordinary boy. He always walked along quietly and this made him the butt of much teasing by other boys; still, I never saw him get angry. He would often, but not always, try to avoid this teasing by taking a long way around."[7] Pete's childhood had its fair share of suffering.

By placing his remarkable patience alongside the occasional slips into an angry reaction makes it clear that this patience was not just shyness or fear or insensitivity, but was a virtue into which Pete had to continually put effort and prayer. His peaceful nature was a gift of God, but one he had to take care of.

So we can see our Pete as young man of his time and place, a "Poor Young Weaver." Poor he was, both in health and in goods. Young in everything but faith and love of God. And a weaver, not the best, but dedicated for the good of his family. Within this young man, nevertheless, was a dream that overwhelmed all these years: "God wants me to be a priest."

III

THE PRIEST WHO COULD NOT BE

William James, the founder of the science of experimental psychology, was fascinated with the phenomenon of faith and religion. In his most famous work, *The Varieties of Religious Experience*, he suggests that there are two basic patterns of religious experience. One is of those who experience themselves as being "Twice-Born." These are the ones who, like Augustine, Ignatius Loyola, or John Newton (author of "Amazing Grace"), experience a "second birth" of spirit transforming them from an unbeliever to a faith-full person. The religious experience of others is of being "Once-Born." These people have experienced the presence of the divine from the very beginning. I recall a fellow priest saying once that, even as a young child, he "always enjoyed being good." To *enjoy* being good seems to be the heart of this experience.

Certainly, Pete Donders is a member of the "Once-Born" choir. There seems to be no time in his life when Pete was not deeply aware of the role of God in his life. But his awareness had a special feel to it. And we have Pete himself to tell us what it was in something he wrote a half century later.

When a person enters the novitiate of the Redemptorist Congregation, he is asked to write a brief account of his vocation. For some unknown reason, Pete did not write this account or *curriculum vitae* until about seven years later. Perhaps this delay was due to an oversight since he was the first novice the mission in Surinam had to deal with, and so some of the formalities might have been overlooked. In some ways, this *curriculum vitae* is similar to a job-seeker's resumé in which he or she recounts past experience and training for the position being sought. The difference is that a novice's *curriculum* is to give an account of the experiences and events of his or her life that led to the decision to ask for admission to the religious congregation. Probably, when this oversight was noticed, his Redemptorist superior thought it worthwhile to have such a document, and asked him to prepare one in 1874. He was asked again in 1879 to write a second curriculum, why we are not sure.

From these personal recollections of Pete, we see clearly what filled his mind and heart as a child. He begins his first account: "I was born in Tilburg in 1809. It pleased God to give me at an early age, about five or six, a burning desire for the priesthood to work for the salvation of the souls he loves so dearly." Not another word said about his youth for he immediately moves on to speak of his entrance into the seminary at age twenty-two. Pete sees his entire childhood wrapped up in this overwhelming purpose.

In his second account he states, "The Good God, to whom I cannot be sufficiently grateful, preserved me from many dangers to which my salvation might have been exposed. He gave me the grace to pray often and a sure, although still imperfect love and devotion to his Mother Mary, to whom after God I ascribe my vocation to both the priestly and religious states of life."[1] If we recall his statement about his avoidance of military service mentioned earlier, we understand why he saw in it the special providence of God: it was meant to allow him to follow his life calling.

Ann Mary Van Dijk, thinking back some seventy-five years to when she and Pete were about six years old, knew the Donders family well enough to have been present as Pete's mother received the last rites. She recalls, "On the day his mother received Extreme Unction, he picked up the book the priest had been using from the table. As he handed it to the priest, Pete said he hoped that one day he would have a book like it himself."[2] It does not seem farfetched to suppose that God opened the grace of a calling in answer to a mother's dying prayers.

Whatever the unfathomable ways of God may have been, we know that surely from this time the great desire in Pete's heart made him find joy in prayer and obedience. He tried to pay a visit to the Blessed Sacrament every day. He was always at the Sunday Eucharist, going early to church and staying long afterward. Other companions of his mention, "He received communion every Sunday," and "I know for a fact that Pete received every Sunday and twice a week besides."[3] (Recall that in this era, Catholics considered even monthly communion proper only for the most observant.)

His little brother Martin told a woman once, "Pete was always the first in church and the last to leave....It felt like he spent his whole Sunday there and [he] used to tell me 'That's what Sundays are for.'"[4] It's hard to say whether Martin was all that happy about his brother's pious ways. Another young fellow, whole family name was Biezemortels, told how Pete would come to his house to rouse him at daybreak so they could go to church together. He recalls how Pete had a big prayer book he always carried to Mass. Martin also admitted that at bedtime, Pete would remain kneeling in prayer next to their bed far into the night, even when it was extremely cold. All youngsters spend hours in daydreams; it seems Pete's were usually lost in God.

Another of Pete's relatives was a much younger man, Michael Van den Brekel, who later would recall how his father told him that "Pete was a model of piety in church. Everyone looked on him as a holy boy. The parish priest, Father Van de Ven particularly thought a great deal of him. Others would also frequently praise him, especially on the subject of his edifying behavior. [Was this possibly brought up because of Michael's not-so-edifying behavior?] They would add that it was a pity that his great poverty prevented him from becoming a priest."[5]

All through Pete's youth, the idea of going to a seminary seemed to be completely out of reach because of his poverty. There was no way his family could scrape together enough to pay for the twelve years of studies he would have to undertake. This would especially be true when the family would lose the income of Pete's own labors, which would cut the family income almost in half. All through the first twenty-one years of his life, Pete lived under the shadow of this poverty whenever he thought of becoming a priest.

This remark brings us to the great suffering Pete felt in his childhood years and during his youth. This great desire that burned in him was for something well beyond his grasp. First, he was poor. Second, he had a very limited intellectual capacity. "Humanly speaking," he wrote in his second *curriculum*, "Even as a child I had a strong desire to someday become a priest... although humanly speaking it seemed impossible because my parents were poor."[6] Still, and this is a basic key to Pete's spirituality, "The Good God, who willed all of this, consoled me along the way and I obtained the firm trust that someday I would be a priest and a missionary. 'Thank God, who consoles us in all our troubles.'"[7] So he never stopped praying and thanking God for his blessings.

And, of course, God surprised him. "By the marvelous dispositions of Providence (when I lacked the necessary means to take up the studies and was already twenty-two years old), I came to obtain the means to accomplish it in an extraordinary manner, or better, a miraculous manner."[8] What seemed to have been the turning point was Pete's final rejection by the military on February 3, 1831. Soon after this, Pete must have decided that prayer alone was no longer enough, and that he should get up and do something. "So, right after Pentecost, I made up my mind to write my confessor, who was my parish priest, and ask him to help me begin the study of Latin."

Father W. Van den Ven was curate in the little parish of De Goirke near Tilburg where Pete lived for a few years when Pete was about eleven. He returned as pastor in 1826, so six years later, when Pete put his mind into writing, Father Van den Ven knew him well, and surely had a good idea of this longing. Late in life, Pete always considered this man one of his greatest benefactors because he put his faith in Pete's calling. Pete called him "the first instrument God made use of" to allow him to pursue his vocation.[9]

The first thing the venerable pastor did was the hardest task for most priests; he asked for money. He went around to his friends and parishioners in search of enough to provide for Pete's admission to the seminary. He faced some rejections. "If I thought I had money like that, I would spend it on my own children," one indignant parent responded. ("Later on, my grandfather often expressed his regret over this," his grandson would say.)[10] Nevertheless, he had success with others, especially Father Gerard Walter van Someren who knew Pete (and who preserved for us some of Pete's letters) and Mrs. Mutsaerts who paid most of Pete's expenses all through the seminary.

Finding the money was not easy, but getting the seminary to accept Pete was just as hard. The president of the preparatory seminary (roughly equivalent to secondary school and junior college), Rev. John Henry Smits, had to be convinced it was worth the effort to allow this ill-prepared young man to enter S. Michiels-Gestel. It is difficult to determine on what grounds an eventual compromise was reached. Was it that the rector could not agree to the straightforward admission of such a poor student? Was it the rather sure opinion of either Father Smits or Father Van den Ven (or both) that he would never make the grade and so would have had to return home in disgrace? It does not seem to be the issue of finances since that had been taken care of. In any event, the rector agreed to accept Pete into the seminary, but not as a student! No, he was to be a servant who could attend classes part time! If he could manage his studies, he could then become a regular seminarian.

Father Aegidius Vogels, a curate in the parish, brought Pete the news of his "acceptance" into the seminary. Mary Mathijsen says, "I never saw him as happy as on the day he got word of his admission to the seminary."[11] Pete himself tells us of it in a letter he wrote to Father Vogels from Surinam forty years later. "It was you who brought me the happy news that I would be able to enter the minor seminary in hopes of completing my studies there, according to the inscrutable plan of God and in spite of my unworthiness, so as to receive priestly ordination and finally become a missionary."[12]

So it was that in the fall of 1831, Pete was taken to S. Michiels-

Gestel in the wagon of a neighbor named Van Son, who later said that when he returned he found Pete's mother cleaning up some of her stepson's things as she remarked, "He was always dreaming of becoming a priest." Pete carried a letter from his pastor to the rector which said, in part, "I am sending you this young man that you may do with him whatever you think best; Tilburg is not the place for him."[13]

IV

SERVANT OR STUDENT?

That was Pete's quandary: was he a servant or a student? He quickly found out he could not be both. If he was going to get anywhere in his classes, he would have to spend a great amount of time studying. He also found himself with an immense amount of work to do as a servant. The seminary staff was small, largely due to the fact that most young men his age had been conscripted for the political turmoil in the Low Countries in this period when Belgium was gaining independence from Holland. So the administration decided that for at least six months, he should work full time as a servant. Studies would have to wait. Pete tells us that, despite this setback, "I felt certain that I would one day be a priest."

It seems the other servants were suspicious of him because of his unusual status at the seminary; they thought he might be some kind of spy for the administration. So they were slow to include Pete in their friendship. After six months, another servant was found so Pete began to have a chance to attend classes. This did not help his position with the other servants who were sure he was up to something. To add to this, his classmates did not let him forget "his place," since he was still a servant. We should also not forget that most of his classmates were much younger than he, still teenagers. Here was this old fellow of twenty-two trying to untangle Latin verbs that they could catch onto rather quickly.

His anomalous servant-student status was there for all to see. Father Louis Verhulst, C.Ss.R., who had been a fellow student, says, "His place in the chapel was behind the students and professors with the servants and maids. One would be deeply moved to see him coming from there slowly and reverently up the length of the chapel to the communion rail."

This mixed-up situation was its own cross. Even when he finally was allowed to start his studies, he had little time to attend to them outside of classes. The administration and other servants saw him primarily as help, at least during his first years; his studies held a distinctly secondary place in their eyes.

He was teased and tormented when he had to wait on table as well as when he got confused in class. Years later when some of these same young men (now in their eighties and nineties) had to recall those days, they had to admit, "He was a marvel of patience." "He met extreme rudeness with a pleasant smile....At times, when things were going too far, he would just say quietly, "OK, that's enough," and never said anything stronger than "Oh, you guys."[1]

He did once get very upset with the teasing. He went knocking on the rector's door, as he was in conversation with Professor Spierings. "What's the trouble?" "Father, I really have to complain about the students." "Why? Are they swearing at you or using foul language?" "Worse, Father. They keep yelling at me 'Saint Pete, Saint Pete.'" The professor upset Pete more when he burst out laughing. The rector said something to the students about this and one of the culprits came over to Pete later and said, "Pete, listen to me. Saint Pete you are, and Saint Pete you'll always be, but I'll never call you that again. Instead, I'll call you 'Donders Pete.'"[2] (Donders in Dutch means "Thunder"; so this phrase means something like "Pete the Thunderer.") At least, we can say that this nickname was more delicate than another one we are told he had for a time: "Stinky!"[3]

One anecdote that seems to have been a favored memory of this teasing was a challenge made by one of the students when a group of them were hiking in the country. "Pete, if you will jump over that irrigation ditch, I'll give you a dollar for the missions." The young man was well aware of Pete's love for the missions as well as the impossibility of the challenge. Without hesitation, Pete took him up, stepped back for a good run, leapt and—landed waist deep in the water and mud! Everyone rolled over with laughter and Pete joined them—after he got the dollar for the missions.[4]

The transition from the warmth of his home and friends into what seems to have been a very chilly atmosphere for Pete must have been painful for the young man. But there was no turning from his goal: he was going to be a priest at all costs! While much of this teasing was from adolescent malice, some of it was out of admiration and fondness, at least as time went on and the youngsters began to sense the gift they had in Pete.

Pete gradually won them over. "At last we came to realize that the object of our jokes was a most loveable young man and that all this teasing fell far from the mark. Slowly but surely Peter Donders won his way into our affections."[5] A former classmate recalls that his memory long endured at S. Michiels-Gestel. "Even after he left, the name 'Pete' was given to students of exceptional piety."[6] Father Odenhoven,[7] who later knew Pete in Surinam, had been told by several of Pete's schoolmates that

> He was generally among the lowest in the class; the lack of time for his studies is sufficient explanation. Examinations on the Bible were an exception, as he usually came first or close to the top. The students teased him but were generally fond of him. They supplied him with writing materials, books and so on, and they helped him with his lessons, mathematics, history, and the rest.[8]

It also seems that as he got more time for study and more accustomed to the academic life, he began to improve, although the reputation of being ignorant seems to have been branded into his mind. Father Kamp, who later became rector of the seminary, said, "Peter was by no means at the tail of his class, but he gave the leaders some competition."[9] Still, throughout his life, Pete speaks of himself in very low terms when considering his academic abilities.

He seems to have kept his servant role during much of his

seminary career. When the other boys could use their free time for games or hiking, Pete spent it at some manual labor or housekeeping task. Perhaps the difference in ages to some extent explains this. Or perhaps he wanted to reduce some of the expenses of his stay for the sake of his benefactors.

Pete did have the consolation of his friend, Father Van Someren, who had helped him pay for his education, since the priest now served as a professor of philosophy on the faculty of the seminary.

Pete's saddest moment of his preparatory seminary career occurred on December 28, 1834, when his father, Arnold, died at the age of seventy-nine. From all we know of Pete's love for his father, this must have made a deep wound in his heart.

The next year, for some reason, Pete's brother, Martin, decided to give up the home where they had grown up. Perhaps it was because their stepmother decided to move back to Enschot to be closer to her family. In any event, the house was torn down and the property sold on August 21, 1935. This left Pete with no home of his own. After this, when he returned to Tilburg for summer vacation, he usually stayed at the rectory, even though he was constantly being invited to stay with families in the town. He probably felt he could be more prayerful in the rectory rather than in private homes.

During his early days in the seminary, Pete, of course, did not lose any of his dedication to prayer. This was noticed by others. One student testified, "It was our impression that his prayer was unceasing, and that his thoughts were always on God, even during his work and when he was waiting on us at table." Another said, "It is my belief that Peter usually lived in the presence of God."[10] He continued his practice of going to communion a few times a week in addition to Sundays. He received the sacrament of penance once a week as was the practice of the time for reverent communicants.

V

THE UNWANTED RELIGIOUS

Pete completed his work at the preparatory seminary and moved on to the major seminary at Herlaan on October 4, 1937, when he was nearly twenty-eight. But not without a slight detour.

It was widely known that Pete had a great desire not only for priesthood but also had some interest in serving as a missionary in a foreign land where priests were few. The president of the major seminary must have had wind of this, because in Pete's last years at the minor seminary the priest had copies of the *Annals of the Propagation of the Faith* sent to him regularly. This was a publication from the Vatican office that was in charge of missionary activities and recounted tales of the adventures and ministries of priests at work in areas outside of Europe. Much of the material at this time related to the work in North America among immigrants and native peoples. Pete read each issue carefully and the tales began to fill his dreams with new desires.

One feature of this missionary work was that it was mainly conducted by religious communities since these areas were not under the care of dioceses and the question of financial support and replacement of personnel was a major consideration. So the president of the major seminary recommended he seek admission to one of the religious orders in Holland that was providing missionaries to the New World.

Pete tells us quite frankly, "At this time and later, I felt no special desire for religious life, but only to become a priest and work for the salvation of souls. Nevertheless, out of obedience to the Very Reverend President [of the seminary], I visited the Jesuits in Belgium...."[1]

Pete recounts his efforts at joining a missionary order in both his curricula vitae. (We shall combine elements of the two accounts here; the actual texts are found on pp. 216–217 and p. 22.)

> ...the Jesuit provincial decided that I did not have a vocation to their order because I was already twenty-six years old. Thus, I set off again the next day early in the morning. When I had gotten home, the president wanted me to go again, this time to the Redemptorist Fathers at S. Truijen; he said these did almost the same [missionary activity as the Jesuits]. I obeyed. I asked the regent for a letter of recommendation which he gave me. The president added, "If these do not accept you, there are monasteries of other orders in S. Truijen where you should ask whether they will accept you." This I did.[2] I went with that to Saint-Trond, stayed there for a few days and received a scapular of the four confraternities from the rector who sent me with another postulant to the provincial superior in Liege [rather the visitor, Father Frederik von Held], who is still alive. Again, he judged, after consulting with Father Bernard [Hafkenscheid] (because I did not know how to speak French and the provincial did not have command of Dutch), that I was not called to the Redemptorist community. I then went to the Franciscans.[3]

The Franciscans could not figure this young man out and were suspicious because his recommendations had all been opened. So they told him to "come back next year" when he had finished his philosophy. (Was this a polite "Don't call us; we'll call you?")

So Pete had to walk back to the seminary to report that no religious community was interested in him. Most young men would have been ashamed and saddened, if not angry, at these failures. And Pete seems to have felt these same emotions at first, but his great faith in God's call came to the fore again. He tells us,

So again, with nothing accomplished, I returned but I had the comfort of knowing I had obeyed the president and had acted as he had recommended. The Good God, who willed all of this, consoled me along the way and I obtained the firm trust that someday I would be a priest and a missionary. "Thank God, who consoles us in all our troubles."

At this point it was established in my mind that I was no longer to think of the Franciscans because that was certainly not my vocation, and so with the others I took up philosophy and later theology.[4]

Today's world preaches constantly that, with effort and determination, we can be anything we wish to be. How many young people has this doctrine led to despair and meaninglessness because they could never gain perspective on their own limits and realities? Pete offers a different message. We can be anything God calls us to be. The painful road Pete followed to priesthood and, eventually, religious life gives us a sense of how to balance the little we are with the much we can be when we place ourselves in the perspective of trust in God.

VI

A Call From Over the Sea

Pete entered the final phase of his preparations for ordination when he began his theological studies at the major seminary at Herlaar. Happily, he was among older students who seemed to accept him more readily. The excessive teasing of S. Michiel's was a thing of the past. The theology students also had a much higher regard for his personal piety. He came to be not just appreciated but respected by his peers. For the time being, at least publicly, he was no longer "Pete" but "Mr. Donders," as was the proper form of address among the students.

His fellow students who were still alive after his death remembered him as humble and dedicated, especially to prayer. This sometimes proved to be the source of a little envy. One student confesses,

> His fervor touched every moment of his day and made it holy. He began early. For five years, I tried to get down to chapel in the morning before him. No luck!
>
> I did not know him in the preparatory seminary, but in the theology school he was so attentive to duty that we all looked on him as a saint. I have to say that I never saw him do anything wrong. I always admired him. It was not that he tried to stand out, no, not at all. On the contrary, he took an artless and quiet pleasure in our innocent fun. His usual gentleness and peace simply charmed us. I never remember him getting angry or even put out.[1]

Perhaps these recollections best sum Pete up. It is not easy to describe a holy person and not make it sound maudlin or otherworldly. Yet there was a tangible joy here that quietly surrounded the man, a sense too subtle for human words.

The students respected this about him. One of them said, "None of us would go bursting into his room without knocking. Yet no one would refuse if he said, 'Come in and have a smoke.'"[2]

Pete smoked! This was the most formidable objection to his sanctity brought up at the process of his beatification. The Defender of the Faith made a great to-do about this "vice" as a sign of his self-indulgence and fault of character. Of course, the modern-day understanding of smoking as a serious health hazard to oneself and others was a discovery far in the future. At Pete's time, in most of Europe and especially Holland, pipe smoking such as his was seen as the normal practice of an adult man. It was seen as an ordinary end to a meal and adjunct to the conversation that followed, as much as a cup of tea or coffee. The defender of Pete's cause pointed this out. The debate was hot until the commission discussing the case had the sense to cite the adage, "All good things in moderation," and agreed it could see no reason to consider his pipe smoking as any reason to question Pete's complete dedication to God and his mission.[3] Thus, throughout our story of his life, we shall find Pete doing good to the most abandoned, even with his pipe in his hand.

Pete was overjoyed to find that the study of the "sacred sciences" of theology, liturgy, Scripture, canon law, and pastoral practice gave him little difficulty. "Thanks be to God, these studies were more successful than learning Latin during the study of the humanities, etc."[4]

Pete continued to be an example of cheerful piety as we can see from the words of a very close companion. The students shared rooms in their dormitory. One of his roommates during this period tells us:

> We shared a room and one morning when I came back to it, I found the whole floor covered with water. I couldn't believe it until I saw that some practical jokers had got it

into their heads to put a huge block of ice in front of our fireplace. I got furious and turned to Peter who came in right after me, "Look at this dirty trick someone has pulled." Peter just smiled, opened the window, and threw the ice out. Then, he mopped the floor. And with not a word of anger, he sat down with me to our studies. Since I was the younger, I couldn't say anything. He did not allow me to do things for him, even though as his junior, I was supposed to follow his directions. I think he used to straighten up our room even before I got up. He was the one who was always ready to help me quite humbly. He was very honest and generous and thankful for the smallest kindness.[5]

When vacation period came around, he would go back to Tilburg. Since he no longer had a home there, he continued to stay in the rectory. This left him free to spend time in church, usually from early morning until noon. People would remark on his ability to spend this time on his knees lost in prayer. He used no book and seemed unaware of what went on around him. Furthermore, the locals were concerned to see that he got enough to eat and that his clothes did not get shabby since he did not care to spend what little he had on new clothes.

His theology years seem to have gone very smoothly since he was doing well in his studies and his kind benefactors saw that the necessary bills were paid. There was, however, a very decisive event that occurred in his second year at the major seminary. It was to lay the foundation for the rest of his life after his ordination.

We remember how much interest Pete had in the work of the foreign missions. The general awareness of the expansion of the Church in the New World was a constant theme in this period of European history. Surely Pete had continued to read of the adventures of the missionaries in North America and elsewhere in the *Annals of the Propagation of the Faith* and other sources. At this time, however, his friend, Father van Someren, called his attention to the need for priests in Holland's own colonies in

America and the East Indies. Pete writes in his second *curriculum vitae*:

> Since the professors knew that I wanted to be a missionary and at the time everyone was going to North America, Professor G. van Someren, who is now the dean and parish priest in Eindhoven, said that our Dutch colonies were in great need of priests and it was only fair that we give preference to our own colony. If I was not very averse to going to Surinam, I could then speak with the Prefect of the Surinam Mission, J. Grooff, who was to visit the seminary in a few days.[6]

Rev. James Grooff was born in Amsterdam August 3, 1800, and was ordained August 19, 1825. He landed at Paramaribo on February 8, 1826. He was quickly recognized for his extraordinary zeal and for his kind affection for the lepers. With him had come Bishop van der Weyden, who was named Apostolic Prefect of Surinam. The following year Father Grooff took over this post, when Monsignor van der Weyden died after only eight months. One of the new prefect's tasks was to promote the mission in Europe by seeking funds and personnel. This was the reason for his presence in Herlaar that providentially provided his meeting with Pete.

Obviously the pilgrimage of Monsignor Grooff did not bring much in terms of the numbers of personnel he was able to acquire, though he was more fortunate in obtaining some funding. Still, if a saint is worth even ten ordinary ministers, he reaped a bountiful harvest. Pete tells us, "He indeed came and we agreed I should go there as soon as possible, with the proviso that I first complete my theological studies and be admitted to the priesthood. This was decided in 1839 at the major seminary in the town of Haaren."[7] From that time on, Surinam was not far from his mind. "He would often speak of Surinam to me," one of his fellow students recalls, "it was his favorite topic, and he would tell me how anxious he was to get there and convert the unbelievers."[8]

During Pete's time in the major seminary, the numbers of students were growing and so a new site had to be found. The same year as Monsignor Grooff's visit, the seminary was moved to a new building on the road between 's-Hertogenbosch and Tilburg and the students and faculty moved to it on July 16. But a new residence was not Pete's concern; the final hurdle on the way to ordination lay in obtaining the required benefice. Unlike the present day when priests who are not members of a religious order receive salaries from their diocese, in Pete's day a candidate had to show that he had some source of ongoing support such as a family inheritance, a benefice (a type of trust fund), or similar stable source of income. This was to assure that he would not become a beggar or burden to the Church. Again, Pete's friends, especially his pastor in Tilburg and Father van Someren, managed to provide some form of sufficient backing for their protégé.

Less than a year later, Pete received tonsure, minor orders, and subdiaconate at the hands of Cardinal Sterckx in his private oratory in Mechlin (Malines), April 26, 1840. That he had finally reached the last steps before priesthood filled Pete with inexpressible joy. A fellow cleric who accompanied him writes, "The day we left the archbishop's residence in Malines after receiving subdiaconate—I can still picture it—Peter Donders said to me with the most ethereal look of happiness, 'All my lifelong desires have been satisfied now since, in spite of all my unworthiness, God's infinite mercy is pleased to admit me to the ranks of his ministers at the altar.' As he said this, tears began to fall."[9]

After completing his final year in the seminary, Pete received the order of deacon on April 10, 1841, from Monsignor Van Wijckerslooth, the Titular Bishop of Curium and Procurator for the Mission in Surinam. Two months later, on July 5, 1841, he knelt before the same bishop and, as he says, "by the goodness and mercy of God, I was ordained a priest."[10] Pete was now Father Pete.

VII

WILL HE EVER GET THERE?

As far as Father Pete was concerned, he would have been happy to walk out of the bishop's chapel with the oils fresh on his hands and climb aboard a ship to Surinam. The problem was there was no ship on which he could book passage for several months. In fact, he had to wait slightly more than twelve months. During this time, he continued to live at the seminary and to assist in several parishes in the vicinity.

Father Pete's ministry immediately impressed people. Twice during this year of waiting, Father Pete assisted for a short time in his home parish of Tilburg. In his seventies, Norbert Donders (no relation) recalled the way Father Pete celebrated Mass when Norbert was a server,

> His visible emotion attracted me. It did me good to serve his Mass and many a time I asked my fellow servers to let me take their turn to serve him….On one occasion, when Father Pete was assisting a newly ordained priest at his first Mass, I could not take my eyes off Father Pete….It inspired me with the resolution to discharge my duties as altar-boy with greater reverence.[1]

On the other hand, sanctity does not automatically confer eloquence. Norbert also remarks,

> I heard Father Donders preach two sermons for us. To be candid, he was not much of an orator, but he put his

whole heart into what he said. His words made their way into the depths of our hearts, nevertheless. What proves this is that his preaching was talked about for quite a long time afterwards.[2]

Well, eloquence is not the goal of preaching, inspiration is. So, in this sense, Father Pete was more than eloquent.

Finally, in June 1842, Bishop van Wijckerslooth told him to prepare to depart for his voyage. He returned home to Tilburg to make his farewells. He preached in the parish church, asking the assembly to remember him in their prayers. The congregation was moved to tears as it bid him farewell after the service. Gerard Tudor remembered years later how the new missionary asked the children to pray for him and, to remind them, he gave out small holy pictures on which he had written "Pray for Peter Donders." As children do, many gathered around him and clung to him. "And so did I," said the old gentleman with feeling.[3] That the people of Tilburg had learned to respect this "poor young weaver" of earlier days is evidenced by the fact that they kept sending him stipends for Masses to support his mission. But they always added the condition that Father Pete was to say the Mass himself, or at least to pray for the intention the donor specified. No secondhand prayers would do!

The hardest moment came when he had to say goodbye to his brother Martin and his stepmother, Jane Mary. He was especially concerned for his handicapped brother, who was then a skilled worker for one of the tradesmen of the town. The daughter of Martin's employer recalls that her mother "gave Father Pete her word that we would take good care of Martin, and this assurance allowed Pete to leave reassured."[4] Pete never forgot his brother. He wrote him some affectionate letters and even a few times sent him gifts from Surinam of crates of oranges or preserved native fruit. As we mentioned, his stepmother moved into her family's home and Pete had no worry that she would pass her life in good hands.

God would still not give Father Pete an easy time. Martin accompanied Father Pete to 's-Hertogenbosch where he was to catch a boat to Leiden where his ship was to dock. But when he got there, he learned that the ship to Surinam was delayed by bad weather and would not reach Holland for a few months. Again, he had to return to Tilburg. Bishop van Wijckerslooth, however, asked him to come and live with him, so he and Martin again returned to 's-Hertogenbosch where Martin bade his older brother farewell; they were never to see each other again.

Since the bishop did not wish his anxious young priest to sit around, he sent him to a small parish in nearby Warmond to help a priest who was there alone. Father Pete spent several weeks there. During his stay, he sent a little note from Warmond to his Ordinary, Bishop Henri den Dubbelden, Vicar Apostolic of 's-Hertogenbosch, to let him know how his days were being spent. There is no better way to sense the young priest's joy over ministry and peace of mind during the delay than to read this short letter itself.

This letter is found in Part II, Chapter Two, #1, page 101.

We can leave Father Pete biding his time in Warmond, and take a few minutes to introduce you to what is surely not the best-known country in the world, Surinam, as well as to a little of the history of the Catholic Church's presence that awaited Father Pete's arrival.

If you go to very top of South America, next to Venezuela, you come to three small countries, different from all the rest of the continent in that neither Spanish nor Portuguese is the official language. These were originally known as the Guianas. In colonial times, these three countries were named (moving east to west) French Guiana (site of the infamous Devil's Island penal colony), Dutch Guiana (now Suriname), and British Guiana (now Guyana). While the country's name is spelled "Suriname" in Dutch as it is also sometimes written in English, the common English spelling is "Surinam."

Surinam is just above the equator, so its climate is tropical. Its northern coast facing the North Atlantic has a narrow coastal plain with many swamps. As one moves south, one enters low rolling hills and finally steeper heavily forested slopes. It is a little more than 160,000 km square (63,000 square mile), about half the size of Italy or slightly larger than the state of Georgia (USA).

The earliest inhabitants were Caribs in the northern coastal areas. Amerindians, whose largest tribe was the Arowaks, settled further inland.[5] The first European settlers were English, soon followed by the Dutch who took it as their colony in 1667. It was taken over by the English during the Napoleonic Wars in Europe, but returned to the Netherlands in 1808.

The Europeans mainly developed the country into sugar and tobacco plantations and the Dutch imported slaves from Africa to work them. Many of these slaves gradually fled into the jungles and formed their own tribes, coming to be known as Maroons. While mitigation of slavery began with the English in the early 1800s, it was not abolished until 1863. For ten years after that, the slaves continued to work these plantations, now receiving a small salary, as the owners began to replace them with contract workers from India. Donders' stay in Surinam spanned these years of change.

Surinam takes its name from one of the Amerindian tribes. Its capital and largest city is Paramaribo, a short distance from the sea on the Suriname River. As of 2002, Paramaribo was the home of about a quarter million of the half million inhabitants of the entire country. In Donders' day, the population of the entire country was estimated at about sixty thousand with perhaps one-third residing in the capital. The only other towns, also along the coast, were more like large villages: Nickerie (or New Rotterdam, far to the west, on the boarder of French Guiana), Nieuw Amsterdam (a fortress where the Suriname and Commewane rivers empty into the sea), and Coronie (not so much a town as a row of several plantations, midway between Nickerie and the capital).

Two Franciscan priests came to Paramaribo in 1683 from Louvain, in defiance of the anti-Catholic laws in force. Another priest and brother joined them, but all four died within three years. It was another whole century before several other priests ventured to the colony. All these spent various short periods there, but it was not until 1817 that two Dutch priests, Fathers Wennekers and van der Horst arrived to begin the mission that has endured to this day.

Their work was not easy. The Protestant Churches were antagonistic. Among them, the Moravian Brethren were the most numerous, counting about twenty thousand members in Surinam in Donders' time. The "Unity of Brethren" began in the early fifteenth century as a group of followers of John Hus (+1415) in Bohemia and Moravia. In the eighteenth century, Count Nicholas Louis von Zinzendorf (+1760) offered refuge from persecution to European Moravians and it was from his estate in Saxony that the renewed church spread to England, Holland, and North America. The Brethren had taken strong hold in Surinam since it was favored by the government and had strong financial backing in Holland. Indeed, the government forbad the Catholics from working with slaves on its plantations or from dealing with state employees and even with the lepers in Batavia.

The Catholics in the colony were also a problem. Since they had for so long cared for themselves, they were not happy at the priests trying to take over leadership roles, especially in financial matters. Some of the Church Building Commission are even said to have gotten into a fistfight with Father Wennekers! To top it off, a fire spread through the city and destroyed the church along with other structures.

Father Wennekers did not paint a very pleasant picture of the moral state of the colony. As far as the Europeans were concerned, he said simply, "Chastity does not even appear in their vocabulary."[6] The Blacks and Amerindians had no more than a vague notion of good and evil. The two priests labored alone for about nine years, and began to gain the respect of the locals, especially in their efforts to restore respect for marriage. In 1826, as we mentioned above, they were joined by Monsignor van der Weyden and Father Grooff. Although Bishop van der Weyden lived less than a year after his arrival, he was able to complete the rebuilding of the church in Paramaribo. Father Grooff succeeded in convincing the government to entrust him with the care of the leper colony at Batavia in 1830. He worked there regularly and built a hut to live in, quickly replaced by a church and small house. In 1832, a law was passed that removed all restraints on Catholics evangelizing and baptizing slaves; thus, he began a regular visitation of the plantations around the city. Over the years, he was joined by four other priests, only three of whom, Fathers Janssen,[7] Schepers, and Kempkes were still there when Father Pete arrived.

This is the country and mission that awaited Father Pete, whom we left quietly enjoying the parish in Warmond. The last week of July, he received the call from Bishop van Wijckerslooth that the ship had finally arrived at Den Helder and he was to return to Amsterdam and begin preparations for his voyage. At last!

VIII

Surinam, at Last

Father Pete arrived in Amsterdam and began to collect the materials he was to bring with him. He vainly sought a chalice that he could use on the trip as well as add to the meager collection of liturgical accessories in the mission. He also had to call upon some of the major benefactors of the mission, especially Sophie Gillès de Pélichy in Antwerp. Then on July 31, he was called out of church unexpectedly to be told that the ship was leaving for Den Helder earlier than expected, in fact, the next day. He had to get up there immediately.

Meanwhile, in Surinam there was a great deal of anxiety because they did not know of the delay of the ship's arrival in Holland and its subsequent later departure. So several months before Father Pete actually arrived, every time word came down the river that a ship was sighted, Monsignor Grooff would rush down to the docks in the hope that the young man he had met over three years earlier would walk down the gangplank. Finally, a few months before Father Pete's actual arrival, he wrote downheartedly to Bishop van Wijckerslooth,

> This morning, June 15, 1842, we were told that Captain Anderson was coming up the river. The flag was already floating from the tower, the finishing touches had been put to the decorations of the altar, the church doors had been thrown wide open, and I was standing at the entrance to the sanctuary, ready to welcome Father Donders. Full of the same joyous expectation, Fathers Janssen and

Kempkes had gone to the riverside to greet him. Alas! Instead of hearing the bells ring out, I had to suffer a cruel disappointment. The *Sophia* had indeed put her passengers ashore, but there was no Father Donders among them. How annoying! I can only hope to have the pleasure of welcoming him soon....[1]

While those in Surinam were anxiously waiting, Father Pete was rushing to Den Helder and arrived just in time to catch the ship. This was unfortunate for his friends in Holland because he had little time to say goodbye. It was, however, very fortunate for us because this meant that within two months of his arrival, he began to write letters recounting his trip and his first experiences of Surinam. They show all the excitement of his new adventure and his great trust that God would see him through this work. His letters also manifest his happiness that he is finding it easy to learn the Pidgin English that is the common language of the slaves, the freedmen, and the poor. But why waste time telling this? Let us allow Father Pete to do it in his own words.

See the letter found in Part II, Chapter Three, #2, page 104.

What a whirlwind tour of the Surinam mission this letter gives us! In the breadth of six weeks, Father Pete had been introduced to three of the four main fields of ministry that would occupy the rest of his life: the city of Paramaribo, the leper colony of Batavia, and the world of the plantations. The only area missing was the last one he was to try his hand at many years in the future, that is, ministering to the escaped slaves and Amerindians in the forests. We can talk about that later. If fact, we will have more to learn about all these fields as we move along. For now we will begin with his experiences in his first days in Paramaribo where he would spend the first fourteen years of his missionary life.

As we have seen from Father Pete's letter, the bishop wasted no time in putting the young missionary to work. On October 31, he preached his first sermon in the "cathedral" of Paramaribo, perhaps a bit of a ponderous word for the small structure, but it was, after all, the only Catholic church in town and (except for the chapel in Batavia) in the whole country! It was not long, either, before he developed a regular routine for his work. A few people who were children at the time of Father Pete's arrival give us their recollections of his life and impact on theirs. Among them is Johan Marius Mehcis who kept a close eye on him:

> I was thirteen when I received baptism from him and I knew him until the day he left for Batavia. I saw him say Mass at seven every morning in the church, which he had reached long before I got there. After a quarter of an hour thanksgiving, he went and took a cup of coffee, and then at eight, he taught school to the boys and girls. First, we had prayers and catechism; then reading and writing. If I remember rightly, I went to his school for three years. At ten o'clock, he would take his hat and go off to visit the parishioners in the most out-of-the-way parts of town.
>
> Father Donders usually returned from his rounds at noon, but sometimes as late as one or even two o'clock—Father Schepers[2] would give him a good scolding then. After dinner, he went to the church to pray. He never took a siesta. If Father Schepers could not take the First Communion class at four, Father Donders took his place, and then resumed his visits. Sometimes, however, he would stay home in the rectory and play the pump organ. At seven, he held the class for adults. Then he spent the rest of the day with Bishop Grooff.[3]

These discussions with the bishop could last rather late. Some years later someone asked Father Pete, "Father, how on earth did you become such a heavy smoker?"—"Oh, ever since I used to sit up (sometimes until midnight) with Bishop Grooff." The bishop suffered from insomnia and appreciated the company.

Dorothy Kustner was nine when Father Pete came to Paramaribo. She remembered how Father Schepers used to tease the children: "I'm going to have to have Father Donders shipped off to Batavia because you are just abusing his kindness. We don't get a moment's peace at the house because you keep coming to the door with your 'Father Donders,' 'Father Donders!' Father Pete would always tell us when we were leaving, 'Remember now, pray, pray, pray.'"[4]

It did not take long to appreciate Father Pete's extraordinary zeal. Bishop Grooff himself wrote to Monsignor van Wijckerslooth on November 14, 1842, "I have not the smallest doubt that Father Donders is going to be a source of great help and consolation to me in the midst of my many worries. It is clearly the one wish of the young missionary to share with me both the heat of the day and the burden of the ministry." A month later, he continued, "May God soon raise us up another Father Donders! He is a great help and comfort to me."[5]

Right after the beginning of the New Year, an outbreak of severe dysentery fell upon the city. Both the bishop and Father Janssen were afflicted with it and had to take to their beds. For nearly three months, Father Pete had to carry on the entire ministry in Paramaribo alone. Not only were there the usual responsibilities, but as a result of the sickness sweeping the city, the numbers of sick and dying were staggering. Father Pete tells us that at the worst of the epidemic, three or four Catholics were dying each day, and this was in addition to those of other religions. The greatest suffering, however, came from the death on March 12, 1843, of Father Janssen. Over this loss of a friend and coworker, Father Pete's pain can be seen in his few words, "It is God's holy Will, and we must adore it in all things."

The bishop slowly recovered and took some of the burden of ministry off Father Pete's shoulders. In June, Father Pete wrote to the rector of the major seminary in Herlaar about the events of these few months and about another setback that the mission would have to face. The best way to bring this chapter to a close is to read Father Pete's own account.

See his letter found in Part II, Chapter Three, #3, page 114.

IX

Two Hurricanes in Paramaribo

Perhaps that is an overdramatic title. Still, the next fourteen years of Father Pete's life often sound like a whirlwind time. One hurricane was made up of the difficulties crowding in from all sides. The other hurricane was Father Pete himself. When Monsignor Grooff was forced to leave the colony a year after Father Pete arrived, he praised Father Pete as the mirror-image of the revered founder of the mission there, Father Wennekers, "the noblest and most energetic, perhaps indeed the most perfect personality in the whole line of apostles of this country....He spends himself in ceaseless work day and night, winning everyone's heart as much by his example as by his many activities. I say this without wishing in any way to depreciate the zeal and charity of my other assistants."[1] A hero among heroes.

Father Pete has told us of the plague that hit the colony and took away the life of his fellow missionary, Father Janssen. An even greater loss had already been in the offing. At the beginning of 1843, rumors had reached the colony that the Holy See was planning to advance Monsignor Grooff to the office of Vicar Apostolic of the much larger colony of the Dutch East Indies (today, the island nation of Indonesia). Unlike most rumors, this one proved true and Monsignor Grooff received his new appointment. All four other priests were upset and heartbroken. They begged the influential people they knew to try to change the Vatican's mind. Then came Father Janssen's death. So within a few months the mission force was cut almost in half.

Though Father Pete was saddened by the loss of Father Janssen, the Prefect's departure seems to have been an even deeper pain. From what we have seen in the last chapter, Monsignor Grooff and Father Pete were close friends. The older missionary and his young newcomer were a great mutual support for each other, almost a father and a son. Father Pete calls him "father." While this may have been a formal term of respect for clergy at the time, one feels there is more than that when Pete calls him his "never-to-be-forgotten father," and describes the departure as "a painful and irreplaceable loss."

At Monsignor Grooff's leaving, he named Father Schepers his temporary pro-vicar, with the other two priests, Donders and Kempke, his assistants, Donders in Paramaribo and Kempke in Coronie. Fortunately, in December, Father Gerard Heinink arrived. (His stay in Surinam was not to be very long since he died six years later.) As we saw in his letter to Father Cuyten in the last chapter, Father Pete quickly set about becoming a promoter of missionary vocations. His letter may have contributed to Father Heinink's arrival. Father Stephenus Meurkens also came to Surinam in December 1844, bringing the number of missionaries back to five.

This number is obviously small for the possibilities. There was a concern, for example, to begin to educate the poor of the colony in literacy and practical skills. But how? A little of Father Pete's frustration is seen in his reply to a letter from the head of a small circle of benefactors who were offering help to establish a school, an offering, however, he could not yet accept.

This letter is found in Part II, Chapter Three, #4, page 117.

The pressing issue of personnel is again the problem in 1844, when Father Pete wrote to the editor of a Dutch periodical, Joachim Le Sage ten Broek, who published the letter, which ended in a strong call to Dutch priests to volunteer for the colony.

This letter is found in Part II, Chapter Three, #5, page 119.

Unfortunately, it does not seem that Father Pete's letter had any effect. Until the arrival of the Redemptorists twenty-two years later in 1866, only three other priests came to the colony, Arnold Swinkels in 1854 (he left when the Redemptorists came), Peter Masker in 1859 (who departed with Swinkels), and Johan Romme in 1864 (who became a Redemptorist with Pete).[2]

Father Pete's letter opens our eyes to the immensity of the task he and his companion faced in Paramaribo. When we read the little routine schedule remembered by John Mehcis in the last chapter, it may have given the impression of a somewhat leisurely, well-ordered life, such as could be enjoyed in a quiet European village. If so, we can suspect that we are not taking into account the very oppressive climate of Surinam, the size of the mission, and also, perhaps, the rather idealized memories of John sixty years later. In any event, one has to imagine the schedule was more flexible than it sounds when the words of Father Pete tell us what was actually going on in Paramaribo at the time.

There was more, however, than just "work" in the life of Father Pete. There was the great interior world of his personality and his relationship to God. When we turn to this world, we find the creation of a sacred center which forms the eye of this spiritual hurricane called "Donders." First, we will look at one facet of it that Father Pete himself reveals in a letter of 1846 to his good friend in Holland, Father van Someren.

This letter is found in Part II, Chapter Three, #6, page 125.

What a remarkable bit of social analysis imbued with spirituality do we find in this letter! The whole structure of sinfulness is traced to its core in a social structure. Slavery creates not only the sale of a body to a master, but the chaining up of the souls of both slaves and masters. Until that chain can be broken there can be no freedom, either of mind or body. The overpowering greed upon which the system of slavery is based destroys the slave's freedom to make the most basic decisions of a person's life: its purpose, its morality, its beliefs. It prevents the freedom of God's children. For the masters, it unleashes callousness to human life, cruelty, lust, murder. And it captures the whole social scene into its workings. How clearly Father Pete sees this and how all of his sense of God's presence rebels against it.

The spirituality Father Pete preaches in his words shows itself in his actions. One of the great signs of the apostolic spirit is one's detachment from material goods, not a spurning of them, but a freedom to choose not to keep them when others need them more. We are told Father Pete had a great trick to help the poor. When someone with a special need came to the door, he would see what he could get out of the Prefect. If he was being refused, he would say, "Well, I guess I will have to sell my watch since I have to get some money." Finally, one day the Prefect had nothing to give, and Father Pete had to find something for a family in extreme distress, so he went and pawned his watch![3]

The Jewish pawnbroker, a Mr. De Vries, had no intention of keeping the watch and soon brought it back to the Prefect and told him to forget about paying to redeem it. That night, at supper with Father Pete and the workers who lived with them, Monsignor Schepers announced that someone had donated a watch to the parish and he had decided to draw names to see who should get it. A rather unsurprised Father Pete found himself with his own watch in hand.

The parish carpenter who lived in the rectory tells how the woman who did the wash kept complaining that Father Pete's clothes kept disappearing! The Prefect's admonishments on the matter had only short-term effects. Before long, the shirts and trousers would again be appearing on some poor persons of the neighborhood. But the result was that Father Pete gained access to everybody's heart. No one felt they could not trust him. Monsignor Schepers once wondered out loud how he could ever manage without him since he "managed to worm his way into every nook and cranny."

Matthew Bernhards, a longtime sacristan for the Paramaribo

church, has preserved other instances of Father Pete's dedication to the poor. He recalls for us a conversation he overheard. Monsignor Schepers, after another request for aid, threw up his hands saying, "Father Donders, you are always giving, giving, giving. What will you do when I die?" "Oh, don't worry, Monsignor, God does not die!"[4]

His admirer, John Mehcis, testified that this generosity meant that he became the most popular confessor.

> He had more penitents than the other priests, and although—to be candid—he was by nature rather on the strict side, his words were always well taken. I would not like to say that he was exactly a good preacher, but he let his heart go, and that is why, I think, great numbers loved to go to hear him.[5]

This deep sense of indifference to self was, as we have already seen, because of his great sense of his value in the eyes of God. He had no need to enrich himself; he was rich already. The stories of his childhood are repeated of the man. Bernhard's recollections show us the root of Father Pete's life:

> At the time, we had no Stations of the Cross. I noticed, however, that Father Pete used to go around the church and kneel in certain spots as though the stations were actually there.…When I opened the church each morning at six, he was always there ahead of me. He would be kneeling at the communion rail with a book in his hand—his breviary, I presumed. His devotion to the Blessed Sacrament was beyond words, and his good example did much to contribute to inspiring us with a deep reverence for the mystery. Nearly all of his free time was spent before the Blessed Sacrament.[6]

Perhaps a word should be said about his views on Protestantism. In our age, we have come more and more to recognize the communalities of Christian churches and seek to bring these into the open as bridges between us. In Father Pete's day, it was not yet that way as the bitterness of the Reformation and its aftereffects were still burning. Yet his remarks are rather mild for the time. Especially worth noting is how the main complaint he makes is their lack of attention to the Incarnation and nature of God. This suggests that he did not see enough of the God of Love in their teachings and enough of detachment in their way of life. He also did not see the opposition to slavery that he found was inseparable from a Christian view of life.

In 1851, the city of Paramaribo was struck by a plague of yellow fever. Father Pete again became an angel of mercy, visiting the overflowing hospital two or three times a day as well as attending to many sufferers in their homes. He finally fell ill with the sickness as well. Matthew Bernhard, the sacristan writes, "I was the one who nursed him....He never murmured and bore all with unfailing patience."[7] To the great relief of all, after four weeks in bed, Father Pete had recovered enough to get up and slowly again took up his ministry.

We would not have a clear picture of the ministry of Father Pete in Paramaribo if we did not move on to the other great apostolate involved in it: ministering to the slaves on the plantations. Before we do so, however, let us record a special happiness that did come into his life in June 1847. Pete's "Father," Monsignor (now, Bishop) Grooff returned to the colony. In February of the previous year, all the Catholic clergy were expelled from the Dutch East Indies by the government. He was again named Vicar Apostolic for Surinam, where he again took up his apostolic work in Paramaribo, but spent a great deal of his time with the lepers in Batavia, his preferred home. The bishop continued to minister until he died of a stroke on April 29, 1852.

X

Plantations of the Spirit

We remember how the first quick tour of the Surinam mission under Monsignor Grooff introduced Father Pete to one of the plantations and how impressed he was with the faith of the slaves he met. Nor can we forget the strong condemnation from Father Pete's lips a few years later after he had spent much of his time caring for these suffering people. We can now take a few minutes to look at this work that formed part of the routine of his life for the whole period of his assignment to the capital city.

The majority of the plantations were within a few days journey of the three larger settlements (Paramaribo, Nickerie, and Coronie). At the time of Donders' arrival, there were some fifty thousand slaves on plantations in Surinam. Father Pete and the Monsignor cared for the plantations closest to Paramaribo on the Commewijne and Suriname rivers, both of which emptied into the sea at the capital city. Monsignor Grooff had begun with two plantations in the 1840s and his successor, Monsignor Schepers, had put new efforts into the work, such that by 1852 the visits included twelve plantations with some 1,145 Catholics on them.

While Schepers was the driver behind this growth, Father Pete was the workhorse. The chronicler of the mission wrote:

> Father Donders was the first priest who, on taking up his residence in Paramaribo, undertook the systematic visitation of the plantations on the Lower Suriname and on the Commewijne, and on a less regular basis of the Upper

Suriname and the Saramacca [River]. Other priests, indeed, visited individual plantations, but the fact remains that Father Donders was the first to take an energetic initiative in this important work and to ensure its stability.[1]

By the time the Redemptorists arrived in 1866 to take over the mission, the number of plantations being served stood at forty, with about three thousand Catholics. During the years prior to the order's arrival, outside of the occasional assistance of the Monsignor, Father Pete carried on this work. Father Heininck assisted him for six months and Father Meurkens for two years; that is all. Father Pete was the backbone of this enterprise. His simple and generous dealings with both slaves and masters gradually broke down many of the walls of suspicion or hatred between them and the Catholic Church.

In the last chapter, we read Father Pete's scathing analysis of the plantation system of slave labor. He was still serving in Surinam when the Dutch government outlawed slavery in 1863, but for the first twenty years of his stay in the colony, he had to deal with the situation. The first demand of this ministry was that of getting to the plantations by boat once or twice a month. The usual procedure was that immediately after the morning Mass in Paramaribo, Father Pete would board a tentboot, a large, four-oar boat with a low wooden cabin at the stern. In addition to the four seats for the rowers, there was a plank seat for the passengers while the captain steered from behind the cabin. The trip upriver could last one to several days, with landings on shore to pass the nights. A cabin boy attended to the travelers and there was also a cook on board. There was little to protect the passengers and crew from either sun or rain.

While the boat was well provisioned for Father Pete, he used to take very little and gave most of the food to the crew. He usually let the cabin boy sleep on his mattress while he slept on a plank. His cabin boy for some of these trips, Gisbert Rups, recalls that he sometimes had nightmares and would cry out, "Mamma, give me a drink of water." Father Pete would wake him with a cup of water to drink.[2]

Plantations of the Spirit

Most of the trip, Donders would spend in quiet prayer and meditation; he made few demands on his crewmates. They in turn held the man in special awe, at least for the most part. Later, we will see one incident that was "the exception that proves the rule."

When the boat landed at the plantation, Father Pete would speak to the owner or the overseer to ask for time to hold a religious service. At many plantations, he would be curtly refused because of prejudice. He would not immediately give up but argue that this was to the advantage of all on the plantation because it brought more cooperation and responsibility, or some similar argument that might appeal to the person. If this was to no avail, he would move on but would not neglect to try again on his next trip. Gradually he wore down resistance and the number of refusals grew less.

If he was given permission, he and his boat crew would immediately find a hut or barn to prepare for a chapel. Here he preached, instructed, gave the sacraments—whatever was needed. His pleasantness and gentleness, but above all, his evident holiness, endeared him to the slaves and gradually made their owners and overseers even glad to see him arrive at their dock.

A story is told of one overseer known only as Menalda, a rough fellow, who had no use for anyone—except Father Pete. Though not Catholic, Menalda always had a dinner for the priest when he came, invited the neighboring planter, and had a sizable credit line with the owner of his plantation for these soirees. Father Pete, however, would hardly eat anything. Finally, one night when Menalda was trying to get him to eat more for his strength, Father Pete said, "They [the slaves] don't eat meat or drink wine either, and yet they are pretty healthy." Menalda replied, "If you don't eat more, you will turn me into a thief!" "Why?" was the surprised Donders response. "Every time you come, Father, I get ten florins for the expenses and you hardly eat a quarter of a florin's worth! So you are turning me into a thief!" "Well," said Pete, "just give back the extra nine and three-quarters."[3]

The planter who recounted this story, tells us, "There was one man—and only one—for whom Menalda, and many others besides—including me—professed great esteem and affection, and that man was Father Donders."[4] The grace of God followed Father Pete wherever he went and gained him access to places no one else could reach.

The routine followed by Father Pete and the other missionaries usually meant that they spent about two days at each stop. There would be instructions on the first evening after the laborers returned from the fields. The next day the slaves were usually freed from all work. Thus, about seven thirty there would be Morning Prayer with a sermon, Mass, confessions, followed by another instruction. In the afternoon, baptisms and marriages were celebrated and further instructions given until evening when the missionary would prepare to leave.

We should not forget that Father Pete carried on this ministry for almost forty years, continuing it after being assigned to the leper colony and after becoming a Redemptorist. He is often referred to as "The Apostle to the Lepers," and compared to his contemporary, Father Peter Damian of Molokai. Such a title, while true, is only partial. Long before he took up that worthy apostolate he was an "Apostle to the Slaves," and when they were emancipated, he continued to serve them as an "Apostle to the Poor." He had to face the difficult task of working with these Blacks as they were freed from sheer dependence on their owners to a new life for which they had no preparation and few skills. The vast majority could neither read nor write, had no education, and were only trained in the most basic types of heavy labor or service work.

In order to gain a sense of how delicately Donders dealt with those whom he served, we can jump forward to a letter he wrote in 1871 when he was already a Redemptorist and had moved on to his work among the lepers that we shall speak of in the next chapter. In this letter, Father Pete describes for his provincial superior, Father Johan Schaap, what he has learned from his years of experience in this ministry.

This letter is found in Part II, Chapter Four, #11, page 143.

XI

AT HOME IN BATAVIA

The first time Father Pete saw the lepers confined to the Batavia leprosarium a few weeks after arriving in Surinam, he longed to be able to give himself to their care. But the Prefect Apostolic assigned him to work in the capital and among the plantations for the first thirteen years of his ministry in the colony. So Father Pete quietly awaited God's will. There had been a history of difficulties with the assignment of personnel among the lepers. Outside of old Bishop Grooff who had gone there until his death, the other priests had run into opposition (one was even poisoned by a man whose public sins he had condemned). Toward the end of 1855, Monsignor Schepers asked his small band of priests if any would volunteer for the work. The words were hardly out of his mouth, when Father Pete jumped up to offer his services.

If one tried to find Batavia today, all that would be encountered are a few old grave stones and some foundations of the leprosarium buildings. A boarding school and small chapel were built after the leper colony had long been abandoned at this site where the Coppename and Saramacca rivers meet shortly before emptying into the sea some fifty miles west of Paramaribo. The site was established in 1824 when a leper colony begun thirty years earlier was judged to be too close to a developing town and was moved to the site. It continued until 1897 when the Redemptorists opened a foundation for lepers in Paramaribo and the Moravian Brethren and state government did the same in Great Chatillon. Until these foundations were established, the lepers got little care from the secular nurses; the first doctor only came in 1850. Bishop Grooff had constructed a small church and respectable cemetery, and he and his successor chaplains, especially Father Pete, worked to provide more decent housing.

It is unfortunate that none of Father Pete's correspondence during his first stay (1856–1866) at Batavia has come down to us. We have many short ones from his second period there (1869–1882); however, he had a confrere to assist him during this period so much of Donders' correspondence concerns his new venture to reach the Amerindians in the jungle rather than his work among the lepers. Thus, most of our information must come from his confreres and others who helped him.

Father Van Coll, C.Ss.R., wrote,

> Batavia, where Father Donders usually resided for twenty-five or thirty years, has no charm to boast of outside of its location which is indeed beautiful. A visitor enters into a cloud of suffering. The majority of those who have been sent here are of the lower classes; among them are Catholics and non-Catholics, Blacks, Chinese, Hindus. All, every single one of them, is stricken with the same dread disease. The very sight of it makes you shudder. Its repulsive odor makes you sick. Its contagiousness, while not so great as it once was, terrifies you. Your ears are full of the groans of those poor wretches who see their members being eaten away little by little by this pitiless scourge....[1]

Father Pete would spend his time visiting every last one in this ever-changing community where new patients and the death of others kept the population at about three hundred during his years there. No sooner would a boat arrive with a new group of sufferers, and Father Pete was at the shore to meet them. His openness and the absence of any holding back in the face of their dangerous condition quickly won their trust. Few were the exceptions whose hearts he could not win.

The pattern of his day was not much different from the one he tried to follow since his arrival on the mission. He was at his prayers in the chapel by six o'clock. Mass was celebrated at 6:30 AM and then he would continue his prayer until around eight o'clock when he had a little breakfast. After this, he began his rounds of visits to the sick in their huts. At noon, he had lunch and then spent the heat of the afternoon taking a nap, working in his little garden, cleaning the cemetery, and, of course, in prayer. When the day had cooled a little, he held prayers in the chapel at 7:00 PM, which included rosary, instruction, night prayers—all of these interspersed with hymns. Three times a week, there was the procession to the little shrine to Our Lady at the river's edge as we mentioned earlier (see pp. 109–110). Then he spent a long time in personal prayer, in the chapel or in another favorite spot, before the large cross in the cemetery.

We should not think that his rounds of the sick were simply to offer words of consolation. He always tried to bring any alms he could, even if it meant cutting into his own personal supplies. Food, clothes, money—all went to help. He often upset his cook by sending his supper to some sufferer and taking just some bread and drink for himself. Once, when the bishop came for a visit, Father Pete told his cook, Cornelia, to put together a suitable meal. Then the bishop accepted an invitation to eat with the colony's doctor; Pete was happy to take all this specially prepared fare to some of the lepers. Someone was heard to remark that Father Donders only fault was that he was too generous!

Father Pete would hound the government for aid. Though his constant petitions, he was able to have wooden floors put in the leper's huts, better beds obtained, and a form of laundry set up for those who could not do their own. One of his great concerns was to provide education for the children of lepers for whom there was nothing in the colony that offered them any way of being able to leave it and live on their own. We can see his early thoughts on this from a letter he wrote to one of his fellow priests a few years before Donders took over his ministry in Batavia.

This letter is found in Part II, Chapter Three, #7, page 133.

From the testimony from lepers he had cared for we know that he would fetch water, chop wood, sweep out and clean huts, change bedding, dress wounds, remove burrowing fleas from their feet. Many times others would warn him against all this close contact for fear of his being infected. "Don't worry; there is nothing to fear" was his usual reply. If it was God's will—we can be sure this was his meaning—then so be it; it is still nothing to fear. In fact, despite this close contact with infected patients for twenty-six years, he never contracted the disease.

Still, Father Pete was not a cold stoic. One of his lepers tells us that one day he was to have a gangrenous finger amputated. Father Pete, unable to watch, had to leave the room, but returned as soon as the operation was over to comfort him. Yet he could be fearless. It was not unusual for him to have to break up fights, especially if some rum was smuggled into the settlement; and in doing so, he occasionally took a few misdirected punches.

Perhaps Father Pete's most difficult task, but the basic one that he had come to fulfill, was to bring some peace and hope to these tormented and helpless lepers. One of his first biographers says:

> Since the lepers had lost all hope of being cured and since their bodies were doomed, Father Donders reminded them of this truth of Faith, that the patient bearing of their pains would cure their souls and save them from eternal death. It was not long before discontent gave way to submission to the divine Will; murmuring ceased, and their poor disfigured faces reflected the joy and serenity of their souls.[2]

While this description of the situation may be a little over-zealous, Father Van Coll could simply say, "A great many learned from Father Donders how to lead a holy life and die a holy death."[3] Father Pete instilled great reverence for the dead in their burial and care of their graves; he insisted that all attend the funeral rites and thus helped these dying sufferers to sense the sanctity and honor of everyone, especially themselves, even though society had no use for them.

Beside the inherent self-mortification in the ministry itself, Father Pete practiced his own freely chosen acts of self-denial. He generally slept on the floor and limited his sleep to what was necessary, spending much of the night in prayer. One of his assistants, Andrew Gerling, tells us that he usually limited his meals to the native fruit and vegetables along with bread. If any meat was given to him, he usually distributed it to his helpers or to the sick. He only drank wine or beer when he had a visitor; and then, he just sipped a little.

As we said, he was the cross of his cook, Cornelia. Father Kuyper wryly remarks, "She ruled the roost in the presbytery and, unless I am mistaken, she must have afforded the servant of God many a chance to practice virtue. She told me herself that he was most abstemious in food and drink and never insisted on any preferences."[4] Another friend, Amarantha Tijdig says, "Cornelia told me that some days she had no cooking to do, as these were days on which he fasted. In any case, he ate little. Sometimes, when eating his soup, he would say, 'This is too salty,' and tell her to take it to the sick, or he would say that the meat is too tough and send it the same way. Cornelia knew what he was up to, 'He didn't fool me. My soup wasn't salty and my meat sure wasn't tough!'"[5]

Father Pete's sense of the dignity of the slave, the leper, the downtrodden is at the heart of all of these actions and attitudes. We should attend to the oft-repeated phrase of his, "Jesus shed his precious blood for them just as much as for us," to understand his sense of the equality of all created in the image of God. Someone once chided him that he did not assert his dignity enough. For example, they said, he should not take off his hat and bow to a leper as he did when he entered their hut or room. His reply was, "Is it all right if I do it on account of the person's guardian angel?"[6]

Bishop Schepers had found all his hopes for the leper colony fulfilled in the ten years that Father Pete served there. The whole atmosphere of the establishment changed for the better. Even the Moravian Brothers who knew him held him in high regard. One of these who visited Batavia often made a point of seeking out

Father Pete to visit with him. He always left remarking, "He's surely a holy man."[7]

Meanwhile, in Paramaribo, significant events were unfolding that would radically affect Father Pete. On November 27, 1863, Bishop Schepers died, after a long, fruitful period of leadership in the colony. He was succeeded by Father Meurkens as pro-vicar apostolic. This new head of the mission quickly realized that the work would never be able to continue with any success unless it could be guaranteed a steady injection of personnel. The many requests for volunteers among the secular priests of Holland had provided only four priests after Donders; at the death of the bishop, a total of only six priests remained. Thus, Father Meurkens began to recommend to the Holy See that it seek some religious order to take over the staffing of the mission. Father Pete's work in Batavia would soon be interrupted.

XII

THE LATE VOCATION

Teresa of Calcutta used to say that founding the Missionaries of Charity was her second vocation or her "vocation within a vocation." After many years as a Sister of Loreto, she discovered that God was calling her further into the religious state and to a special ministry to the dying. Something similar is true of Father Pete. We recall how he was refused acceptance into three religious orders when he was a seminarian, and how he said he felt no particular call to such a life but was only following his rector's recommendation.

Now some thirty years later, he finds himself at the same point of asking admission to one of the orders that refused him, the Redemptorists. He was discovering his second vocation or his "vocation within a vocation." How did this happen?

When Bishop Schepers, the Vicar Apostolic of Surinam, died on November 27, 1863, he was succeeded by Father Meurkens, who had served on this mission for several years, as pro-vicar until a permanent appointment could be made. The work had grown immensely due to the freeing of the slaves that year, as well as the beginnings of the forays into the jungles to the nomadic natives. Yet the number of missionaries had remained stagnant. After several months in his new post, Father Meurkens made a trip back to Holland and ultimately to Rome to recommend that the vicariate be transferred to the care of some religious order so that it might be stabilized and guaranteed a future. After several months of negotiations, the Vatican's Congregation for the Propagation of the Faith arranged for the assignment of the mission in Surinam to the Redemptorists. On August 31, 1865, the decree of transfer was published designating the Provincial Superior of the Dutch Province, Father Johan Swinkels, C.Ss.R., as the new vicar apostolic and named him a bishop; he was also assigned to be the religious superior of the Redemptorists who were to go there. He was ordained bishop in Holland on September 12, 1865, and on October 15 set sail for his new post along with three other Redemptorists, Father John Baptist van der Aa, Father John van Rooij, and Brother Lambert Swinkels,[1] his blood brother. After five months at sea, they arrived in Paramaribo on March 26, 1866.

With the arrival of the Redemptorists, Father Meurkens decided not to return to the mission. Two of the other secular priests who were there, Fathers Arnold Swinkels[2] and P. Masker, also decided to use this opportunity to go back to their homeland. They left on the second of July 2. The remaining three—Fathers Kempkes, Romme, and Donders—agreed to stay as secular priests working with the new religious priests and brother. Brother Lambert died August 6, 1866, five months after arriving in Surinam. Father Kempkes returned to Holland in 1869.

At first, Father Pete was content to stay on as he was. A few years before, however, he had happened upon a book that contained the story of the founder of the Redemptorists, Saint Alphonsus Liguori. This biography deeply impressed him because of the saint's total dedication to the will of God and to the care of the most neglected people of his area of southern Italy. The parallels to his own life and desires did not escape Father Pete. After much prayer, he decided that he would ask to become a Redemptorist. This must not have been an easy decision since the memories of his earlier refusal must have made him feel many misgivings. Still, he discerned it was God's will; if he was wrong, he would soon find out.

Therefore, about a month after Bishop Swinkels' arrival, he found Father Pete on his doorstep, not just to pay his respects and welcome the new vicar apostolic (Father Pete had been in Batavia when the bishop arrived), but to ask to be admitted to the Congregation. Monsignor Swinkels was taken aback and suggested that Father Pete give it more thought and spend a few weeks with him and his community in Paramaribo to see how he would feel as a religious. Father Pete found himself so much at ease in this new setting and the bishop was so overjoyed at the type of person he found in Father Pete that at the end of the two weeks the bishop agreed to admit him as a postulant.

Father Romme, who had been in Surinam for about four years, heard of Donders' decision. The news made him begin to think the matter over and he discovered stirrings of a desire to follow his friend's example. So, before long, the bishop found another postulant at his door. Years later, Father Romme wrote,

> I always thankfully recall how, after God, it was in great measure to Father Donders' example that I owe my vocation. It was four or five months after Bishop Swinkels' arrival that I heard Father Donders had been accepted and that I thought seriously of applying as well. Up to that time, as far as I can remember, the idea never crossed my mind.[3]

Father Pete could not leave Batavia to begin his novitiate until a replacement was sent and trained. Likewise, Father Romme had to finish his visits to the plantations. Father Pete was formally received as a postulant on July 24, but then returned to Batavia after a few days to await Father van der Aa as his replacement. (One can try to imagine poor Father van der Aa, arriving in a tropical country, not knowing Pidgin English, suffering a bout of dysentery, and then being assigned to a leper colony—all in the space of seven months! It is no wonder the man died within six years, in 1872; he did, however, outlive his confrere Rooij by one year. Father Pete was not the only saint in Surinam!) Finally, on November 1, 1866, the "Reverend Brothers" Donders and Romme began their year of novitiate.

Well, not quite a year. Church law is rather strict about novices spending a full year in prayer, study, and instruction before taking their religious vows. The situation of the mission was such, however, that there was no choice but to have the two men assist in the ministry in Paramaribo during their novitiate. After several months, the bishop realized that he had two tried-and-proven missionaries, and even uncanonized saints, on his hands and so he petitioned the superior general of the Redemptorists to allow them to be professed after only eight months. Thus, on June 24, 1867, the feast of Saint John the Baptist, the two elder Apostolic Missionaries professed their religious vows and became two young Redemptorists.

In his 1867 report to the Provincial of Holland, Father Konings, Bishop Swinkels describes Father Pete:

> Peter Donders was sent to the Batavian mission in 1856 and has never ceased being a source of edification by his utter self-sacrifice in the service of the lepers. Here he is looked upon as a saint. Prayer, mortification, and almsgiving are his joy. The poorest, most depraved, and most revolting sinners are his favorites. He is as docile as a child and blindly obedient. The only outward evidence of fallen nature I have ever detected in him is a flush that mounts to his cheek whenever I criticize him in public. He is by nature very vivacious—though virtue has made him imperturbable—and to be with him is a delight. I only wish he were several years younger. He exercises a marked influence over all classes—Jews and Protestants, rich and poor, even over the governor and highest functionaries. His health is excellent and it is not easy to tire him.[4]

The bishop gives a similar glowing account of Father Romme, but ends it saying, "He is much given to prayer and is no less given to mortification; and yet Brother Donders excels him in both."[5]

This brief account of the bishop is one of the best portraits of our Father Pete. Mortified but pleasant, prayerful but lively, active but contemplative, powerful but simple. The descriptions of him at this age tell us he was short and a little stooped. His auburn hair, always worn short, was now gray. He had clear and penetrating gray eyes, but had lost all his teeth and so his lips had fallen inward slightly. He was soft spoken but charming. Despite his frail infancy, he had remarkable health and endurance in later life. His friend Amarantha Tijdig mentioned that "whenever he got a slight attack of fever [malaria?], he would simply say, 'This fever came on its own, and it will leave the same way,' so he took no medicines."[6] The bishop once called Father Pete's health "indestructible."

Prayer and good works walked hand in hand for him. We can jump ahead to an example in a letter Donders wrote to his missionary confrere, Father van Coll in 1880.

This letter is found in Part II, Chapter Seven, #30, page 181.

Father Pete's temper, the weakness he had to continually confront before God's eyes, was never far away. Yet he was known as the gentlest of souls. After all, the anger was only the reverse of the unswerving constancy he had been given by God as well. He also never lost the mischievous twinkle in his eye that made him an enjoyable companion. He was happy to be in a community and enjoyed the give and take of jokes and banter, even if he was teased himself. He always became part of the crowd. As one confrere remarked, "How nice it is to see Father Donders lighting up his pipe at recreation and puffing away at it."[7]

The day of Donders' and Romme's profession, June 24, 1867, thus proved to be an outstanding day of blessings. For the Redemptorists it meant the admission of two men outstanding in holiness, one of whom the Church would one day formally recognize as "Blessed." For these two newly professed men, it brought an unexpected blessing in entering a company of missionaries to be their support and friends. Father Pete wrote his own reactions to his friend, Father van Someren, a few days after his profession. The same sentiments appear in almost every other letter Father Pete writes from this day on; as we can see in his next three letters.

These letters are found in Part II, Chapter Three, #8, #9, and Chapter Four, #10, pages 135–142.

Within two months of his profession, Father Pete is back on the river to Batavia. Again, he is on his way to his beloved lepers and Amerindians, but now with a whole new joy and outlook. He was not alone; he was a Redemptorist.

XIII

BACK IN BATAVIA

Father Pete's first assignment as a Redemptorist was to return to Batavia as he had hoped. He went there two months after his profession of vows and arrived on August 13, 1867. He will remain there for the next fourteen years with different confreres. Father van Aa who had substituted for him was replaced by Father Verbeek.[1] We can thank him for a few brief descriptions of the life of the two Redemptorists there:

> We are living over the church in fairly large apartments, but infested with vermin and rats, which we have no hope of getting rid up. We have a population of about 160 to 170 people—adults and children—among whom there are one hundred lepers, including some very advanced cases. A number of them lead the most scandalous lives.
>
> ...We rise punctually at five. Before I was professed, I found it dreadfully hard to get up so early. In Batavia, I must admit—and I thank God for it—that it does not cost me anything. Whenever I do not happen to hear the bell, the next moment [Father Donders] is standing by me waking me or I hear him coming. He is punctual in everything. I hear that during the night—perhaps every night for that matter—he goes to pay a visit to Jesus in the Blessed Sacrament.
>
> As soon as we are dressed, we go down to the church to visit Jesus. At 5:30 we go upstairs again for meditation.

At 6:30 and 7:00 we celebrate our two Masses, during which the people recite the rosary aloud followed by other prayers. At nine, Father Donders gives the instruction to the handful of children we have here, as the older ones are sent into town by order of the government through fear of infection. He then begins visiting the sick. This task falls on me every time Father Donders is away visiting the plantations or the Amerindians—which means ten or twelve days a month, sometimes even more.

After noon Angelus comes the Particular Examen, followed by dinner. At 1:30, we take siesta; at two, Vespers, visit to the Blessed Sacrament and the Blessed Virgin, followed by the Way of the Cross. At three, there is spiritual reading and meditation with Matins at four. At 6:30 we pray privately until the people in church have finished their night prayers. We then recite the rosary with them. Next comes the instruction for the adults, followed by one or more hymns in Pidgin English. Singing is their very life. Father Donders says, "If singing could get them into heaven, not one of them would be left outside."[2]

One can see in this account an image of the well-ordered life of a religious community in the service of a well-established and well-run parish. There must have been frequent, if not daily, departures from this schedule for emergencies, feast days, special events or needs, and so on. But it provided a healthy routine as the background for daily life.

While much of this schedule was what Father Pete knew as a secular priest for years, it is now shared with other persons as supports and companions. There would soon be Redemptorist Brothers stationed with the two priests who could share in the domestic and ministerial life of the community. They did manual chores, taught catechism, and gradually began to teach reading and writing. The liturgical prayer of the Church, recited privately when alone, now becomes truly a communal event. It was this companionship and shared public faith that Father Pete so appreciated and enjoyed as a new religious.

But with the joys of community came the limitations. Where, as a secular priest, Father Pete could make his own decisions about his life and work, now they had to be shared with another. One confrere was always named as "superior" of the community; that is, he was the one to oversee the group's life, order, and finances. It was usually not Father Pete who was the superior of the group, and so the seasoned missionary had to submit to the decisions of his less experienced younger confrere. A simple example was Father Pete's garden that he continued to cultivate in the afternoons as his relaxation and exercise. Before, the people could help themselves to whatever they wanted of its produce. But with the coming of a community, whenever he found someone following the old habit, he had to stop them and say, "Wait. We can't do that any more. I have to ask the other Father's permission."[3]

His confrere, Father Romme, was named the superior in 1870 and remarks, "Though he was my senior by twenty years and had twenty-five years more experience of life in the colony than I, yet he always obeyed me with the greatest promptness and as simply as a child....He never paid the slightest heed to his dislikes."[4] This sense of obedience is easily seen in a short note he wrote to Monsignor Schaap, the superior of the mission, in 1875.

This letter is found in Part II, Chapter Four, #18, page 165.

This should not be taken as if he gave up all responsibility for his actions or simply "did what he was told." For example, once the vicar apostolic told him not to visit one of the Amerindian encampments on his trek. On returning, Father Pete told him, "Since I did not have your leave, I did not go near the Amerindians; nevertheless, I should just like to mention the matter so that you would be so kind as to think the matter over again."[5] A very polite way of showing his disagreement with the vicar, and a very proper way of exercising the obedience of religious life.

Since Father Pete always lived a life of poverty, the only difference was that he no longer asked the bishop for funds or alms, but his religious superior. He had long lived a life of chaste celibacy, so there was no change here. He was not a man without temptations against this chastity. He admitted having temptations, especially of thought, occurring most frequently while reciting the prayers of his Office. He was modest in his actions. The girls noticed that he never eyed them "like other men." While he made efforts to change the Amerindians' nudity, which especially troubled other Europeans, Father Pete got to the point of being able to simply ignore most of it.

Two other characteristics of religious life were also part and parcel of his day-to-day living: prayer and self-denial. As we have said, his prayer was rooted in conventional prayers: rosary, office, verbal prayers. As one author says, Father Donders' prayer was typically Dutch: in nothing extraordinary, but extraordinary in its ordinariness. We hear of no visions, levitations, miracles. Only rarely did anyone ever notice what may have been periods of ecstasy. His confreres, for example, found him one day kneeling at the communion rail, motionless, with head bowed. They called to him and shook him, but he did not respond until at last, on his own, he gave a deep sigh and raised his head. On two occasions, two different Good Fridays, during the procession of the cross, his usually pale face shone brightly and he stopped and stood absolutely motionless for almost fifteen minutes staring at the crucifix.

Yet he told his religious superior one day,

> If you ask me whether I am dry or fervent in prayer, I answer that from time to time I am fervent, but that dryness is my usual state. The best I can do, then, is humble myself before God at my inability even to think a good thought without his grace; or, following Your Reverence's advice, I go through the Stations of the Cross mentally. This is what I generally do during the evening meditation.[6]

As to his mortification, beyond accepting patiently all the trails, the climate, the roughness and lack of necessities of mission life, he kept a constant check on his desires, especially in sleep and food. He always spent a portion of his night in prayer, usually before the Eucharist, or in his favorite spot, the cross in the cemetery. He practiced the usual mortifications of a religious order: special days of fast or abstinence, silent times, and so on. He was careful in his eating. While he had a hearty appetite and ate sufficient food to keep his health, he had practices such as limiting his breakfast to a cup of coffee three times a week. He also avoided wine or beer except when hosting guests. He would finish off leftovers rather than eat fresh food. He ate what was put before him. His famous cook, Cordelia, was queried about how she got along with Father Donders. "Not good at all! He doesn't take the slightest notice of what I cook for him; everything is always 'good, too good in fact.'"[7] He limited his pipe smoking to the after-meal relaxation period with his confreres.

And so life went on in the leprosarium at Batavia for the decade and a half that he spent there as a Redemptorist. "All I could do there was pray and visit the sick," he once told a confrere. Still we know how the intertwining of these two actions not only advanced his sanctity but brought the power of God's grace to the most abandoned of souls. What is surprising in his correspondence from the time he returned to Batavia is how little he speaks about this ministry to the lepers; his letters are taken up with the other half of his life, his missionary journeys to the Amerindians. Why this silence? We can only guess. Had he grown so used to it that he did not notice it? That was his response when someone questioned him on how he could work so closely with these sufferers. Was it because he was tired of repeating it? Is it because, now that he could rely on others to care for these people, his attention was focused on those to whom no one would minister, the Amerindians? We don't know. He remained silent.

We have to rely on the information of others about the painfulness of this work among the lepers. We do not intend to recount extensively the sufferings of these poor people that the missionaries had to share, since we are all aware of the results of this disease in past ages. Still, we cannot ignore this basic element of Father Pete's life. We will just quote from Bishop Grooff when he returned to Surinam after he was exiled from the Dutch East Indies:

> I must admit that the first time I was called upon to exercise my ministry soon after my return to Surinam, I could not help shuddering. I saw before me a leper whose right leg was entirely eaten away. The poor fellow, who was in his agony, lived in a wretched hut open to rain and sun alike. The only comfort the dying man had was a wooden log left smoldering to drive off the mosquitoes and a little river water to quench his thirst. Two birds were pecking at his running sores. He was lying on the floor, the pallor of death on his face, banana leaves his only bed, a log his pillow, and nothing but an old strip of sail-cloth for a covering. A sickening odor came from that body which was one huge sore and which showed hardly one sound spot I could anoint....As I have had to discharge the same duty again, twice and even three times a week, I have succeeded in getting used to it, thank God, without suffering any ill effects. Thus I am as happy as can be to be able to devote myself to such glorious work.[8]

We recall that Father Pete did much to better the living conditions of these lepers when he arrived, still, this scene was frequently replayed for him as he ministered in both body and soul to these sufferers.

One of the constant tasks of the missionaries was dealing with the superstitions in which these people had grown up. For this reason, Father Pete insisted on the use of sacramentals, concrete objects to aid devotion and to take the place of the charms and talismans of the witch doctors. He recommended the scapular and rosary, but especially the use of holy water. "There should be holy water in every hut," was his motto. Father Pete tells Father Schaap, the Redemptorist superior, of the great day of the dedication of the colony to the Sacred Heart of Jesus.

This letter is found in Part II, Chapter Four, #20, page 168.

We should not think that Father Pete created a sinless congregation with all his labors. He had to face the sadness of regression as often as anyone. The New Year's Eve of 1874 was especially memorable. Liquor had been brought into the encampment and a wild party erupted. It lasted well past midnight. The missionaries thought they could get it to wind down by going out to express their disapproval. Quite the opposite happened; the crowd was too far gone and so booed and jeered the religious back to their rectory. The party went on until sunrise. The result was that Father Pete organized a parish mission for the Jubilee Year of 1875 that the missionaries used to reintroduce the virtues of a holy life into the colony.

One of the great concerns that Father Pete had for the lepers was the care of the children of lepers who had not contracted the disease. Around 1873, the governor of Surinam began a process to take these children from their parents and send them to Paramaribo in order to prevent them from contracting the disease. While the concern was noble, the problem was the break up of families and the assignment of the youngsters to orphanages. When the officials started to exercise the law, they began forcibly removing the children. This initiated a near riot in the leper colony. Parents began hiding their children in the forests. The officials got nowhere, so they returned to Paramaribo to bring the district commissioner himself back with them. While a few children were found, even the commissioner got practically nowhere. So he turned to Father Pete. He realized that this was best for the children. So he sent the officials back to their boat. Then he gathered all the parents and began to speak with them about the well-being of their children, the hope for their future, and the preservation of their own families. Eventually he was able to convince the entire encampment of the expediency of this effort and convinced all parents but one whose sad tale you can read in Father Pete's letter to the bishop.

This letter is found in Part II, Chapter Four, #16, page 160.

Such was one of the heart wrenching tasks Father Pete had to face in this sad world of the lepers. His continuous worry about the children is mirrored in other letters of the time.

See his letters found in Part II, Chapter Four, #21 and #23, pages 169 and 172.

As we have mentioned, now that there was more personnel to care for the residents at Batavia, Father Pete continued and intensified his work among the Amerindian tribes of the forest.

We should realize that Father Pete considered this his ultimate apostolate. He began with those closest to Paramaribo and the plantations, the Arowaks and Warros. Next were the Caribs who lived further up river and were most resistant to his efforts. Later he will extend his reach to those who had least been touched by the knowledge of Christ, the dispersed Blacks, the ex-slaves who had escaped into the furthest recesses of the jungle and who were called the Maroons. This work ultimately required him to navigate five major rivers in Surinam along with their tributaries: the Saramacca, the Coppename, the Tibiti, the Waijombo, and the Maratakka. This probably meant over three hundred miles of shoreline that he visited one or more times a year.

Since his letters during his second stay at Batavia are filled with information on these voyages to evangelize the Amerindians, we have only to turn the narrative over to Father Pete himself.

These letters are found in Part II, Chapter Four, #12, #13, #14, #15, and #17, pages 147–159 and 163.

XIV

BACK TO THE JUNGLES

As we have said, what concerned Father Pete most during this second stay at the leper colony was the care of the native peoples who lived in the tropical forests of Surinam. As we continue to read his letters from this time, we learn more about the very practical issues of the life of any missionary. For example, there was the concern about maintaining the Faith of the newly baptized, something that required some type of on-the-spot continuous attention. The solution would be native catechists, as he told his provincial.

These letters are found in Part II, Chapter Four, #19 and #22, pages 166 and 170.

To give a fuller picture of the surroundings and experiences of Father Pete, we will intersperse these writings of his with a few accounts from people who traveled with him. They mention points that Father Pete, in his humility, would not have considered including in his own letters.

One telling account comes from a letter of a Franciscan Sister, Mary Antonia, to her own relative in Holland, in which she mentions (with perhaps a few too many flourishes) Father Pete's account of the first time he was able to offer Mass at one of the Amerindian settlements:

> Ever since a little native boy had recovered from a mortal illness after he received baptism from Father Donders,

these poor Amerindians brought their children spontaneously to him to be baptized....He promised to return soon and offer Mass for them, which he did shortly after. Splendid and colossal was the temple in which the spotless Lamb was first offered in this country. Giant and venerable forest trees seem to pillar the blue vault of the tropics, while the sunlight, streaming through their foliage broke into countless twinkling stars. Myriad winged musicians, in plumage gay, executed their morning orchestra with more than their wonted sweetness. The Father told us it was impossible to describe his feelings at the solemn moment when, for the first time since the institution of the Eucharist, the Holy Sacrifice was offered in that mighty solitude, in the presence of these human beings who, though purchased by the Precious Blood, knew nothing of him who is their creator and redeemer. And how have we merited knowing him and receiving the Faith from his bounty?...From that day forward, in spite of the hardships of the journey, he continued visiting his children regularly.[1]

In a letter to his superior, Father Pete tells us of the constant swing from success to failure and back again, but always with that sense of trust in God that left no doubt about the divine care present in both cases.

This letter is found in Part II, Chapter Four, #24, page 174.

These journeys up the rivers were not pleasure jaunts. The major rivers of Surinam are not streams; some measure miles across at some points. There was also open sea to traverse at times to reach the mouth of one of these. Of course there were boating incidents. One boat sprang a leak and almost sank under him and his crew. Once the boat grounded in a swampy area. The crew said they could go no further. Donders told them there were people on the other side. "Were there but a single person there, I must go." So he took off his shoes and stockings, fastened them to a stick and crossed the swamp with the stick over his shoulder.

Another time the crew was getting anxious to return home after a long trip and tried to convince him that the country further up the river was uninhabited. As he was deciding, he noticed some banana skins floating down the stream. "Look at those! Isn't that a sign that there are some people further on?" On the way they went with no further discussion.

Sometimes, a trek away from the boat meant a night spent sleeping in a hammock between two trees in the forest. When he mentioned this once to one of the sisters, she asked him if he were not afraid of all the wild animals. He laughed and said, "Not at all; they know very well that I would not make a good meal. I'm too thin and tough!"

This perseverance finally began to show more clearly the power of his faith though which the power of God could pass. Later letters show us some of these results, as we see in this report to his provincial superior.

This letter is found in Part II, Chapter Four, #25, page 175.

Unmentioned in any of his letters are some of the powerful experiences others felt in his presence or due to his prayers. For example, we have the account given by Anthony Felixdaal, his boatman, that on one occasion:

> We were returning from the Wayombo by the Coppename. It was nine o'clock at night, and we were in the great bend above Batavia. There was still a breeze blowing and the waves looked threatening. Though we were pulling for all we were worth, we were taking in so much water that we thought we should sink. The captain cried, "Father, come out; we're sinking!" Father Pete came out of the cabin and replied, "Not at all, Joseph, we're not going to be lost. God will protect us."

> He thereupon began to pray and to bail out the water with a bowl. Suddenly, he raised his hands to heaven and cried out something in a loud voice. I did not understand him; I guess it was something in Latin. At once, the water subsided. "Father," Joseph said, "God has heard you; otherwise, we were goners for sure." Father replied, "God hears everyone who prays with faith." He expressly forbade us to say anything about what happened, since he did want human praise. To God alone be all honor and glory.[2]

Donders was not at all happy that some people felt he could do extraordinary, perhaps even miraculous, things at times. He once said that in his opinion miracles would be counterproductive in Surinam. The natives would be too prone to see them as magic and to make their doer the object of some form of pagan devotion. Still, there are times when it seems that God may not have been of the same opinion. In his later years, there are stories told by eyewitnesses that suggest God allowed him to be the instrument of some extraordinary signs of divine presence.

His boatman, Anthony Felixdaal, also tells that

> One August there was a very prolonged drought. The water had receded as far as the Maratakka, and the people were obliged to fetch fresh water from the Upper Maratakka; that meant a week's journey each time. One evening Father arrived and the next morning as he was preparing for Mass, some of the Amerindians came up and told him of their great plight. "What can I do? It is God who has willed it. So let us pray." After the Mass, they spent some time in prayer. Then he said, "Now, get everything ready to collect water. God has heard us and will send rain." In a short time, it began to rain in torrents from eleven in the morning until seven in the evening.[3]

Still, despite his extraordinary work and prayer, there was one thing that Father Pete ultimately could not overcome: his body. He was now entering into his seventies. One of his biographers remarks about one of his trips in the later years:

> He said, "The distance is too great and walking through forest and swamp over hundreds of fallen trees is too painful. Besides, carrying a Mass-kit is out of the question." But he soon went back on these words and was already planning a new expedition. However, as he was getting ready to go alone—his first boatman refused to accompany him—the bishop forbade him and sent another priest in his place by another route.[4]

One of Father Pete's confreres wrote down that he had been speaking with one of the Amerindians about him and the man gave this opinion of Donders, one shared by his people:

> Father Donders was the first to go in search of the Amerindians. He sought them out, he followed after them. He was sometimes stuck chest-deep when going through the swamps. Father Donders loved the Amerindians.[5]

Still, this work was done intermittently while he continued to work among the lepers.

See the letters found in Part II, Chapter Four, #26 to #30, pages 177–183.

XV

THE FINAL FRONTIER: THE MAROONS

There was one final summit for Father Pete to reach, evangelizing the Maroons in the upper reaches of the rivers. These were the escaped slaves and their descendants who over the years had run away from the plantations and formed bands in the most inaccessible parts of the upcountry. Because of their unfortunate background they had become exceedingly fierce and vengeful. The different clans engaged in bloody feuds. Superstition and their ancestral religious practices were common among them. They were also, obviously, very leary of any Europeans who ventured into their lands.

As far as we can tell, Father Pete made his first contacts with them around 1869 when he reached two camps on the Saramacca and Auca rivers. One lesson he immediately learned was tact. On his first visit, he threw down a religious object offered him. This infuriated the people and it took all his gentleness to ward off serious injury. From that point on, while he preached against the continuance of these practices, he was careful not to show disrespect to the symbols until such time as the Blacks themselves realized they no longer had power over them. Then he would gather the objects and take them away to put them in storage until such time as they could safely be destroyed.

Over the years, Father Pete tried to visit them as often as he could. This was, however, very infrequently because of the great distances and the lack of easy access to them. Most could not be reached by the tent-boat on the large rivers. He was required to go by canoe up smaller tributaries to reach them. He was almost drowned one day when his canoe capsized. Fortunately, there were some men on the shore who jumped into the river to rescue him. When they got him to shore and tried to get him to rest, he joked, "Don't worry. I'll dry out."

At first, he was awed by the distance between the Maroons understanding of life and the Christian view. When he offered Mass for the first time with a group of them, and turned to say "Dominus vobiscum" ("Peace be with you"), he could not be sure what answer he would get. Sometimes, he heard "And good morning to you, Father." Or one might come up to the altar and light his pipe from the candle there, as one old fellow did.

While these differences were more amusing than dangerous and were eventually overcome by Father Pete's patience and good will, the anger below the surface of many of these people was a different matter. There were many times when this anger surfaced in drunken moments or at some unsuspecting action by the priest and it became life-threatening. One day, for example, he was off alone praying in a quiet clearing when a newly escaped slave came upon him and tried to kill him. Father Pete begged him to wait so that he could finish his prayers. He then talked the man into letting him go. His boatman later told everyone he could see the marks around the priest's throat on his return to the boat.

Bishop Schaap mentions that Father Pete spent almost all of his annual allowance of twelve hundred florins to pay his boatmen to take him on these extraordinary long trips to the upper reaches of the rivers.

Father Pete was disappointed in how little he was able to accomplish with these unfortunate people. Toward the end of this stay in Batavia, he began to think that the situation was changing for the better when a small group of the Blacks asked him to begin to visit them more and help build a chapel. Unfortunately, this plan never worked out. Four years later, another small group moved nearer to Batavia because of dangers in the settlement. Father Pete immediately began to visit them. He hoped this was a sign that others would follow this lead; something that did not prove to be the case, at least during his lifetime.

This work slowed down in late 1879 when he was again the only priest, along with a lay Brother, in Batavia. The routine of his daily spiritual care of the lepers is seen in letters from these days.

See his letters found in Part II, Chapter Four, #31 to #36, and #39, pages 183–189 and 191.

Later missionaries began to find a more abundant harvest; many of these later converts remembered the "holy Father" who visited them and told of how they asked his prayers for their harvests in dry years and felt he had miraculous powers.

The "holy Father" was also not forgotten back in his hometown of Tilburg in Holland. Many there continued to help support his work in Surinam, particularly a group of women who formed a confraternity to provide for the needs of the mission as we see in some of his correspondence of the period.

See his letters found in Part II, Chapter Four, #37, #38, and Chapter Five, #44, pages 189–191 and 198.

XVI

The Way of the Cross to Paramaribo

We have now reached the last five years of Father Pete's life. Most of them were spent on the Surinam coast in Paramaribo and Coronie. While these years were passed largely in peace and happiness, they began rather sadly.

At the beginning of 1883, he had completed some sixteen years at Batavia, largely spent in his treks to the plantations, Amerindian settlements, and Maroon camps. As we have seen, his reception was always marked by people's admiration for his patience, zeal, piety, and dedication. Universal praise and veneration were the common themes, along with pleasure in his company and welcome for his presence.

Still, as is the case with everyone, there were some who did not share this general veneration. Everyone knows that a prophet is not accepted in his own home. While his Redemptorist confreres enjoyed his companionship and zeal, it was those who had to rub shoulders with him in close quarters that seem to be the force behind his leaving Batavia.

As the story goes, Bishop Schaap was making his annual visit to the mission in Batavia when he received a request from some delegates of the leper colony to have a private talk with him. They began to lay out their difficulties but the bishop felt that he could not understand them clearly in their Pidgin English and asked if someone could be found to translate for him. The only person quickly available was Father Pete.

To his own surprise, he found that he had to explain to the bishop that these delegates were requesting that he be removed from the leper settlement. The reasons for his own removal he had to present were that he was getting too old for his work. The people could no longer understand him when he preached, and he had begun repeating himself. Although some say the bishop became very angry at these assertions and others that the boatmen involved were being vindictive because they had been reprimanded sharply by Father Pete on previous occasions, the bishop agreed to the request and asked Father Pete to prepare to return to Paramaribo.

Was this business some type of revenge or was it an act of real concern on the petitioners' part? From what we know, it can be read either way. It could indeed have been the agitation of some malcontents, as some biographers suggest. From the reasons given, however, it could possibly be that Father Pete's age had caught up with him; many a parish has a story or two of a beloved pastor who was allowed to hold his charge too long. In either case, we should look at it as Father Pete did.

When the bishop's decision was announced, the mission at Batavia was in an uproar. There was nothing to do, however, since Father Pete immediately agreed to the bishop's determination. "You see," he told the people, "we are under the bishop's authority and so we must obey."[1] He later told his confreres, "After twenty-six years in the leper station, the bishop was so good as to give me the chance of enjoying the company of confreres, a thing I had not known for so many years." How much interior pain, prayer, and trust in God lay behind these words, we will never know.

What we do know is that in his farewell to his beloved lepers, Donders said, "Though His Excellency is removing me from here, I promise you, in God's name, that I shall return to die among you. On the day of resurrection, I shall be beside my lepers so that I can render an account of them before the face of the Lord."[2]

On February 7, 1883, he arrived in Paramaribo. A few weeks later he wrote to his provincial superior in Holland.

This letter is found in Part II, Chapter Five, #41, page 194.

Donders remained in the capital for about ten months until he "asked for retirement." When someone remarked about this (perhaps in jest), Father Pete was quick to respond in a way that suggests his retirement was at the bishop's suggestion, maybe to save the mission the costs of this elder confrere by letting the civil government pay them as it did for other citizens.

See his letters found in Part II, Chapter Four, #40, and Chapter Six, #46, pages 193 and 202.

Contradicting the notion that Father Pete was a man losing his faculties, his superior in the community, Father van Coll, wrote another confrere, "Father Donders is back in town again; he is working like a young man and is bringing many people back to God."[3] He goes on to mention how Father Pete visits the sick, works hard with fallen-aways, and uses his spare time for prayer. His care for the poor was not forgotten; Father van Coll continues, "Every day our house is surrounded by the poor and handicapped."[4] Again, he was seen in every neglected corner of the city looking for those in need.

"I was about ten years old," one government employee wrote, "Every time my parents saw Father Donders, they would point him out to me and say 'Look, there is the holy priest.'"[5] A quasi-proverb grew up in the city, "If you find something to complain about in Father Donders, you condemn yourself."[6] Father Pete's own view of these months is expressed this way:

This letter is found in Part II, Chapter Five, #42, page 195.

A month after he wrote this letter, Father Stassen, the assistant at Coronie, fell sick. The bishop asked Father Pete to take his place temporarily and so he did on November 2. Father Pete was happy with the opportunity as he points out in a letter he wrote soon after he arrived.

This letter is found in Part II, Chapter Six, #43, page 197.

Right before Christmas, Father Romme wrote of his own joy in having his old novitiate-mate with him.

There is no need to tell you...[that] he is a source of great edification. Though he is now seventy-five, he still goes out every morning and afternoon to seek the lost sheep. Not only does he never complain of being tired, but he shows no signs of it after going out for two or three hours straight in this tropical heat. May God bless his labors abundantly.[7]

Still, the fact was that Father Pete was getting old. Less than a week after Father Romme's letter, Donders was laid low by a high fever. He asked the community to make a novena to Saint Joseph for his recovery, but the good saint waited until the novena was over to answer; the fever broke the day after the novena ended. Then, less than three weeks later, he was bedridden again with a painful ulcer on his left knee that required lancing and another two weeks of bed rest.

As the size of the towns of Paramaribo and Coronie grew and plantations on their outskirts spread further, it became necessary to maintain a series of smaller chapels. From the time of the Redemptorists' arrival to the time Donders moved there, the Catholic population in Coronie had almost doubled to fourteen hundred. Father Pete, who had never ridden a horse, began to insist on learning to ride the one the community owned, but Father Romme would not let him because the horse was skitterish and hard to manage. Uncharacteristically, Father Pete was put out when the rainy season came and he could not take a horse and cart to one of the chapels; whenever Father Romme returned on the horse, Father Pete was after him asking if the water had not subsided enough for him to go there using a cart.

Father Pete's undeniable persistence in evangelizing can be seen in one story from this period. There was a European who had made his first Communion as a child and had long ago ceased to practice his Faith. He had for a long time lived with a woman. One day he joked to someone that if he ever went to confession, it would only be to Father Donders because he was a saint. Someone who overheard this remark told Father Pete about it. Suddenly one day, he showed up at the man's house (far on the outskirts of the settlement). "Here I am. You asked for me." Despite the man's assurance that he had not requested Father Pete's services, Donders went through all the reasons he should have requested it. The man gave all his excuses, until Father Pete said, "Look, my dear fellow, I came all this way expressly to see you. Surely you are not going to allow these poor old legs of mine to have carried me all this way for nothing."[8]

What could the man do but give in? He received instruction, got married, and with his wife returned to the Church; they remained faithful ever after. There was no resisting Father Pete if you had any sense of sin or virtue.

Brother Alphonsus (Antoon Koenen) lived with him most of the time when he was in Coronie. The Brother later detailed the daily life of Blessed Donders in these late years of his life. Despite his age, he maintained the same time schedule we detailed earlier. He retained practices of penance that he had developed years earlier: prayer vigils during the night, sleeping on the floor, use of the customary penitential practices of the era, ignoring the constant pestering by mosquitoes, and so forth. He made sure he was present for the prescribed community gatherings for prayer, meals, common recreation. If it were possible, during these days his confidence in God seems to grow even stronger.

See his letters found in Part II, Chapter Six, #45 and #47, pages 200 and 203.

He was taken aback with appreciation when the community celebrated his seventy-fifth birthday. A few days earlier, he had written to his confrere, Father Antoon Hengst of his good health. The celebration made him so happy, so appreciative of his community and of all God's gifts, that he wrote his provincial of it.

These letters are found in Part II, Chapter Six, #48 and #49, pages 205–207.

The following year, Father Pete wrote his last letter from Coronie, for in November 1885, Father Van Coll returned to Holland and the bishop asked Father Pete to return to Batavia to substitute for him. Despite his love for the leper colony and his promise to return to die there, he confided to Brother Alphonsus, "I had hoped to end my days here [in Coronie], but may God's Holy Will be done."[9] The letter congratulated his provincial superior on his anniversary of ordination.

This letter is found in Part II, Chapter Six, #50, page 207.

XVII

All Things Work Together

Whatever the reasons why Father Pete had been moved out of Batavia three years earlier, he was welcomed back in no uncertain terms. Brother Wilfrid, who now cared for the community house for Father Pete and Father Jan Bakker[1] (who would soon contract leprosy himself), relates, "I cannot describe the affection the people displayed at seeing him again. I, too, was delighted to have such a saintly superior as Father Donders."[2] One of the leper women later stated, "The moment we heard that he had arrived, we all rushed together to the shore, and kneeling asked his blessing." His friend Gisbert Rups testified, "The whole parish paid him the honors usually reserved for the bishop and led him to the church amid the singing of joyful hymns."[3]

Father Pete immediately picked up the routine of care for the colony. We have few details of his work among the lepers during these last years of his life. Since Father Bakker could only give limited help, most of the day-to-day work of the parish fell to the seventy-plus-year-old man. Eucharists, instruction classes, catechism, daily visits to the sick and dying, confraternities, et cetera, et cetera, made up the never-ending ministry. Of course, Father Pete's life of prayer and community were not neglected. We have only three letters from this final period in Father Pete's life. The first is a simple letter to his confrere, Brother Alphonsus, which shows this old man was the same Father Pete we have known over the years.

This letter is found in Part II, Chapter Seven, #51, page 209.

Still, he could not limit his ministry to the routine of the leprosarium. There were still the Amerindians and Caribs of the forest who needed his attention. It is about these that his next letter deals, another report to his provincial superior.

This letter is found in Part II, Chapter Seven, #52, page 210.

It was soon after this letter that Father Pete began to admit that he was not feeling well. Sometime around October 1886, he mentioned to Father Jan that he was beginning to feel intermittent pains in his abdomen, especially when he needed to urinate. But he continued to work as best he could. Father Jan would frequently inquire about his health, and the usual reply was "I feel fine" or "I am much better." It was in this vein that he wrote his final letter, again to his provincial, to wish him a Happy New Year.

This letter is found in Part II, Chapter Seven, #53, page 212.

It is obvious that Father Pete is either being polite in not wanting to worry Father Oomen or that he is just being modest and stretching the truth. His health was clearly not what he made it out to be. In just two weeks, things would take a turn for the worse. He seems to have managed until New Year's Eve, when he preached to the people and made no allusion to his illness to his confreres in the evening. On New Year's Day, however, Father Jan was forced to write Bishop Schaap in Paramaribo:

> On this first day of the year, it is my painful duty to inform you that Father Donders is seriously ill. He preached last evening without showing signs of anything wrong. So much so, in fact, that had I not offered to do it for

him, he had made up his mind to wish a Happy New Year to the people himself. But I had scarcely gone to bed when he entered my room and told me he was in great pain. I need not tell Your Lordship that I immediately went for the doctor. He immediately saw the seriousness of the case. He even thought that he detected signs of senility in the patient. Around six in the evening he became greatly alarmed and advised that the sick man be moved to Paramaribo if at all possible. As Your Lordship can guess, I fully concurred with this suggestion.[4]

When the bishop received this information the following day, he sent Father Odenhoven by boat to meet the patient as soon as possible and accompany him to the city. Unfortunately, passing by the Caledonia Plantation on his way, Father Odenhoven was told that Father Donders was feeling much better and so he did not go to Batavia. It did not matter, however, since that same day Father Jan wrote:

> Contrary to our expectations, it is not possible to move Father Donders. The patient is better, it is true, but the doctor is of the opinion that he is not up to making the journey. Nephritis (acute inflammation of the kidneys) is the problem; the case is serious.[5]

When this note, after some delay, made its way to the bishop, he sent Father De Kuyper to Batavia along with another doctor. He wrote the provincial, "I think we must be prepared for the news that it has pleased Our Lord to summon his most faithful servant to his reward. What a blessed lot awaits the man!"

The evening of January 5, Father Pete asked for the last sacraments, which Father Jan administered at once. He later reported that the dying man told him:

> I have nothing to dispose of; I have nothing to settle; I have nothing to say. They may bury me where they wish. I only desire two things. First, that you ask pardon in my

name from the people for any offence I have given them. Second, that you let them know the great grief I feel at the bad lives many of them are living in spite of my exhortations and of my desire that they should realize how evil sin is.[6]

This was the last will and testament of Father Pete. Father Jan reported these words to the congregation at the Eucharist on the Feast of the Epiphany the next day.

Father Pete's last action was unusual. It was occasioned by Father Jan. The medical officer assigned to Batavia was a troubled individual, given to drink, nervous impatience, and neglect of his duties toward the lepers. He did little in Donders case beyond writing a prescription for the wrong medication and advising the move to the city. That was the last seen of him. Father Bakker turned to the young assistant doctor who had no authority without the permission of the head doctor. This young man took it upon himself to care for Donders and give him medications on his own, activities that could bring about serious reprisals. This situation of medical neglect, something of long duration before Father Pete's sickness, so angered Father Jan that he sat down and wrote a letter in Donders' name reporting the medical officer and defending the assistant. He figured that such a letter from a man like Father Pete would correct the situation and protect the assistant. When he took the letter to Donders, the sick man insisted the letter be read out loud to him and then signed it. It was for him the only just and charitable thing to do for his lepers.

The assistant doctor later testified under oath,

> I attended Father Donders to the very end. Concerning himself, the servant of God was satisfied with everything and displayed indifference. These words were constantly on his lips, "May the Holy Will of God be done! May the Will of God be accomplished in me!" Whenever someone asked if he were in pain, he would respond with a smile, "No, no, not at all." I never in my life attended a

patient like him. I was still a Protestant at the time and I said to myself, "Father Donders is the first, and will surely be the last, I shall ever see so perfectly resigned to the divine Will."[7]

On Wednesday, January 12, the same assistant doctor visited Donders and asked how he felt. "Very well," he replied, "I have no reason to complain. All I ask is that you put up with me for a little longer. I shall die on Friday about three o'clock." The doctor continues,

> On Friday, at quarter to three, I called to see the Father again. He was fully conscious and was praying silently. Father Jan was kneeling and praying, I presume, the prayers for the dying, I am sure without any idea the end was so near. Not to distract the two priests, I thought it better to leave. Had I foreseen how soon the patient would breathe his last, I would certainly have stayed. I was just entering my house when I heard the knell sounding.[8]

It was three thirty, Friday, January 14, 1887. An hour later, the boat with Father De Kuyper docked.

> Father Jan approached us and said, "It is too late; Father Donders died an hour ago." We went to the church first and then to the house where the body lay and recited the *De Profundis*. The deceased was dressed in his Redemptorist habit and lay on a mat on the floor looking quite peaceful. The people stayed in the church all night, praying and singing the whole time. I went to the dead man's room to take something as a relic, but, search as I would, I could not find the least thing worth keeping, everything left was so old and worn-out. The lepers had already gotten there before me and had taken everything they wanted.[9]

The next day, the body was brought to the church and all day the lepers kept vigil. They kept lamenting and begging their Father Pete to pray for them. Fortunately the deceased did not hear their unkind comments to the ones who had complained about him to the bishop three years earlier when he was removed from Batavia and sent to Paramaribo.

At five o'clock the burial was held. All who could walk accompanied the body to the cemetery, and those who could not, crawled along. There Father Pete was laid to rest, at the foot of the large cross before which he often knelt to pray at night. He was buried next to Father Heinink, the man who had begun the apostolate for the lepers. In the cathedral in Paramaribo, Bishop Schaap held a solemn funeral service which he began:

> *"Be wise as serpents and innocent as doves"* [Matthew 10:16].
>
> I am sure, my dear friends, that we shall never find a man who has better fulfilled that precept of the adorable Savior of us all than the venerable servant of God just taken from us by death. A lovable simplicity accompanied by heaven's gift of prudence, that is the basic quality we find in Father Donders' life.[10]

In April 1887, Father Romme, his fellow novice of years ago, wrote a letter to the provincial with his recollections of his friend and confrere. He concluded it by saying,

> It is no wonder that everyone thought highly of Father Donders and that many even called him Holy Father Donders....As a priest and religious, he was for our little community and for the faithful an example of every virtue....Insofar as I can, I spend a little time each day at his grave....I am sure that by his intercession great blessing will come to Batavia, the mission of Surinam, and to the whole Congregation.[11]

XVIII

Rest in Peace?[1]

One thing a holy person recognized as a saint or as blessed can count on is that he or she will not be allowed to rest in peace. Such a holy one can be assured of constant pestering by prayerful people and disturbances to their graves as relic-seekers or church processes come around.

Father Pete is no exception. The leper colony at Batavia where he was buried was effectively closed in 1897 when the government opened a new and better cared-for institution at Groot-Châtillon, near which the Moravian Brethren opened a similar institution in 1899. Catholics, under Bishop Wulfingh's leadership, had founded St. Gerard Majella House in Paramaribo for the care of lepers in 1895. Batavia was left to decay. So Father Pete's remains were moved (along with the large cemetery cross) to Paramaribo in July 1900. On July 28, the bishop oversaw the solemn laying of coffin and remains in the sacristy of the cathedral. The body, faithful to its owner's lifelong commitment to go where he was sent, was moved again to a new monument in the nave of the church near the St. Joseph Altar on January 27, 1921.

As in life, so poor Father Pete did not have an easy time after his death. The official process of determining whether this holy man deserved to be honored in the Church as a saint was begun both in Paramaribo and in 's-Hertogenbosch in 1900, during which the testimony of 127 persons who knew the diseased was recorded, fifty-one in the colony, and the rest in Holland. The documentation wound its way through the Vatican offices and, when all was seen to be suitably in order, the actual "Introduction of the Cause" (or Case, in the juridical sense) was approved in 1913. This meant that the Vatican office (the Congregation of Rites, at the time), whose task was to study and verify all this material, began its work. The first step involved was reexamining many of the witnesses and determining whether Father Pete's virtues were truly "heroic" (this lasted until 1919).

They say Rome is eternal, not because of its age but because of how long it takes to get things accomplished! When all this material was finally examined, collated, translated into Latin and published it was the end of 1933. At this point, the final examiner felt that there were still lacunae in the material, and ordered the process to be repeated! When this was attempted, in March and April 1936, only four witnesses were still alive! So its only effect was to delay things almost four years.

What were the problems that caused all this delay? The first culprit was Father Pete himself. He was so "ordinary," unobtrusive, quiet, humble, to the point that it seemed there was nothing "heroic" about him. Prejudice and bureaucracy, however, seem to be the real causes. The Roman examiners did not feel they could trust the uneducated people who knew him. As one note of an examiner says, "Many of these are uneducated and very old people, who do not judge the internal, but only see what appears!" Another problem was that the questionnaires required by the Vatican were not used, and so the witnesses were not asked the pointed questions these contained; they were only told to "tell what you know" about Father Pete. Another issue was the very strict view that a saint's holiness must extend over a long, continuous period. The people in Holland, however, had not seen Father Pete after he left at a young age. In Surinam, he lived alone for a long time and in different places. Thus there was no continuity! The Redemptorists in charge of promoting the cause (Father Pete's defense attorneys) were fortunately able to counter these arguments. But not without time passing; the case was not finally approved for presentation to the head committee of the Congregation of Rites until 1941, and to the entire Congregation until 1943.

Two of the cardinals of the Congregation were opposed

(mainly because of the issue of Father Pete's pipe-smoking!), so Pope Pius XII had the two dissenters meet with two other favorable cardinals for a final discussion. Fortunately, this turned out favorably. Thus, on March 25, 1945, the pope declared that Father Pete had lived a life of heroic virtue.

There still remained the question of miracles. At the time, the process for the beatification of a person required that at least two well-attested "preternatural" (that is, beyond explanation of natural processes or medical interventions) miracles have occurred after the death of, and at the intercession of, the person being considered. Several people had told of outstanding occurrences during the life of Father Pete and at his intercession, but none of these cases were clearly seen to be more than hear-say or truly beyond the realm of ordinary possibilities. More than another dozen were claimed after his death.

Of these, one was the cure of a two-year-old child, Louis Westland, from a life-threatening bone infection in his right knee. The swelling from the painful infection gradually grew over two months as the family doctor tried to treat it. Finally, the three doctors who became involved agreed on the evening of November 6, 1929, to operate as soon as a surgeon was available. The next morning, the mother awoke to find the child standing in his crib; she took him out and put him on the floor where he stood without pain; all sign of swelling had disappeared. The parents later testified that from the beginning of the illness they had prayed for the child to be healed through Donders' intercession.

The medical commission of the Holy See then began its careful investigation of the supposed miracle. It examined the testimony of the doctors and radiologist, as well as the x-rays taken shortly before and after the event. The examiners finally agreed that this was indeed something beyond the ordinary course of nature or medicine and they approved the event as a miraculous intervention due to the intercession of Father Donders. It was 1975 by the time all of this was resolved, and finally, on August 5, 1976, Pope Paul VI approved the decision that it was indeed a miracle.

With the death of Pope Paul VI, the process was further

delayed. The promoters of Donders' cause then presented seven cases of healings that had been gathered in the preceding years, including one from an advanced case of gangrene. A special commission was established to consider these cases, which were judged to present sufficient evidence of the intercession of Father Pete. They submitted a request to Pope John Paul II to dispense from the detailed examination and proof of a second miracle in this case. He did so on September 11, 1980.

Finally, Father Peter Donders, C.Ss.R., was to be officially recognized as a sure model of outstanding sanctity and as one believed to reign with God in glory. Pope John Paul II solemnly proclaimed it so in St. Peter's Square on May 23, 1982, and set January 14 as his memorial day in the Church's calendar.

There is no doubt that Father Pete would have been embarrassed by all of this concern and adulation that followed his death. Still, whatever the Holy Will of God wants....He would surely be happy to know that even now he can continue to work "for the honor and glory of God and the salvation of souls."

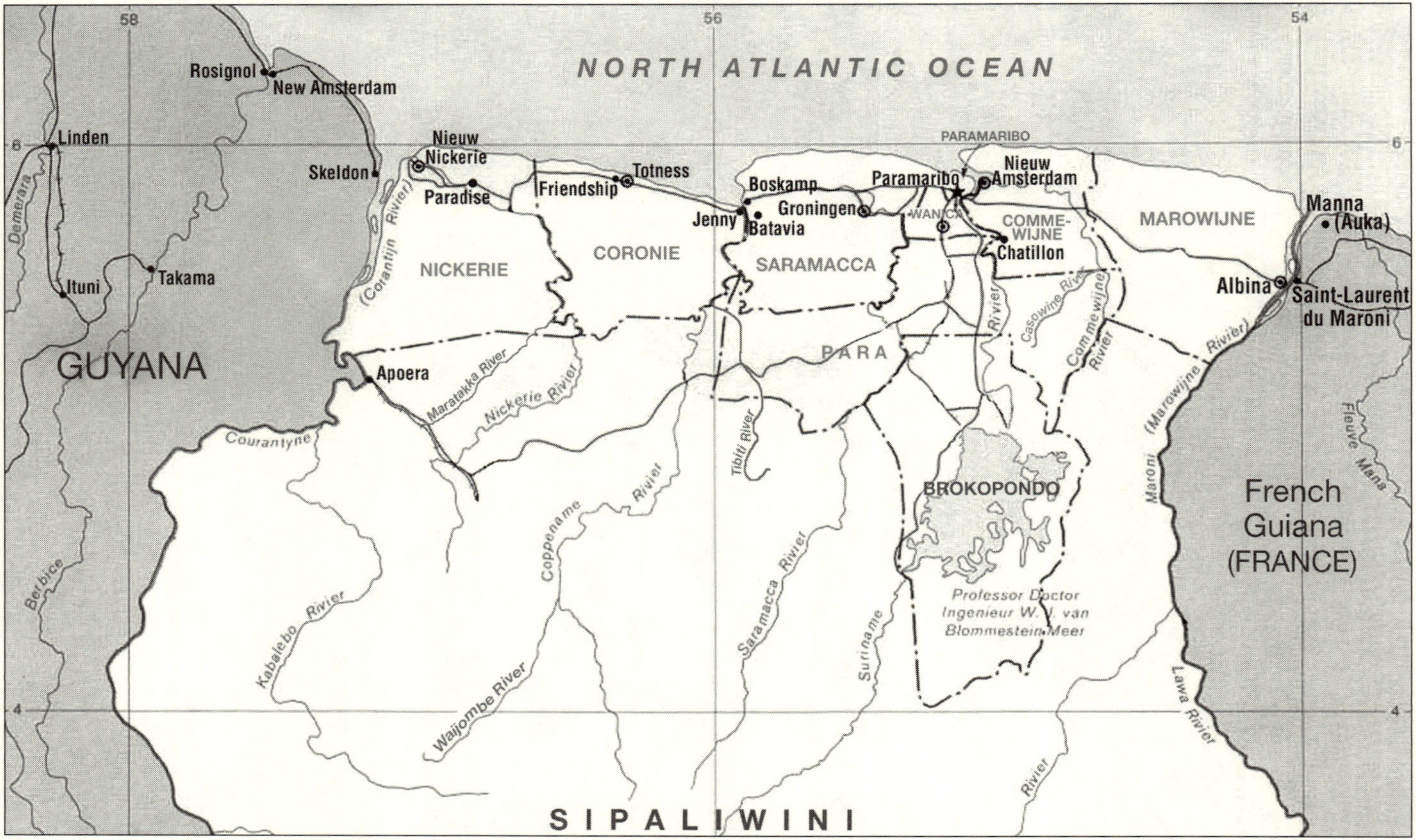
NORTH ATLANTIC OCEAN
58
56
54
6
4
PARAMARIBO
Rosignol
New Amsterdam
Linden
Skeldon
Ituni
Takama
Demerara
Berbice
GUYANA
Nieuw
Nickerie
Paradise
Friendship
Totness
Boskamp
Jenny
Batavia
Groningen
Paramaribo
WANICA
Nieuw
Amsterdam
Chatillon
COMME-
WIJNE
MAROWIJNE
Manna
(Auka)
Albina
Saint-Laurent
du Maroni
NICKERIE
CORONIE
SARAMACCA
PARA
BROKOPONDO
(Corantijn Rivier)
Courantyne
Apoera
Maratakka River
Nickerie Rivier
Coppename Rivier
Tibiti River
Saramacca Rivier
Suriname Rivier
Casowine River
Commewijne Rivier
(Marowijne Rivier)
Maroni
Lawa River
Fleuve Mana
Kabalebo River
Waijombe River
Professor Doctor
Ingenieur W. J. van
Blommestein Meer
French
Guiana
(FRANCE)
SIPALIWINI

PART II

Blessed Peter Donders: His Letters and Writings

Chapter One

THE WRITINGS OF BLESSED PETER DONDERS

An Introduction by J. Robert Fenili, C.Ss.R.

I. Introduction

There is no doubt that the most important insights into a person come from his or her own writings. Unfortunately, Blessed Peter Donders wrote little; he was an active missionary, not an author or frequent correspondent. He kept no diary or journal. We are left with fifty-three letters and two "accounts of conscience," short spiritual autobiographies. Because of the scarcity of such material, it is easy to produce a complete presentation of his writings. This, however, is only at the loss of much deep penetration into his heart and thoughts.

There is a complete listing of his letters in "The Letters of Blessed Peter Donders" in SD (see Section II below) written by André Sampers, C.Ss.R., pp. 133–136. The article also contains information on where the critically edited Dutch texts are located as well as an interesting account of how these were collected and edited (pp. 131–133). There seems to be little hope that more material will be found, since all known possible sources have been searched.

In this chapter, we present an English translation of all his known writings. Donders wrote only in Dutch with occasional standard phrases in Latin. No known English translations have been made directly from that language, except possibly for the short passage found in the official translation of the *The Liturgy of the Hours*.[1] This present translation is based on a Spanish translation that had been compared to the original Dutch for accuracy.[2] Likewise, this English translation has undergone the same scrutiny through the kindness of Rev. Ignaz Dekkers, C.Ss.R.[3]

The letters have been translated into contemporary English; no indications have been made of spelling or grammatical errors in the Dutch originals. Donders' wrote in common Dutch of the period, but as he grew older his mastery of the language grew weaker, probably because he used it so little once he reached Surinam. He also began to use many words that were not even Dutch.

Each of Donders' writings below is prefaced by a short introduction based on those prepared by Fabriciano Ferrero for his Spanish translation. These explain the period and context of the letter as well as some brief information of the person to whom the letter is addressed or who requested the two short spiritual autobiographies.

II. The Sources of Donders' Writings

There are two basic sources for the original letters. They are critically edited articles in two publications.

> PDR = *Peerke Dondersreeks,* volumes 11 and 12, Tilburg, 1947. (This is a journal dedicated to Blessed Peter and was the first place where his letters were published.)

> SD = *Studia Dondersiana. Beato Petro Donders CSSR Leprosorum apostolo in solemni beatificatione obsequii fratrum munus,* Volume XI, *Biblioteca Historica Congregationis Ssmi. Redemptoris* (Rome: Collegium S. Alfonsi de Urbe, 1982. (This was a special publication of the Redemptorist Historical Institute on the occasion of Donders' beatification.)

CHAPTER TWO

HOLLAND

**1. July 3, 1842, Warmond, Holland.
To Bishop Henri den Dubbelden, Titular Bishop of Emmaus, Vicar Apostolic of 's-Hertogenbosch, at S.-Michiels-Gestel.**[1]

This is the first letter of Peter Donders that remains for us. The original of this letter is kept as a relic in the Redemptorist monastery at Wittem, with a copy in the provincial archives.

Donders writes this letter during the period when he was awaiting transportation to his assignment in Surinam. In June 1842, Donders had been told by Bishop Van Wijckerslooth, the Procurator of the Mission in Surinam, to go to 's-Hertogenbosch for a boat to take him to Leiden from where he was to board a sailing ship for his ocean voyage. The ship, however, was long delayed by weather, and since Peter did not wish to remain idle for heaven knew how long he asked the bishop to be assigned some work. The bishop sent him to assist in a parish in Warmond. Donders served there for about a month before new arrangements for travel had been worked out.

At the midpoint of his short stay in Warmond, Father Pete wrote this letter to the bishop in order to be helpful. The parish priest seems to have been a bit eccentric. Still the letter's pleasant and chatty tone induces us to smile at the excitement and simplicity of this newly ordained priest over his first pastoral experience.

Your Excellency,

Taking advantage of the Reverend Parish Priest of Warmond[2] [coming to visit Your Excellency], I venture to write you some lines.

I heard that Your Excellency promised to the Bishop of Curium [Monsignor Van Wijckerslooth] to send a vicar once I leave Warmond for Surinam but that Your Excellency well understood that not everyone is compatible with the parish priest of Warmond. And since this short period of experience enables me to judge somewhat why it has to be someone who will be like the parish priest, I will try to explain this briefly to Your Excellency.

The parish priest, Your Excellency, is a God-fearing and virtuous man, such as I would not have expected to find here in Holland. I know that what he desires is to get a pious priest permanently as vicar, with whom he can live as a brother. He does not want anyone to ever visit someone in the parish, except in the case of sickness (it can be done only with the professors in the seminary). It is easy for me to observe that and I feel comfortable with it. The reason he gives for this are based on the perfection of our state, as anyone easily understands. Still, one does not have to spend his entire life in his room. Besides having a garden, the parish priest owns an adjoining wood, in which there is plenty of room to roam. We spend a good part of the day together. He keeps his house in perfect order and the servants are very kind. The parish priest says his Mass at half past seven. On weekdays, I then say mine, but on Sundays and feast days, I sing the ten o'clock Mass so he need not do so as he is rather frail. We have breakfast together and a smoke. From twelve to half past we are together and we continue together from midday until around two o'clock. At two o'clock, I take a stroll in the garden as often as I like. We have tea at four and smoke a pipe. Then each one goes to his room. We meet again at eight and say matins and lauds together; then follow supper after which we say night prayers with the servants.

The parish is very small—there are scarcely four hundred practicing members in it—confessions are not very heavy.[3] Four times a week I teach catechism. On Sundays, we go for a whole hour before vespers, which I then sing. I teach for two hours on Wednesdays: one in the morning, the other after dinner. I also spend an hour at it on Friday morning. On Sundays, I sometimes preach a sermon, sometimes a homily, and all this gives me plenty to do because it means a good deal of study for me.

I feel quite happy. There is no lack of work and the parish priest is a delightful character. I am picking up a lot from him. This was the plan of divine providence in bringing me here before I should reach my definite workplace.

Forgive me, Your Excellency, my too great freedom to write you this extensively. I wished to do nothing more than to give Your Excellency information so that you can discern who Your Excellency could send here after my departure and thus respond to the desire of the parish priest to have a pious priest here permanently with whom he can live as a brother.

Imploring your episcopal blessing, I remain the obedient son in Christ of Your Excellency,

P. Donders,
Warmond 3 July 1842

Chapter Three

Paramaribo

2. *November 13, 1842, Paramaribo.*
To the Very Rev. Gerard van Someren, parish priest and dean, at Eindhoven.[1]

Gerard Walter van Someren, who had been chaplain in Tilburg (1826–1829), was well acquainted with the Donders family. Later, as professor of philosophy in the seminary, he helped Pete to enter and later encouraged him to volunteer for Surinam. He became pastor in Eindhoven on August 31, 1842.

Donders wrote this letter about two months after arriving in Surinam and two weeks after preaching his first sermon there. His description of his voyage and first impressions of the mission give us a hint of his nervousness at the task he was beginning. His description of the visit to Batavia, the leper colony, where he had spent two weeks the month before, offers insight into his compassionate heart. The boyish surprise of the slow student at how easily he is learning Pidgin English is a joy to read.

A.M.D.G.

Your Reverence,

    It would have given me great pleasure to fulfill my promise to send Your Reverence a letter before I left Holland, but it was not possible since, against all expectations, the ship left so quickly.

Besides, I had to travel as fast as possible from Amsterdam to Antwerp to visit Miss Sophía Gilles, a benefactor of our work whose own deceased mother so willingly aided the mission. This and other matters kept me from writing Your Reverence. I hope, after [hearing] all this, you will pardon me and not think that I forgot you. No, Reverend Father. I could not forget your many kindnesses and the sincere friendship that you have shown me for such a long time. That is why I hope I will never be unfaithful to my promise to always pray for Your Reverence and to write you from time to time. I know that our charity is not affected by distance and the boundless ocean cannot break it or weaken it.

On July 31, I left Amsterdam for Den Helder where, that evening, the parish priest gave me the warmest welcome. I was sure of having time there to write Your Reverence. But the Good God, who knows all things well, had entirely different plans. The following morning, while I was in church, I unexpectedly received notice that the boat would leave immediately. I left the church—since it was God who was calling me—without being able to celebrate the holy sacrifice I grabbed my breviary and left, abandoning myself into the hands of his divine providence to which I recommended myself.

We pass through the Channel. It was August 1, the feast day of [my patron] Saint Peter in Chains, a consoling thought for me. After a voyage of forty-six days, we arrived at our destination, safe and sound, on September 16. I found the voyage very uneventful and we never ran into any real danger. The only problem was that we were often caught in calms or contrary winds. We had a very large and rapid ship that belongs to Mr. Rothuis of Amsterdam. There were eight passengers in all, among whom there were two Lutherans and three Calvinists. The rest were Roman Catholics, along with the captain, G. van Medevoort. I would gladly have said Mass from time to time since I had received permission, kindly granted me by Bishop Ferrieri. However, I did not have a chalice, although an altar and the rest of the things were available. Moreover, it would have been very difficult not to place the Blessed Sacrament in danger of the ridicule of those who believe differently. Still, in this I also recognized the wisdom of God who did not wish me to find a chalice in Amsterdam.

As I was deprived of this great favor and grace, I tried to make up for it with other prayers and meditations. Oh, what a consolation I got from the *Ave Maris Stella*, etc.! Especially when I could make my meditations on the feasts of the Assumption and Birth of Mary in the middle of the boundless ocean. What a sense of consolation I had resting in the hands of the caring Father who had called me.

I often thought of my travel companions with the greatest sympathy, as they try to do everything possible to pile up a temporal treasure but who have no care for God and their eternal happiness. This proved to be a motive that urged me to sacrifice myself for God and for the salvation of souls as much as these poor souls were doing for what would bring them unhappiness both in time and in eternity. Anyway, as far as temporal benefits go, there really is not much in the colony worth thanking God for.

The longed-for day finally arrived, Reverend Father, when we could exchange our surroundings for a walk on dry land.

Hardly had we dropped anchor off the city, when I had the happiness of seeing the Reverend Apostolic Prefect come aboard in order to welcome me and take me to the church so we might thank the Good God for our many blessings. Your Reverence will surely understand that these were moments of joy and emotion for me now that I had arrived at my destiny and could visit the House of God in this new land.

We started walking, accompanied by a multitude of every skin color, while the faithful gathered in the church praying the rosary as they waited for our arrival. As we drew near the church, they rang the bells. When we arrived at the church door, I put on a white stole which they presented me. Then the bishop passed me holy water. Immediately after that, we entered (the Most Reverend Prefect, the Reverend Fathers Janssen and Kempkes, and I) into the House of God and we went up to the altar where the bishop prefect blessed me with the Blessed Sacrament. Then we sang the *Te Deum* in thanksgiving for all our blessings. Afterward, my [new] father and brothers in Christ gave me a cordial welcome along with all of the faithful.

I can say, Reverend Father, that I reached the destiny to which the Lord called me and "his right hand upholds me." "Blessed be the God and Father of our Lord Jesus Christ, the Father of mercies and the God of all consolation" (2 Corinthians 1:3). I see the promise already fulfilled that our Sanctifier gave us in the gospel, "Everyone who has left…brothers or sisters or father or mother… for my name's sake, will receive a hundredfold" (Matthew 19:29). I have abandoned parents in the spiritual life, my true friends at the seminary and elsewhere; but the One whose promises never fail has returned them to me.

After resting for a day at the advice of the Monsignor, I celebrated a solemn mass on Sunday, my first one in this new land. I was assisted by Fathers Janssen and Kempkes, while the Most Reverend Prefect preached on the text, "Go out and preach…" (Matthew 28:19). During it, he exhorted me to help him and his assistants, in his words, to carry the iron cross.

On October 7, I left with my Most Reverend Father for the institute at Batavia, his beloved place. We arrived by boat in the afternoon of the 8th. I cannot hold back sharing a few words about this place with you since I am now so wonderfully delighted with everything here.

As we approached the place, the Most Reverend Prefect commanded that three salvos of gunfire be given so that the lepers would know that their father had arrived. When they heard these, they began to sound the church bell and the sick people began to go down to the riverside to wait for us.

When I saw these poor lepers drawing close, Reverend Father, I could not hold back my tears. Among other things, the Bishop showed me (there were tears in his eyes, too) the cross that the Most Reverend Prefect M. van der Weijden, of happy memory, had raised there on the shore of the river in 1826. It was the place where this zealous man had found, when he arrived in the country for the first time, a sacred tree that he cut down to replace with this, our Redeemer's cross.

And what else do I see on the river's shoreline, but a small chapel dedicated to the Blessed Virgin Mary. Inside, high on the wall, is her image under the title, Health of the Sick. This was recently placed there by our Most Reverend Prefect out of his indefatigable zeal and dedication.

Between the cross and the little chapel you can see the church built in honor of Saint Roch. This was constructed with planks on a mound built up of sand and small sea shells just like the church in the city.

We anchored and went ashore in sloops. The lepers kept greeting us again and again, saying in Pidgin English "Odi Fadri" ("Hello, Father"). The bishop blessed them and then we began to walk through the main street to the church. The lepers followed us as they sang the "Wi Fatta" ("Our Father"). We entered the church to give thanks to God. The lepers followed still singing. After a brief pause, we began to ready the altar (the gift of Miss Gilles of Antwerp) for celebration the next day which was a Sunday. We adorned it quite well because the Most Reverend Prefect wished that I celebrate my first solemn Mass, which I did at nine o'clock, with the Most Blessed Sacrament exposed, while the lepers sang some times in Latin and other times in Pidgin English. They know how to sing together very well.

It is very moving to look at these poor misshapen people: one without toes on his feet, another without fingers on her hand or with them all gnarled, the third without a nose, and another, blind....Others have enormously swollen legs, as if they were monsters. Others find their tongues are beginning to rot in a way that does not allow them to speak.

Despite all of these sufferings, they come to the church morning and night if they can, hobbling along or using a stick, in order to pray morning and evening prayer together and to assist at Holy Mass when they have the joy of a priest being with them.

The poor lepers, who are usually slaves from the different plantations, are sent there as soon as the first signs of leprosy appear. All of them (with the exception of a few free Whites) live in wooden shacks roofed with straw or branches which, especially inside, look more like a pig sty than a human habitation.

The supplies and the food that they receive from the government are meager and poor.

Yet, how good is God and what great care his paternal providence gives! For many, this disease is their unique path to reach eternal happiness. Here many have learned to know and adore the one true God whom they otherwise never would have known and adored. Here many find the most beautiful occasion to do penance for their sins by putting up with their infirmity, pains and miseries until they reach eternal happiness in this way. Furthermore, they have a father, the Most Reverend Prefect, who not only consoles their hearts but who also takes care of them bodily, sharing with them the pious alms from Holland and other places that have been given him.

He has also taken care to see that they have a lovely church and a very well kept cemetery. Against all hope, he began to construct this church, even when he did not have enough money for it and in spite of the fact that construction, as everything else, is very expensive here. Indeed, we have every reason to say that he has given his life for them because he has come here by sea and leaky boat with danger to his life in order to preach to these poor people the word of God and to comfort them with the holy sacraments. Likewise, for more than ten years, he lived in a wooden shack and celebrated Holy Mass outdoors. Even with all this [being said], it is not possible to sufficiently appreciate the zeal, self-denial, and resignation that prompted him [to do all this] for the honor and glory of God and for the salvation of souls. This is why it is a blessing that God has given me such a zealous man as my father. I hope that it will be God's will that I can spend some time under his paternal care and be guided by him in everything since he now has seventeen years of experience. Indeed, here it is particularly necessary [to listen to] what the Savior said when he sent out his disciples, "Be prudent as serpents" (Matthew 10:16).

Three times a week, they hold a beautiful celebration here among the lepers. On those days, after evening prayers and the rosary, a priest, preceded by the cross, goes in procession from the church to the chapel of the Virgin on the bank of the river. The lepers follow, singing the Our Father or some other hymns.

When they arrive at the chapel, they ring the bell so that all those who cannot come and have remained praying at the church know [that they have arrived at the chapel]. Then the priest sprinkles the image of the Virgin with holy water and incenses it, and everyone kneels and prays the Our Father and the Hail Mary five times, asking that idolatry and lust be stamped out of the colony through the intercession of the Most Holy Virgin Mary. Finally, the priest returns to the church where he had begun the procession to the chapel, and everyone follows singing.

I have to admit to Your Reverence that this ceremony deeply impressed me the first time it took place. Imagine if you can this scene: a lonely place far from civilization, a quiet river, a full moon. A priest vested in surplice and stole; before him our Redeemer's cross. Finally, that crowd of poor, suffering sick people of all ages, children and adults, venerating the Holy Mother of God with prayers and songs. And all of this, over the ruins of paganism....Oh, that our Good Mother hear their prayer.

In the face of all this in this place of misery and some times of consolation, I had the satisfaction of baptizing three children and two elderly men. Afterward, as I offered the solemn Mass, for the first time in their lives I fed three old women and a girl of eleven with the Bread of Angels. The girl was very much infected and would probably not live much longer. After Mass, I married a couple that had almost no more fingers.

On October 20, we left this place of the mercy of God and returned again to the city with a government boat, after a farewell full of many tears. Still, the Good God provided them with another priest since Father Kempkes had already arrived to take our place.

Upon our return, we went to one of the plantations to catechize the slaves, some of whom have now been baptized. As a general rule, we usually dedicate one Sunday a month to their instruction. Every trip costs us forty florins.

I was much edified at the diligence and attention with which they attend the religion class. The plantation owner who had given them permission to attend the instructions was also present. This owner, although he is a Protestant and formerly—it seems—

not too kind to us, has now made a complete reversal. He finally realized that all his slaves are beginning to become Roman Catholics. He prefers that we instruct them rather than the Moravian Brethren.

We could not continue our trip completely through the channel because the water was low due to the dry season. Here, in fact, the year is divided into four seasons: the long dry period and the short one, the long rainy period and the short one. Therefore, we had to find a small canoe. Then we had to go on foot by almost impassable roads, we reached a high tide and were able to make it home on Saturday at ten o'clock.

During the trip, we passed a "kakanti," a tree that is famous because there the devil is venerated and the Amerindians adore it as a god and offer it eggs from their chickens. Profoundly saddened and full of pity, I gazed at the place and prayed to God.

Now Your Reverence has a short report of my first voyage through this colony. In a few days I hope I can again make another trip with the Most Reverend Prefect, namely, along the seashore, on the occasion of the consecration of a new church dedicated to the Most Holy Virgin where the zealous Father Schepers is now working to great effect.

As you see, we now have three churches by the work and blessing of God. Indeed, if God assist us with his help by sending us more workers for his vineyard, and at the same time giving us the means, the Most Reverend Prefect would like to also build a chapel on the seacoast and a church in Nickerie where he has already baptized many pagans. Finally, but later, build a small church in Fort New Amsterdam at the mouth of the colony.

It is clear that all of this has to be done slowly since construction here is very costly. We hope and firmly trust that the One who has begun this good work will also bring it to completion for his greater glory and exultation as well as for the happiness of many souls and the displeasure of the demon who used to have here a secure throne, which now, by the grace and power of God, is beginning to crumble.

As to my health, Reverend Father, all is going along very well now. This hot climate does not bother me much: I sweat more, but that is all.

As far as the English of the Blacks is concerned, I understand it with manifest ease and, with God's help, I will manage it quickly. Since my return from the Coppename River, I have begun to teach the children catechism every day in the Pidgin English of the Blacks, something which pleases me a great deal. This language is not the same as that spoken in Curaçao, which I saw before in a little book.

Let me write out a few of the words in the Pidgin English of the Blacks that will certainly make Your Reverence smile: "Na nem va Fatta é va Oejueb é va Santa Jéjé" are the words of the sign of the cross.

The Our Father goes like this: "Wi Fatta. Joe disi dee na hemel! Joe nem moessoe dee santa. Joe kondre moessoe kom. Joe wanni moessoe dee na gron tappo, so leki na hemel. Gi wi tideij wi deijbrede, é gi wi pardon na wi paiman, so leki wi toe de gi pardon na den disi ben meki paiman na wi. E no kjori wi na ini teensi, ma loessoe wi na da ogriwan. Amén."

This is the Hail Mary: "Odi Maria, foeloe va gnade. Masra dee nanga Joe. Joe de na blessi morro leki alla oema, é na blessi dee ka pekien va Joe bele Jesus. Santa María, Mama va Gabo, begi foe wi zondari nagaso, é na dagoeroe va wi dede. Amén."

That is enough for now, Reverend Father. Later, when I have spent more time in the interior of the colony, I can write about all this again. I do not want to close without first thanking Your Reverence again for all the kindnesses I was able to receive so abundantly from you. May the good and omnipotent God be your recompense for this throughout all eternity. On my part, I will not cease to remember you every day in my prayers, doubtlessly weak as they are, along with all the other good works that, by the grace of God, I may accomplish here.

Again I recommend myself to your holy prayers, because, believe me, here we need them for ourselves on one hand, so that we may remain firm in the midst of so many dangers, and on the other hand, so that we may work successfully for the conversion of so many unbelievers and so many indifferent Christians. I recommend myself cordially as well to the prayers of my seminary companions, that they may pray for me and for so many souls still in such straits. Let them pray as well that the Lord send more workers into this vineyard, men according to the heart of God, enlivened by his Spirit, who will offer themselves totally for the glory and honor of God and the salvation of souls.

It is true that not everyone can work as a missionary in this vineyard; indeed, it is the Lord who must call them for this. Nevertheless, all can surely help with their prayers and alms. What prayer could be more agreeable to God and beneficial for one's own salvation than this prayer for the conversion of souls for whom Jesus Christ himself gave up his life?

The Most Reverend Father Prefect, Jacob Grooff, cordially sends his greetings to Your Reverence, to the rector [of the seminary], and to all the rest. [He wishes] to let them know that if his many occupations permit it, he will write the rector. Please be so kind as to give him my best wishes. I would also like to express to him once again my most heartfelt thanks. Similarly, above all, to Monsignor den Dubbelden and to Reverend Wilmer, his secretary. Finally, greetings to all the professors, as well as to all the theologians, and especially to Fathers Swagemakers and van Baast; in short, to all those from Tilburg. And if it is not too inconvenient, also to the priest in charge of the minor seminary and to all of its professors, etc.

Again, may Your Reverence accept a cordial expression of thanks and greetings from the one who calls himself

A very humble servant of Your Reverence,
P. Donders, Apostolic Missionary
Paramaribo, November 13, 1842

PS: In the event that Your Reverence would have the generosity to write me, something which would please me a great deal, remember that the kind Mr. Rothuis has promised to bring us at Paramaribo all our letters from Amsterdam free of charge. Goodbye.

3. *June 5, 1843, Paramaribo.*
To Father Jacob Cuyten, the rector of the major seminary at Haaren.[2]

> *Cuyten was rector of the major seminary at Haaren from 1837, precisely when Donders arrived there to study theology.*
>
> *Now, almost a year after leaving Holland, Donders writes him to describe the epidemic that afflicted Surinam and to tell him of the death of one of the priests. Because of this, Donders begs his help in sending some students from the seminary who are willing to come as missionaries.*
>
> *Donders does not present the tropical climate or the amount of pastoral and social work as a drawback but as an inducement for which he thanks God. Nor has he had difficulty in learning the language.*
>
> *This letter gives us a sense of the tremendous pressures being put on the personnel of the mission as well as Donders' calm trust in God. Again, we can sense his surprised joy over finding that, the poor student he had always felt he was, he has had no difficulty in learning the native tongue.*

Very Reverend Father Rector,

I hope that Your Reverence does not hold it against me that I have not written earlier, for I have written Father van Someren and I am sure that you would have read that letter. Still, I do not want to miss this opportunity, not only to fulfill the desire Your Reference expressed but also because my duty and gratitude toward you urges me to. Your Reverence already knows the success of my arrival here, the place of my destiny, as well as of my short journey to the colony at Batavia. Thank God I enjoy good health and the hot climate does not bother me.

The islands neighboring this area have had a dreadful misfortune, as Your Reverence is aware, due to a violent earthquake.

Here we experienced a great shaking as well at the same time, but without causing any damage, thank God.

Another calamity, arising from God's justice but from his mercy as well, had befallen us here: a serious epidemic called dysentery. For the last four months it has mercilessly afflicted us and brought many to their grave. There have been days when we had to bury three or four of our people at one time (and that is not counting the unbelievers, Lutherans, Calvinists, and Moravian Brethren).

Nevertheless, this chastisement of divine justice was for many a grace and mercy of God, since many, especially the children of unbelievers, had the chance to be baptized. Adults and elderly people as well, after having received instruction and converted, had the joy of receiving baptism.

Moreover, this scourge has fallen upon the pastors. Father Vitus Janssen was laid low by the sickness as well as the Monsignor Prefect, the father of us all (whom, as Your Reverence must already know, Pope Gregory XVI named Vicar Apostolic of the East Indies and Bishop of Canea, i.p.i. We all hope, however, that at his own request, His Holiness will relieve him of this new appointment, if it is God's will. Still, this hope is not without fear [that the request will be refused]). Blessed be God! The Prefect, after a long convalescence, has started to get better and is now recovering. Unfortunately, Father Jan Vitus Janssen died this last March 12. It is God's Will and our own that we must accept all of this. Father had worked on our mission for nine years. Thus, this is a great loss.

You can easily understand, Reverend Father, how much our work has grown. We are, in fact, only four priests for the entire mission. Also, the Very Reverend Father Prefect is often sick and has many tasks and much correspondence. Moreover, it seems the moment has arrived to plant the cross of Christ in all corners of our mission since the new governor looks on us very favorably. Indeed, he has given the Prefect full liberty to go wherever he wants, and says that he has no objections against us. This is so true that, at the request of the captain of Fort New Amsterdam, the Prefect was asked on May 14 to offer the Holy Sacrifice for the first time for the soldiers and slaves, something that had been forbidden us for many years by a disastrous decree. Instead, now we go there two Sundays a month according to an agreement we have. The Fort is located on the shores of the Suriname River an hour from the city.

The Prefect sent Fathers Schepers and Kempkes to the coast and they have an abundance of work among the new and promising peoples. They must also start working in Nickerie.

I have already spent some time with the Prefect in the city where there is also a great deal of work, above all, in educating the children and, in the evening, the catechumens. As well, I frequently have to take care of confessions.

In spite of it all, so much work does not depress me. On the contrary, I thank God because he has satisfied my desires and has willed to use me, unworthy as I am, to work for sinners and unbelievers. The God of Goodness has granted a special help in learning Pidgin English. I did not find it difficult and I could quickly teach the children and visit the sick. It has reached the point were I can now speak equally well in Dutch or Pidgin English.

Still, since there are only two of us, we cannot do everything. The poor lepers number more than four hundred. For the greatest amount of time they are without a priest. In addition, we are responsible for the Johanna Catharina plantation, seven hours from the city, etc. There are many things we could do if we had the manpower.

I have written, at the insistent request of the Most Reverend Prefect, to the students in the theology program and I ask you as well to help obtain, as soon as possible, two priests from the seminary to come to assist us in this vineyard. The Prefect has written in the same way to Bishop Wijkersloot, the Mission Procurator. I trust that Your Reverence will help us to obtain two priests who are suitable for this great task so we can continue the mission and bring the good work begun to a successful completion. I am sure that Your Reverence, along with your companions, do not cease to pray to God that we be worthy to give increase to what has been planted and watered. Pray for me as well, unworthy as I may be; I do not forget to pray for Your Reverence.

I acknowledge myself affectionately as your humble servant and son in Jesus Christ,

P. Donders, Apostolic Missionary,
Paramaribo, June 5, 1843

PS: Please give my best wishes to Bishop den Dubbelden and Zwijsen, to Father Director and all the other professors, and above all, to Father van Someren.

4. October 5, 1843, Paramaribo.
To Miss Johanna Cornelia Manni at Tilburg.[3]

> *Johanna Manni was an acquaintance of Father Pete from his hometown in Holland. She became a benefactor of his missionary work when he went to Surinam and organized others in contributing. We do not have her letter that he is answering. It is obvious that she was offering assistance in founding some type of school, a matter that Father Pete had obviously given thought to but could not see a way to accomplish at the time.*
>
> *The letter shows that he sees his spiritual concern for the people is one that is not separated from their basic human needs. Education and ability to provide suitably for one's life as well as that of one's family are a necessary part of offering a person eternal salvation. Pete's compassion, like Christ's, extended to all that was human and humane.*

Ad maiorem Dei gloriam
The Peace of the Lord be with you.

Dear Spouse of Christ,
 I received your letter of February 12 in excellent condition. I thank you cordially for what you sent and for the zeal and care you have for the mission. The Good God will repay you a

thousand times and I, for my part, will not omit to pray for you as well as for others who have contributed.

As far as regards your wish, be sure that I, on my part, will not omit doing everything to meet it, as well as to contact you for it, if it pleases the Good God. For the time being, the moment has not yet arrived to start something like that here. If we could open a school here like the one at Curaçao and get Sisters for it, then it could be a good opportunity for you. But when will that be? For this, we have to wait for the bounty and mercy of God. God grant that we can do this soon.

In the meantime, go on praying with your children for us and our people; by doing so you can sometimes offer more help to us than with activities. Moreover, your desire to sacrifice yourself totally for this work pleases God already. And he will always recompense you for it since he considers the will as valuable as the work when it does not depend on us to do it (as Saint Bernard says). So go on praying and submit yourself in everything to the holy will and dispositions of the Good God who knows how to dispose everything for the best at the proper time.

This is enough for now; for the rest I trust that you read also the letters that I write to my brother.

For now, I recommend myself again to your pious prayers since, believe me, I need them; the burden of the souls becomes every day heavier for me. May the Good God, in his infinite mercy, sustain me, unworthy [as I am], and strengthen me so as to promote his honor and glory and the salvation of souls, for whom he wanted to shed his precious Blood, and may he also sanctify my soul so that after having preached to others, I myself will not be rejected.

Also be sure that I will not forget you in my poor prayers. Accept once again the most cordial thanks and loving regards of him who calls himself

Your servant and friend,
P. Donders, Apostolic Missionary
Paramaribo, October 5, 1843

5. September 24, 1844 (with postscript of October 8), Paramaribo. To Mr. Joachim Le Sage ten Broek.[4]

Ten Broek was editor of the review De Godsdienstvriend *("The Friend of Religion") a periodical with wide circulation in Holland. After his appeal to his fellow seminarians in his letter to Father Cuyten (# 3 above), Donders made a wider appeal in this description of the mission that ended in his strong call for missionaries. These appeals had some success because on December 28, 1844, Father Stephen Meurkens joined the mission.*

We can feel in the letter the great sense of urgency he feels for the good of the people he serves in Surinam. His modesty does not cause him to hesitate to mention the great difficulties and pressures he is under in order to excite the desires of some committed and venturesome priests to come to this poor land. Especially in his concluding remarks, we can sense his endless commitment to his call from God.

Paramaribo, September 24, 1844
To the Editor of the *Godsdienstvriend*

Dear Sir and Friend!

Since I know your zeal and care for the Surinam Mission and that you like to communicate something about us and our mission from time to time, I feel urged to satisfy your religious aspirations (I spoke with the Very Rev. Pro-Vicar Apostolic G. Schepers, who encouraged me since his Excellency is impeded from doing so himself due to many tasks, though I too am burdened by many continuous activities). [I write all the more because I hope that this will contribute to God's greater glory and the well being of our mission.

You are already long aware of the painful loss that our mission, as well as we [personally], suffered by the fact that Monsignor Grooff, our beloved and unforgettable Father, was moved and taken away. You have undoubtedly regretted this striking and irreparable loss along with us. What will I say? It is God's Holy Will since he gave him to us; he too took him again from us; however painful it might be for us, may his Holy Will be done. The ever Good God wanted to chastise us in his mercy and justice, but he did not want to destroy or leave us. He supported us weak and futile creatures with his omnipotent grace so that we may continue, and even expand, the work begun by our unforgettable Father as you will see from what follows.

In the first place, at the coast where, a year ago last March, the new Church of Our Lady was blessed. Rev. Kempkes has been working there now for a year and a half after the departure of Most Rev. Schepers. I hear it is going very well. The slaves show a great deal of zeal in attending the Christian instruction so that even their great distance from the church—sometimes they have to walk five hours on very bad roads—does not prevent them from coming to catechism and the services in church as much as possible. I have already heard that the new Church of Our Lady is becoming too small to hold them all.

With the lepers, the place so loved by our unforgettable Father, Monsignor Grooff, everything is going as wished. Rev. Heinink (who followed the call of the Lord and came to help us at the end of last year) has been living there for three months already and he is very satisfied because these poor, ailing people are very keen on receiving instruction. A considerable number of them are preparing enthusiastically to receive baptism and an even greater number is preparing for admission to first Communion. In a word, they do their best to find their only comfort and satisfaction with God and religion.

Yes, dear friend, one needs to see it for oneself (a privilege I had twice during my stay here) to appreciate their misfortune and at the same time the happiness religion is giving them.

I am the pro-vicar's only assistant in the town. I have, moreover, the Johanna Catharina and the Toledo plantations, as well as Fort New Amsterdam, to look after. Yet the town alone would be more than enough to keep us both going. Last year, we baptized 210 souls here—including a few individuals on the plantations—and according to my calculations, the total for the current year will not fall below 300, as so far we have more than 200. Now I am speaking only of baptisms. All this involves instructing these children and adults, especially since the slaves cannot read! Apart from one or two kind souls who give us a little help in instructing the sick and infirm in their homes, we have all this to do by ourselves. Furthermore, we have over a hundred adult pagans coming for instruction every day in preparation for baptism, when they are not prevented by lack of time or the pressures of work.

On Holy Saturday, I had the happiness of solemnly baptizing a good thirty adults. There were a few more on the Eve of Pentecost and I hope to baptize a great many on All Saints' Day. We had a large number of first communicants this year, and a great many more are being instructed for it. Moreover, we have had the joy of seeing a large number of Protestants coming over to us and entering the bosom of the Church. There is one noteworthy circumstance connected with these. Eight of them were admitted to first Communion, six of whom who now suffer from leprosy used to be among the most important people in the town. There are still many of them who have not yet been admitted, but they are preparing carefully. As for the unfortunate lepers—who see everyone shunning them with horror through fear of contagion—their joy and courage on experiencing the consolation of belonging to the true Faith are indescribable.

I am firmly convinced that God in his mercy has sent them this trial only to bring them back to the straight path. How admirable are the works of God! In this land, my dear friend, there is not a Jew, pagan, or Protestant who can deny that it is only in the Catholic Church that these afflicted lepers find strength and consolation. They would look in vain for such priceless benefits elsewhere. Oh, all the proofs I could give you. But I fear making my letter unduly long. All this gives us a deep comfort amid our many activities and a pleasant prospect for the future.

Fort New Amsterdam, where we go every fortnight, has corresponded with our efforts beyond all our expectations. Even if we do not count the slaves from the country districts, several of whom have already been baptized while many more are preparing for baptism—and their number, we trust, will go on increasing.

[In addition to these,] we may count a great many soldiers who made their Easter duty, and I feel sure that all—about fifty—will make it. To give them every opportunity, we are about to build a church there. Big? Small? The almighty goodness of God and the generosity of the mother-country will not fail, let us hope, to help us to realize our plan. Monsignor Grooff, our unforgettable Father, has already undertaken the project, for he keenly desired to have a church there in order that Mass might be said regularly.

The Johanna Catharina plantation, on the Saramacca, ten hours from the town, gets a monthly visit from us. Now we have the satisfaction of seeing that our trials and sacrifices bear excellent fruit. The slaves show great eagerness for instruction and baptism. Those that have already received baptism are numerous; most of the others are preparing for it, and we entertain the well-founded hope that before long, with God's grace, all will enjoy the same happiness. Here, too, they are imploring us to build a little chapel with a cemetery. The cemetery has already been completed and blessed. It will not be long—at least that is our hope—before that chapel will rise from the ground.

From what I have said, you will gather how burdened we are with work and worry. There are the town, the fort, the plantations, and, to care for it all, there are only the two of us.

Add to all this the material cares resting on the Most Rev. Pro-Vicar's shoulders over all the buildings made out of wood, which therefore need constant repairs at enormous expenses. The church here in town is becoming too small—it is so already—to contain the number of faithful, which increases from day to day. Thus, we will be forced to enlarge it, the sooner the better; it also needs to be painted (postponed for a long time for serious reasons) since otherwise it will totally collapse. Where will we get the means to do all this? This, dear friend, sometimes discourages the Monsignor and not without reason. Still, we put all our trust in God. It is the work of him who directs everything and to whom everything belongs; it is for his honor and glory, and these thoughts encourage us.

But there is still more. Where are the workers we will need here? *Messis quidem multa, operarii autem pauci.* [The harvest is plentiful, but the laborers are few.] Sure, the harvest is big but the laborers are few. How much there needs to be done here beyond what has been mentioned already! How many plantations, which we can't reach since there are no priests! Still so many thousands of Amerindians who are still sitting in the darkness and shadows of death and do not yet have the good fortune to see a priest to show them the right way to heaven. How much they long for it since they have asked several times for priests, as Monsignor has told me. What shall we do? How much I pity them! For the moment, I can't do anything more than help them with my poor prayers and recommend them to the infinite mercy of God.

To you, Priests of the Lord, do we appeal. For the love of God and for the love of Jesus Christ, who once left his Father's throne to save us who were all doomed, come to our assistance, we implore you. Do not let us sink beneath the burden; for indeed we can bear it no longer. Think of and have pity on Most Reverend Monsignor Schepers who, these last fifteen years, has been bearing the burden and heat of the day. I fear for his life, when I see his difficulties and worries increasing daily. Have pity also, we beg you, on so many hapless beings who will be lost unless you come to their rescue. Are not they redeemed by the Precious Blood of Jesus Christ as well as we? If, then, there are some to be found among you who will hear the voice of God, harden not your hearts, I beg of you. Do not be afraid. There is nothing to fear as long as you have God and the salvation of souls alone in view. We cannot, it is true, promise you earthly goods, joys; but God himself, I hope, will be our reward as well as yours.

We beg and beseech of you, then, to come to our assistance at once. Send us two priests at least: one for the coastal region, where he could not be more needed than he is, and the second to give us a helping hand in the town. If these indispensable reinforcements are not forthcoming, I fear His Reverence will soon succumb.

You, beloved people, assist us also by your prayers, to begin with, that the Master of the Vineyard may send us laborers and that, meanwhile, he may deign to bless our sweat and labor and grant us the grace to win those souls that are so dear to him. There is nothing that the collective and persevering prayer of the just cannot effect. Help us also with your alms. How urgently we need them you can gather from all I have said. Unless they, too, are forthcoming, how are we going to save what is still left? How are we going to bring to a happy issue what is only just begun? Many times we have experienced your generosity, and certainly we are not unmindful of the heavy burdens that lie on the mother-country, especially today. All the same, do not forget the Savior's promise: "Give and it shall be given to you." God will bless you and reward your generosity, even in this world, as he did in the case of the widow of Sarepta in the days of the Prophet Elias. If a cup of cold water given in his name will not go without its reward, what will not your reward be in eternity?

Dear Friend, we trust in your goodness to collect alms for the love of God. Meanwhile, the angels of heaven will present your care, fatigue, and generosity before God. For our part, we will not cease to remember you in our prayers and sacrifices.

Sending you best greetings also from His Excellency, I am honored to call myself your servant and friend,

P. Donders, Apostolic Missionary

PS: Today, October 8, just as I was about to seal this letter before the departure of Captain Andresen's ship, the *Sophia Maria* (who will take this letter to you), we received with the *Jacoba Maurina*, under Captain Kernkamp, a beautifully painted portrait of Monsignor Grooff, our unforgettable Father, in a marvelous frame, presented to our mission from Holland. How striking it is! But what memories, what feelings for all of us; God's will be done; all come here to see it.

6. September 8—December 5, 1846, Paramaribo.
To the Rev. Gerard Walter van Someren.[5]

Four years have passed since Father Pete's arrival in Surinam. Here he presents more details about the religious, social, and material situation of the region. In spite of the difficulties that surround him, Father Pete shows confidence in God and his joy in the work. He also shows his polemic attitude against the other religious confessions, an attitude that was normal in the nineteenth century. Even saints are children of their age.

The prophetic cry which he voices for the liberation of the slaves would only begin to be realized with a decree of August 8, 1862, applied in the Dutch colonies as of 6:00 AM, July 1, 1863. Here, sixteen years before that date, Donders dreams of a society of free human beings. Father Pete cries out that "Faith and morality" cannot progress where there is slavery.

Father Pete's spirituality demands the transformation of a society that exploits human beings and is used as a tool of those who enrich themselves with the sweat and blood of the oppressed. The announcement of the Gospel precedes the arrival of the reign of God, the reign of justice, love, and peace. The true disciples of the Redeemer suffer in their own flesh the oppression of those on the margins and live out their compassion in solidarity with the saving cross of Christ, the Victor over sin and death.

A.M.D.G.
Paramaribo, September 8, 1846

Reverend Father and Friend,

For so long, I have really wanted to write Your Reverence, but could not fulfill my desire, since so many constant duties kept me from doing so. Do not think, my great and unforgettable friend, that I forgot you and the blessings you provided me so often and so generously. No, Reverend Father, not a single day passes that I do not think of you and remember you in my poor prayers and Masses. I hope, by the grace of God, to be able to [remember you] until the day I die. To give you a proof of my thanks and appreciation, I begin this letter, which by the help of God and whenever time allows, I hope to finish. [I write,] on one hand, to fulfill my word given long ago, and on the other, to repay Your Reverence through this detailed narration of the events that have kept me from writing you for so long.

I hope that you received my last letter, written in 1843, the letter that the unforgettable Father Monsignor Grooff took on his voyage to our homeland. In it I congratulated Your Reverence for your nomination as parish priest in Eindhoven and as dean of the district, something I wanted to briefly mention along with the important news of our mission published in *Godsdienstvriend* in January of 1845. Now, to my narrative.

Earlier, I promised Your Reverence that I would tell you something about this colony, which is what I want to do right now in the best way possible. If this following picture does not contain anything to please [you], at least I hope Your Reverence will receive it kindly.

To give you an idea of this colony, think of a great and widespread forest, such as the Creator made to spring up with his word, *"Ipse dixit et facta est"* ["He commanded and they were created" (Psalm 148:5)]. It stretches wider than a sixty-hour trek [along the coast] and extends back [toward the mountains] I have no idea exactly how far. Imagine, then, that this extensive area is filled with every kind of bush and tree, so numerous in their diversity that they cannot be counted; full of every kind of wild animal: tigers, monkeys, etc. There are, as well, a great number of snakes, many of which are very venomous. Imagine as well that this rugged forest is furrowed by many rivers and torrents with all kinds of fish, including sharks and crocodiles.

Though the country is generally very fertile, still very little of it is cultivated since, up to the present, the cultivation has been done solely by slaves, because the natives and the free people, especially in the city, are too lazy and proud to do this kind of work. Certainly there is a great number of plantations outside the city of Paramaribo, which looks little like a city and at times seems to be buried in the middle of the forest. However, because the number of slaves is diminishing, many of these plantations are abandoned.

The principal products of the plantations are sugar, coffee, and cocoa. Rice and turkey corn also grow here very abundantly. The principal food of the slaves is bananas, which grow on a kind of tree, as well as other fruits, which this year, because of an extraordinarily long drought, have produced almost nothing. Because of all this, we find that heavy poverty has taken over.

The primitive inhabitants of this region are the Amerindians, whose skin is copper-colored. Almost all of these live far from the city and along two large rivers, the Marowijne, which is near the border with French Guiana, and the Corantÿn, which forms the frontier with British Guiana. These people are free, but they live in a completely savage state, and they still lie in the darkness of paganism.

The second group is constituted by the Maroons, with black skin. For a long time, they have been independent of the government.

The third group is formed by the slaves. Brought here from Africa in the past, they are also black-skinned. Now, however, they are of all colors because of their intermingling with Europeans of dissolute morals. In earlier times their number was very large. Now it has greatly diminished and is continuing to grow smaller due in part to their disorderly lives, etc., and also in part (and not a small part) because of the inhuman punishment, which at times one would more properly have to call "torture." Then one adds to this the lack of necessary food for life, above all considering the terribly hard work they have to undertake. All of this has been aggravated this year by the lack of bananas, as I have mentioned above.

To my way of looking at it, however, it is evident that, above all, one has to see here the hand of God who wishes to say, "This far and no more." Oh, if here they took even as much care of the health and well-being of their slaves as people in Europe take of their pack animals, the situation would improve. If only I could recount everything on this topic that I have seen and that I hate.... But I prefer to pass over this in silence because it is beyond anything you can imagine. I tremble whenever I think of them. And so I prefer to limit myself to crying out with profound pity:

> Woe, woe to Surinam on that great day of judgment!! Woe, woe, indeed, a thousand woes to the Europeans, owners of the slaves on the plantations, to the administrators, to the directors, to the foremen (who have authority over the slaves)!!! Damned are those who enrich themselves with the sweat and blood of these unfortunate people who have no one to defend them except God!

It is no surprise, then, that the Holy Father Gregory XVI of happy memory published bulls and petitions trying to completely suppress the slave-trade and to bring these people liberty. You, Reverend Father, will possibly think now that this will threaten to be the ruin of the Dutch government because it does not completely suppress the commerce in slaves....Yes, and God knows it!...

It is not necessary to describe to Your Reverence the moral situation. It is enough to tell you that everything seems to conspire to its destruction without anyone, outside of ourselves, trying to oppose it. Here we find ourselves alone in the fight against the immense torrent of impiety, without any other arms than the cross and our confidence in God.

Idolatry as well encounters few other antagonists than us. Earlier, the government prohibited and punished it. Now, however, it is ignored. This is due to the fact that many Protestants, precisely the most respected, are attached to it to such a degree that one can say they have turned into pagans. O times! O customs!

The different sects present in the colony are: (1) Lutherans, (2) Calvinists, (3) Moravian Brethren, and (4) Jews. The Moravian Brethren are the most pernicious of all. Except for us, they are the only ones who have a concern with the slaves and freed Blacks.

Unfortunately [this is] with great success, since with their teachings and their tolerance, they win over the majority of the slaves. Just to give your reverence some examples. Without any qualms, they baptize those who are cohabiting with four or even five black women, and only require them to promise that, once one of the women dies, they will not take another one in her place. It is true that they have a type of marriage, but they can also dissolve it in their own way, etc. The administration of baptism, above all as far as the form is concerned, is very doubtful as to its validity.

To this we must add that many Protestants, and above all the Jews, all oblige their slaves to attend the instruction of the Brethren. If the slaves were truly free, I believe that less would go, since the Brethren are not the most beloved, at least for many people, because of their avarice for money and because they mix their business into everything. They oblige the slaves, and even the freemen, to buy in their stores, because, people say, they make sure the slaves believe that all of the things they sell are blessed, etc.

Your Reverence may think that, because of all this, [the Brethren] are numerous. No. Here in the city their membership comprises fewer slaves and freemen than we do. Moreover, one must take into account that they have been active much longer than we have. Second, [we must recall] that everyone favors them, both the government as well as the slave-owners. Furthermore, they have access to many plantations, something denied us, but, all things considered, it does not amount to much.

For example, they teach them something to sing, and then they began, as I've heard from others, to read to the slaves a chapter of the prophet Isaiah in Pidgin English, which they themselves translate, instead of first teaching them to know God. In this way, they make them well-read persons. This I have often discovered among the ones who, even after some twenty years of instruction at their hands, ask us to be admitted into the true Church. These persons, who after a great many years of instruction and who many times have participated in the Lord's supper, understand nothing of the mystery of the Incarnation of Jesus Christ, etc., as [is the case] for all Protestants.

Finally, what I can still say in general is that in this colony, fidelity and justice are very rare. Instead, each one tries to cheat the other as often as possible. Lawsuits and bankruptcies are now the order of the day. Yes, Reverend Father, the situation of the colony is so bad that it seems to be very close to complete ruin. It is not surprising that the Good God wishes to chastise such injustices and impiety in his own time. It is not rare to see many who, after enriching themselves by amassing goods through usury and by every kind of injustice and mistreatment of the slaves (including the cost of their sweat and blood), are now completely ruined. Their goods have been sold by judicial order. The houses where they lived up to now seem to be stables for horses and, what is more, they go around bearing the [pain of] their condemnation on their faces. The same is happening in the plantations, many of which are under compulsory administration this year.

At least I hope that, by the grace of God, all this will accelerate the freeing of the slaves. Yes, the God of Goodness, as I hope, in his mercy and justice, will mitigate the condition of the slaves, so degraded, so long oppressed, and will give them the liberty by which they can recognize him as their creator and serve him with sincerity. Oh yes, then we will have open before us an immense field of labor! May the Good God grant us this!

As to the interior of the country, where the morality and customs of the Amerindians and the Maroons reign, I cannot tell Your Reverence very much, since, up to now, we have not yet worked among these people. I certainly hope that we will soon have this satisfaction, something which I have desired for a long time. I've heard it said that the indigenous people who are furthest from the city are very dedicated to agriculture, while many others, on the contrary, are very lazy. What the situation may really be like, I cannot tell you with any certainty. May the Good God grant that we can illumine with the light of Faith these unfortunate people who still lie in darkness and the shadow of death. Then I will send Your Reverence more details about this.

In the meantime, I recommend these unfortunate people to your pious prayer and your Eucharists. From time to time, I see them in the city, living in the neighborhood in small groups. I have verified that they are very happy to wear clothing to cover their nakedness; this gives me much hope that they may become civilized and then converted. I've also heard they cohabit with a single woman and have an aversion to robbery, something very different from the Blacks. Both of these qualities give me great hope for the future, if the Good God, without whom we can do nothing, hears our prayer and blesses our work.

The "European Protestant Colonization" that has worked here for the last two years, as Your Reverence knows, is a less efficient matter. Up to now [it has made] enormous expenditures [that have been] totally useless. The survivors (half of them have died) have accomplished nothing up until now, nor will they. As far as their practices are concerned, they have done badly. Pastor van den Brandhof, who was decorated by his Majesty with the Order of Knighthood, will eventually not come out much appreciated. No, my friend, this is not work for Protestantism; they cannot do it and they never will.

In regard to the well-being and material prosperity of the colony, it is struggling with its last gasps not to disappear. His Excellency, Governor Raders, has found a way of getting the free aboriginals of the city to do manual labor and to gradually accustom themselves to it. This is because it is considered unbearably shameful for a free person to have to work, even though they see themselves obliged to beg for alms. Work was something for slaves. The project consists in digging a canal from the city to Post-Groningen (a European colony).

The Lord Governor entices them by giving them a florin each day and it has to be a silver one (this is more valuable than Surinamese paper money since the silver florins are worth 30 to 40 percent more). Women receive fifty cents a day. The goal is to give them land to cultivate once they get used to work, so that at the beginning they can procure their own food for themselves. Then later, they can cultivate sugar cane, when the forests have been cleared and they can construct an irrigation channel. As I see it, Your Reverence, this is something which seems theoretically beautiful, but nevertheless makes us all ask if it will last. And, moreover, what will result from all this? And so on. Up to now it is going well. The governor solemnly inaugurated this project on August 31 and now 230 men and women are employed on it. They work from six to eleven in the morning, and in the afternoon from three to six to earn their money. Will it continue? This is a question only time can answer. Moreover, there exists another question, what will happen with morality? Will it get better with this work in common? My answer is no. May God grant us the best and preserve what is good.

My Esteemed Sir and Dear Friend, here you have a general sketch of the country and its present situation, a picture, which, as I said at the beginning, does not present anything very attractive. From all this, Your Reverence may gain an idea of the many difficulties we must contend with, and see that Faith and morality cannot advance quickly until the traffic in slavery and the plantation system are totally suppressed, as in North America, where they deal with free persons.

Certainly we have among the slaves and the recently freed many good Catholics. No Sunday passes but that several frequent the Lord's Mass and there are crowds on each first Sunday of the month and holy day of obligation. Also, since my arrival, many are the slaves and recently freed who have married. This is enough for Your Reverence to be able to judge a little about this and that. In case Your Reverence needs more particulars, be so kind as to let me know and to give me your questions. I will gladly answer them.

May I ask Your Reverence for the favor of sharing the content of this letter with the Rev. Father Pastor, W. van de Ven in Tilburg, or even of [passing on] the letter itself once you have read it?

Well, I must conclude. Cordial greetings and best wishes for God's blessings, I remain with a heart full of gratitude to Your Reverence, your most affectionate son and friend in Jesus Christ,

P. Donders, Apostolic Missionary
Today, December 5

PS: Cordial greetings to Your Reverence's sister, your brother-in-law, and their children, and finally, please, if you have the opportunity, to Monsignor H. den Dubbelden, to the Reverend Father Rector, and the professors at the seminary, etc.

7. September 4, 1861, Paramaribo.
To Father Arnold Swinkels, Missionary in Surinam, then on leave in Holland.[6]

Unfortunately, there is a fifteen-year gap in Father Pete's letters that remain to our day. We now find him in the leper colony in Batavia, but as he notes, temporarily working in the capital so that Monsignor Schepers could recuperate from some unmentioned health problem. We notice the changed situation from the last letter where he had to refuse help with a school at the time. Now he is eager to start a new educational project for boys since a group of religious sisters has begun to educate girls. The idea of taking the young children away from Coppername may sound strange, but this refers to children born in the leper colony of Batavia. If they were to remain there, they too would be condemned to the same deadly disease.

Father Pete's concern for the education of the children of lepers again shows the all-encompassing concern his spiritual view has for these people. Since the majority of the lepers were former slaves or poor natives, their children were the poorest of the poor in his care.

Charissime Frater,[7]
I am in the city for four weeks because I have exchanged places with the Monsignor (it did him much good, since yesterday he came back from Coppername feeling very healthy) so I can't let this opportunity of writing you pass by. At Batavia everything is still the same; the Director Van der Hoop is still there and will continue until God disposes differently. It seems the Governor is not in favor of firing him for spoiling everything; since he is already on pension and he can stay on indefinitely.

I have a plan for the children of Batavia if Your Reverence can get me brothers. I hear from Sister Engelberta that her brother Engelbertus, who lives with the Brothers of Tilburg, desires very much to sacrifice herself for the missions. Your Reverence will have already heard where this project could best be established. It would be highly desirable if an organist could be found among the Brothers, and some who know a trade like cobblers and tailors and who are able to teach boys a trade without getting them spoiled.

There are already some orphan girls with the Sisters, and it is going very well. If we had Brothers for the boys, then I would take the children who are four or five years old from Batavia and never bring them back. The Sisters and Monsignor would be very much in favor and I do not doubt that the Governor will allow this, as well as give them the food and clothes just as they get at Coppername. We will pray the Good God meanwhile may fulfill our wishes. I do not doubt that Your Reverence will do everything possible to get capable brothers.

Reverend Kempkes, who is sick in the city, sends you his cordial greetings; so do the Monsignor and the Sisters who all, thanks to God, are well and busy with a project for a convent behind the church.

I ordered some books from Langeveld in Amsterdam. Please kindly pay them for me; we will refund them when you come back. In a few days I go back to Batavia. We celebrated Saint Rosa solemnly in the Saramakkastreet. The Good God may give this community a permanent pastor. Joanne Operalle is still ailing. That is all the news I have for now. You already know that Mr. C. de Jong at Brussels died.

If you go to Tilburg, be so kind as to give my cordial regards to the parish priest Van de Ven, and give my best regards to Dean G. van Someren too, if you visit him. Both of them would appreciate it.

For the rest, let's pray much for one another; so I remain with friendly regards and have the honor to be,

P. Donders, Apostolic Missionary
Paramaribo, September 4, 1861

**8. June 26, 1867, Paramaribo.
To Father Gerard Walter van Someren at the major seminary at Haaren.**[8]

Two days after his religious profession as a Redemptorist, Donders wrote to his great friend in Holland, Father van Someren. He tells of his joy over his profession, made at the age of fifty-eight, and moreover, right in Surinam.

As he speaks of his apostolic work, he emphasizes God's loving will manifested in all events, especially in this step from a diocesan priest to a religious. This sense of change is even evident in the way he addresses his letter. There was a custom at the time to begin a letter with a motto dedicating it to God. The motto of Saint Ignatius, "Ad Majorem Dei Gloriam" [A.M.D.G.: "For the Greater Glory of God"] was commonly used for this purpose. Saint Alphonsus Liguori, the founder of the Redemptorists, however, had the custom of using "J.M.J.T." [(In honor of) Jesus, Mary, Joseph, and Teresa (of Ávila, his favorite saint)]. Later Redemptorists followed his custom but inserted "A" for Alphonsus into it, and it became "J.M.J.A.T." Donders now adopts the Redemptorist custom.

J.M.J.A.T.
Paramaribo, June 26, 1867

Very Reverend Sir and Friend,

I thank Your Reverence with all my heart for the lovely letter and portrait, the likeness of which is excellent. I received both of these though the kindness of the Most Reverend Bishop Swinkels, our dear Father. It has been a long time since I have written to Your Reverence, my great friend, but do not think that I have forgotten you.

Surely you have heard that I have entered the Congregation of the Most Holy Redeemer. What you do not yet know is that on the twenty-fourth of this month, the feast of Saint John the Baptist (the bishop's patron), I made my religious vows along with Father Romme. I ask you to thank God for me, something which I cannot do worthily.

How admirable is his Providence! At fifty-eight, he has accepted me as a religious, right here in Surinam and in Paramaribo! I cannot express to you, my Reverend Friend, the joy and satisfaction I feel.

Pray for me, I beg you for the love of God, that I may persevere until death in the Congregation, as I have promised with a solemn oath. I will always pray for you, my reverend and dearest friend. Since it is probable that we shall not see each other again on earth, I hope that one day I will see you in heaven and then we can eternally rejoice in God.

The change from a diocesan priest to a religious happened with no difficulty. Thanks be to God!

Everything is working together for my good. With the help of God, without whom we can do nothing, we hope that from now on we can be always greater propagators of our holy religion.

The bishop is well enough; he enjoys health and is of very good spirits. We now count more that twenty religious sisters and the number of children to educate increases day by day. The number of Protestants as well who enter our holy religion is great.

For seven [or] eight months now, I have been in Paramaribo where I made novitiate and now, as a professed member, I will perhaps soon go elsewhere.

The Most Reverend Bishop has just administered the holy sacrament of confirmation twice in the city and also in Coppename, Coronie, and on the plantations.

I hope to write you again in a short time in order to make up for the great delay in corresponding. I cannot and must not forget you in my prayers.

Again, many thanks for the souvenir you sent me. I greet you cordially in the Sacred Hearts of Jesus and Mary,

P. Donders, C.Ss.R.

PS: I almost forgot to congratulate you on your beautiful church; I have heard it said that it is the most beautiful of all the churches in Meijerij.

The bishop and all the priests, especially Father van Rooy and Father Verbeeck, send heartfelt greetings. I hear that you look favorably on our Congregation, and this makes me very happy. Goodbye. Let us pray for each other. When we go to care for the sick here in the city and on the plantations, we wear our religious habit and everyone shows us signs of reverence.

9. May 29, 1869, Paramaribo.
To Father Gerard Walter van Someren, Dean at EIndhoven.[9]

This letter is the one promised by Donders in the previous letter and contains a detailed account on the native reality of Surinam. We see his happiness over the way his pastoral work is unfolding in the vicariate that had been confided to the Redemptorists in 1865. He is excited that his work among the Amerindians is beginning to show its first results, especially with the children.

We see how Father Pete's spirituality is based on the popular devotions of his time. His joy lies in vocal prayer and in public manifestations of the Faith, such as the Stations of the Cross and processions. Witnesses tell, "Normally he prayed kneeling or walking back and forth in the church....His prayer was more frequently vocal than mental and it was based on the frequent recitation of the rosary, spiritual reading, and the use of prayer books to nurse his devotion." The foundation stone of his life in the Spirit, however, was his total confidence in God's plans.

J.M.J.A.T.
Paramaribo, May 29, 1869

Very Reverend Father in Christ,
   A promise is a duty, as the saying goes. Therefore, I now want to fulfill the promise that I once made you. Reverend Father Theodore Kempkes, who has labored here in the colony for thirty

years as a missionary, is now returning to the homeland. This is why I am in the city for a few days. Since my last letter, in fact, I have not lived in the city, but at the Batavia leprosarium where I will be returning in a few days.

Now, however, I am no longer alone as I was before, but rather I am with another priest. Therefore, I have more time to visit the plantations and to instruct the Blacks. It is been a year now that, with the permission and at the urging of the apostolic vicar, I have been occupying myself with the natives, the first settlers of this colony, in order to teach them to know and love God.

These native people have copper-colored skin. They go about almost completely naked. They live in the higher reaches of the forests and they cultivate the land for their food as well as work at fishing and hunting.

They're divided into three tribes, namely, the Arowaks, the Caribs, and the Warros. Each tribe has its language, very limited, but still very distinct from the others, for example:

Words	*Arowaks*	*Caribs*	*Warros*
Father	Awawa	Papa	Gima
Mother	Atete	Fata	Dani
Child	Dassa	Kiri	Makka
God	Adjahili	Foroesi	

Many of them understand and speak a little Pidgin English.[10]

I have gained the confidence of very many of them. I baptized some eighty children as well as some adults and sick people. I also married some and admitted them to their first Communion.

Your Reverence certainly understands that we're dealing with a task that develops very slowly. With the Good God's grace, however, without whom we can do nothing, I hope to succeed in gaining all of them for God. Jesus Christ spilled his precious blood as much for them as for us.

Thanks be to God, things are going well everywhere since we now have a greater number of priests. Here in the city, there are now eleven priests and twenty-five sisters dedicated to the education of the children. Just in this city, the sisters have a thousand students in their schools! In Coppename as well, we have children in school. In Coronie, where there are two priests, they have one hundred children. If they had sisters there, Moravian Brother Lerimans would lose everything. The Protestants and the Brethren in the city, according to what I hear, are furious at the loss of so many.

We hope that the bishop has a long life because he is the man we need. The God of Goodness has arranged all this. The day before yesterday, the Feast of Corpus Christi, we had a solemn procession here in Paramaribo with the Most Blessed Sacrament carried by the bishop. This had never before been seen in Paramaribo nor in Surinam. And such things produce wonderful effects. The ethereal Protestantism cannot do this. The procession began with various members of the Confraternity of the Holy Family with their banners from the two parishes, etc. The Protestant preachers and Moravian Brother Lerimans ran through the city trying to hold back their own followers. Afterward, everybody wanted to do the same thing, and this brought about their loss of face. I call them "Protestants," but they really are not that. They believe in nothing, and among them incredulity and corrupt morals reign supreme.

May the Good God, in his infinite mercy, bring it about that there be a total conversion among them. Let us pray that there will be only one flock and one shepherd. Let us also pray a great deal for each other. With prayer we can obtain everything.

Permit me to recommend to your prayers and sacrifices our Congregation, myself, and the poor native people, that the God of Goodness and our dear Mother Mary, who is also their mother, illumine and comfort them to take up and bear joyfully this gentle yoke of Jesus so that they may participate with us in the joys of heaven.

Very Reverend Father, in the Sacred Hearts of Jesus and Mary,
I remain for Your Reverence, son and servant,
P. Donders, C.Ss.R.

Chapter Four

Batavia

**10. December 12, 1869, Batavia [Leper Colony].
To his confrere, Father Aegidius Vogels, in Holland.**[1]

As a young priest, Father Vogels (1804–1877) had helped in the parish at Tilburg and had known Pete Donders as a young man. Father Vogels left Tilburg and joined the Redemptorist Congregation in 1843.

This letter is a response to one Vogels must have written him on the occasion of Donders' religious profession several months earlier. He writes of his "new" pastoral work, that is, one rooted in his profession because this would now allow him to dedicate his efforts to the evangelization of the Amerindians of the forest. He has already organized twenty locations for meeting with them, but he knows that the natives cannot easily adopt a sedentary life.

Although we have heard many of the details of his pastoral work already, and will continue to do so in his future letters, we can begin to feel the complete simplicity of Father Pete in that all of this work and trial flows out with peace and joy from a heart that has found rest in the love of God and a renewal in his profession as a member of an apostolic congregation.

J.M.J.A.T.
The Establishment at Batavia
December 12, 1869

Reverend Father,

I am happy to be able to write to you, Reverend Father, in answer to your request. Your Reverence has every right to receive some few words from me because it has been such a long time that we have not been able to see and converse with each other. It was you who brought me the happy news that I would be able to enter the minor seminary in hopes of completing my studies there, according to the inscrutable plan of God and in spite of my unworthiness, so as to receive priestly ordination and finally become a missionary.

I had spent fourteen years in the city of Paramaribo and on the plantations when God wished that I should work here in Batavia alone for ten years among the poor lepers. Then—who would have suspected it?—to leave this place for ten months while I made my novitiate (or better, my "quasi-novitiate,") in the city, make my vows, and become a Redemptorist. And all of this in Surinam! How absolutely marvelously has the God of Goodness planned all of these things!

Beg God and his Holy Mother that I can persevere in this sublime and holy vocation. I can certainly confide in the help of God, together with the intercession of Mary and of our Father Saint Alphonsus. Still, I hear that so many have abandoned their vocation and their crown. If the cedars fall, the little twig must tremble. Let us pray for each other so that we can persevere.

After my profession, I have once again come to Batavia, but now no longer alone, but with my superior. He is the third that I've had up until now (namely, Reverend Fathers Verbeek, Bossers,[2] and Odenhoven). In fact, however, I spend most of my time traveling, not by train—something unheard of here—but by a tent-boat, and at times on short trips, in a canoe ("corjaal" = a hollowed tree trunk) always journeying by water.

I lived in the tent-boat both day and night on the Coppename and Saramacca rivers as well as on the tributaries, Tibiti, Waijombo,

Combae, Casowine, Watramili, etc., in order to instruct the freed slaves, celebrate Mass, and administer the sacraments on the different plantations. I likewise go among the natives in the far-off forests in order to track them down like wild men and preach to them. There were 125 youngsters baptized and also some adults; six couples were married; eight Amerindians were admitted to first Communion. We move, however, slowly. Please, Reverend Father, every so often say a Hail Mary for me and for the poor natives so that they can learn to know and love God.

Here there are three types of natives: the Arowaks, the Warros, who are the most civilized, and the Caribs who live like children of nature, surrendering to drink because of the situation. They live very far from one another in the forest and in the uplands. Some are thirty-five hours away from Batavia, others fourteen or fifteen hours in these immeasurable jungles. They live by hunting and fishing; they have arrows, bows, harpoons, shotguns, and large machetes; they use the corjaal or canoe. They all know how to swim and run around almost totally naked; nevertheless, the ones I have baptized have already begun to obtain clothes for themselves.

I only began in May of last year and I already have twenty places for meetings: plantations, small properties or Amerindian camps where I give instruction. This way in six weeks I can make a circuit once. For others, I need as much as two months in order to gather each group once. The Amerindians are especially difficult, if not impossible, to gather into groups because they live almost entirely on hunting and fishing treks. This is a nomadic people that are very difficult to gather and organize.

With this, Reverend Father, you have some details I can share with you. I hope that by means of them I have been able to fulfill your desire; I remain, in the Sacred Hearts of Jesus and Mary,

The servant and brother of Your Reverence,
P. Donders, C.Ss.R.

11. February 11, 1871, Batavia.
To the Very Reverend Johan Schaap, Superior of the Dutch Redemptorist Province, then in Surinam for a canonical visitation.[3]

This letter was written while Father Pete was situated in the leprosarium in Batavia but had continued his work on the plantations, although less frequently. His words show Donders' well-rounded grasp of the peoples and cultures with which he is dealing. His remarkable patience with uneducated people is an inspiration. His openness to the role of the laity in the mission is also noteworthy, along with his desire to address not only the spiritual needs of the emancipated slaves but their social condition as well through education. Father Pete's spirituality is neither this worldly nor other worldly, but a firm union of both for the redemption of the whole person from sin and suffering.

To comply with your Reverence's wishes, I am going to open my heart to you to the best of my power with God's help.

I. The Plantations: (1) There are not just a few times that the visits to the plantations bear fruit. (2) How often? (3) How to work there as best we can for the salvation of souls?

II. The Amerindians

III. The Maroons in Auka, etc.

As to (I), The Plantations: (1) Though the spiritual results of the visits to the plantations are not as a rule very visible; (2) still I believe that there are more than a few rare places where the missionary labors fruitfully. This is why it seems to me that these places should be visited every month, if it can be managed, or at least every six weeks.

If the instruction of the Blacks is to bear fruit, it should be characterized by the greatest simplicity and by much patience.

Whenever old men are to be baptized, we should, I think, first have a talk with them individually, in order to help them to examine their conscience and go through a sort of confession. This is in order to find out, first of all, any possible impediments and then to induce true sorrow for sin in those good old fellows by means of fervent prayer. This way they may receive the sacrament of regeneration with the proper dispositions.

After their baptism, each time they are visited their confessions should be heard, as far as this is feasible. I make an exception in the case of many plantations where this is very difficult for want of a suitable place. Above all, a fervent preparation for as early a first Communion as possible should be insisted upon.

They should be urged as strongly as possible to marry, though with caution at the same time, for if there are many immoral families, it is the result of their having prepared badly for marriage and of having started family life under the influence of the devil instead of God's blessing.

Instruction, I repeat, is necessary; but so is prayer. Parents must be frequently reminded of their duties toward their children. It is much to be desired—and this is of capital importance—that we have catechists who are also schoolteachers, for if they lead holy and pious lives, they will be a great help. The Government agrees with us on this subject and would like to see schools opened in every plantation, if possible. It would, moreover, secure their maintenance by a financial grant.

As to (II), The Amerindians: I am very pleased with the Arowaks and the Warros; work among these is very successful. There are very few of the latter. On the Upper Saramacca in the *Kraaijeshoop* territory, they got others to help them build a small church, which was blessed under the invocation and protection of Saint Alphonsus on the feast of Saint Rose of Lima. Nearly all these Amerindians have been baptized, married, and admitted to holy Communion.

So far, those on the Maratakka have had the benefit of only one visit. On that occasion, thirty-six children and one sick old woman were baptized. Their eagerness to receive religious instruction was extraordinary and I was much touched and consoled. It took some among them only a few days to learn the Our Father and Hail Mary, together with the essential truths. The divine goodness will, I hope, let me see them again soon and make a longer stay. I trust I shall thus have the happiness of baptizing and marrying a great number. They are about 130 in all. These live about eight hours from Batavia.

The Caribs are the most numerous, but so far I have nothing good to report, though I hope to have better news later on. I baptized most of their children—almost all, I may say. As for the old people, the women as well as the men, are slaves to drink. Many of the men have two, and even three, wives. Great patience is needed in dealing with them. All the same, I think we are making headway, and I hope, with the help of God, to have better news for you soon. Let us pray, let us pray, and let us put all our confidence in God's power and mercy.

For these Amerindians it would be necessary to have a catechist and schoolteacher for the children; we might even have to stay there to prevent drunkenness. But these Carib Amerindians are dispersed throughout various places: on the Upper Saramacca [River], the Casowine, the Tibiti, the Calebaskriki, and the Waijombo [tributaries of the Coppename River], and various other places. We try to bring all these people together under their chief, Christiaan. Then a station and school could be founded there; their number is five or six hundred.

As to (III), The Maroons in Auka and environment: Auka is situated on the Marowijne River (near Manna, French Cayenne, or Guiana), but far inland up the river. Their numbers are difficult to determine; it could be five or six thousand, a large number. All these people live in the most terrible idolatry, and so far they have not wanted to hear of religion, but it seems that now God in his goodness and mercy begins to enlighten the hearts of some. A few who live here on the Upper Saramacca River are baptized; and a couple also has been admitted to first Communion. They are so well behaved that I can congratulate them.

One of their chiefs, who is still a pagan, is speaking of bringing me to Auka, his native district. One couple, already Christian, is married and they have made their first Communion. They want to accompany me there and even settle in the place, on the condition that we remain for good. Two Negro children of Auka have already received baptism at my hands, and one of them has received Communion. At the present moment they are with their families in Auka, and will, I hope, become the apostles of their young friends. May God have pity on all these poor people and give them his light. *Fiat.* The month of August will be the best time to visit them.

Now about the Nickerie and the plantations on the Nickerie River.

In former times, as you know, we had a church there between the Paradise and Hasard Plantations but because of its unfavorable situation—on a deserted plantation—and the continued sickliness of Rev. Monsignor Meurkens, it has been deserted. But now it would be a good time to start a station again. The reasons which give me now more hope of success are the following:

1. Formerly, that is to say in the old slave days, the Negroes depended on their masters for everything and in everything, even in things spiritual. They were given no choice in the matter of religion, and, in most cases, they were obliged to conduct themselves in accordance with the whims of their owners under threat of formidable punishments.
2. In those days, 1850, there were numerous owners and managers who showed us but scant sympathy, and who, with the connivance of the Government, preferred to see their spiritual interests committed to the hands of the Moravian Brothers.
3. The sickness of Reverend Meurkens and the poor situation of the church on the deserted plantation that was often flooded.

This has now all been changed.

1. The slaves are free, even where religion is concerned.
2. The overseers, the owners, the managers, and the other functionaries are very sympathetic toward us and are anxious to

see Catholic churches rising on their lands. Mr. Findal has even spontaneously offered a piece of land on his Nusserij Plantation that is in every respect a very suitable site for a church. [It is] (1) sufficiently elevated; (2) connected by road with the other plantations above and below it; (3) its personnel and conditions are now more positive.

Another point: if a station could be founded with two Fathers there on the Nusserij Plantation, one could then more easily serve and visit the Amerindians on the Maratakka from there, and also, from time to time, the edge of the city of New Amsterdam.

Now, as far as regards to the Blacks in general, I cannot judge whether things are good or bad.

But God is infinitely merciful and also endlessly mighty. If we put our trust in him and pray humbly to help us and also those poor people, he will be with us.

Such is my deep conviction. I have the fullest trust in God "who wishes that no one perish but that all be saved."

Very Rev. Father Provincial, I recommend myself to Your Reverence's prayers and asking your paternal blessing, I am in the Sacred Hearts of Jesus and Mary,

Your humble son in Christ,
P. Donders C.SS.Red.
The Batavia Establishment, February 11, 1871

12. October 16, 1871, Batavia.
To the Very Reverend Father Johann Schaap.[4]

Donders proposed to periodically send a report of his apostolic activities to the provincial superior. Since he now has another priest as a companion in Batavia, he can once more pursue the work he most desires, to evangelize the nomadic native Amerindians. He can now dedicate the two annual dry periods of the year to them.

> He sees the mercy of God expressed in the welcome some natives are giving to the Faith, as well as in those cases where his efforts are refused. Because of this, it is necessary to continue to pray that the reign of God may reach all of them. While we see his delight in his successes, we find him equally calm in his failures. He also begins a new pastoral strategy: developing some of the Amerindian children into catechists for the rest. His patient spirituality sees all these events in the will of God.

J.M.J.A.T.
Batavia, October 16, 1871

Most Reverend Father Provincial,

Upon my return to Batavia from my trip among the natives of Maratakka, I am now fulfilling my duty of writing you.

We decided that I was supposed to travel during this dry season to the Aukaner Blacks of the jungle on the Marowijne in order to try to bring them into the Faith, but the circumstances and decision of my superiors has prevented this—or better—it was not the will of God that this would happen now. This was because, as agreed, I wanted to visit the natives of Maratakka in the short dry spell. Nevertheless, unexpected downpours prevented this and so I had to postpone the journey to a more opportune time.

Thus, the Very Reverend Pro-Vicar wrote telling me that during the longer dry period, I should go to Maratakka and postpone the trip to the Aukaners until next year or until whenever God wishes it. So August 27, I left for Maratakka and returned on the twelfth of this month after forty-seven days, during which I visited the Caribs on the Waijombo and Tabiti.

Your Reverence recalls that I visited the Arowaks on the Maratakka only once during the past year and, at the time, baptized several children. My plan was now to instruct and baptize some old people as well. Thanks be to God and to Mary! The results surpassed my expectations, since, out of God's goodness, I baptized forty-five native elders and blessed sixteen marriages.

I moreover baptized one old man and thirteen children of the Negro race. In total, fifty-nine.

I stopped first at Maratakka for thirteen days (while I conferred baptism in three different places since they now live spread out). There, in a single day, they built a kind of church. Since they have a great desire to learn about religion, the first thing in the morning, at 6:30 AM, they came with their children to be instructed and to attend holy Mass. They quickly learned the Our Father and the Creed, etc. As is the custom in Batavia, Joseph prayed the rosary with them during holy Mass. They assisted reverently at Mass, between the consecration and the communion they knelt down, and for the Gospel they stood. Then they began working at 8:00 AM; in the afternoon at 4:30 or 5:00 PM, they returned in order to stay until 7:00 at night or later because they are untiring in their desire to learn.

Meanwhile, many send their children in the morning and in the evening. Almost all of them, like the adults, have already memorized the necessary means and precepts as well as the prayers, to the point where they can already pray them. One need only ask and one receives.

I prepare the elders for holy baptism and for the sacrament of marriage one or two evenings. Before baptizing them, I pray the rosary with them in order to acquire from God through the intercession of the Most Holy Virgin Mary the grace of true repentance for sin so as to be worthily baptized.

Yes, these good, simple Amerindians have great faith. Two men, each of whom lived with two women, heard that this is displeasing to God and that they are only permitted to have one wife in the union of marriage after baptism. They were disposed to the point of leaving one rather than being deprived of baptism. Thus, they showed that they loved God more than creatures.

I baptized a piaïman who renounced his superstitious practice. The parents of two children whom I had baptized last year and to whom I had given the names of Peter and Paul asked Joseph (whom you met here in Batavia and who always goes with me on the visits to the plantations and among the natives) that he take care of their children and take them to Batavia so they can attend the school there and afterward be able to teach others. I brought them with me and now have them in Batavia. They knew all of the prayers from memory so well that even during the journey they were already teaching other children how to pray, turning themselves into regular little apostles.

Reverend Father Van Vlokhoven was overjoyed to have these youngsters here. In order to take these children with me I needed to obtain the permission of the director of the Institute, which I have already asked. I wrote the vicar apostolic who, as far as I know, is already back in Paramaribo. In the month of February, the Amerindians of Maratakka will contact me as they promised and then I hope to be able to admit many of them to their first Communion.

Other Arowaks, who live along the Upper Saramacca, as you know, built a small church and have almost all received communion. A short time ago, I admitted five to first Communion. Thus, with the Arowaks, things are going well. Would to God that I could say the same for the Caribs. Indeed, there are still many things left to be desired. Nevertheless, I do not despair. God will convert them some day as I hope. Let us pray fervently, because without his help we can do nothing.

On my return trip, I visited the Caribs of Waijombo and Tibiti. I baptized the children but, on this occasion, they faced me with indifference when I compare them to the zealous Arowaks. I promised them that if they wish to be instructed, be baptized, and renounce magic and drunkenness, I would stay with them for a good stretch. Some accepted and promised to build a church and to call me quickly. I hope, then, to be able to write you a good deal of better news about them.

Tomorrow night I will begin, with God's help, my spiritual exercises. I cannot, Very Reverend Father, forget to thank you with all my heart for the books that you sent and, above all, for the life of our Father Saint Alphonsus and the other works.

I beg you to give my greetings to your brother in Antwerp and to the Reverend Fathers Vogels, Jansen and the other priests and students at Wittem. I ask you to remember me and the

Amerindians in your prayers and pious thoughts. For my part, I will always keep Your Reverence in mind in my prayers, however poor they may be.

I ask your fatherly blessing, while I remain for Your Reverence, in the Sacred Hearts of Jesus and Mary,

> Your devoted, though unworthy, servant and son in Christ,
> P. Donders, C.Ss.R.

PS: In the city there is great devotion to the image of Our Lady of Perpetual Help, which, as you desired, I've placed in the church. On that occasion, I told the people the story of this miraculous image.

13. December 6, 1872, Batavia.
To the Very Reverend Father Johan Schaap, Provincial.[5]

Donders, who was now sixty-three and had spent thirty years in Surinam, has profited from his leisure moments of the last few years to learn to play the accordion so he could draw the Amerindians with his music. In this letter, he thanks the provincial for the pump-organ he had given as a gift to the mission.

His comments on his journeys among the indigenous people continue to show his balanced view of the blessings the Lord has poured out on his apostolic efforts. His successes bring him joy; his failures bring him hope. We also become more aware of his preoccupation with the last group he would seek to evangelize, the Maroon Blacks dispersed throughout the forests.

J.M.J.A.T.
Batavia, December 6, 1872

Most Reverend Father Provincial,

A year has already passed since the last time I wrote you and there is no excuse for me to put off doing so any longer, even more so, since I must thank Your Reverence for the beautiful, indeed I believe, magnificent pump-organ you were pleased to present to Batavia.

I received it in perfect shape, together with the letter from the maker. Many thanks, Very Reverend Father, for this precious gift. May God repay you. Yesterday I played it for the first time and we prayed the rosary for Your Reverence. Every day we will say an Our Father and a Hail Mary in the church for your intentions.

In September, I again visited the Amerindians of Maratakka and in October I returned to Batavia. Thanks be to God and Mary! The trip had results far beyond my expectations. With the help of God, I not only baptized and married some of the Arowaks and Warros in the places I could reach but also succeeded in hearing the confessions of those whom I baptized last year and in giving first Communion to six of them. Moreover, a group of them moved to the Waijombo, an area much closer to Batavia, so that now I can visit them more frequently and the majority of them can communicate easily. It is my hope that later the others will follow their example and live closer to Batavia.

I again had the joy of baptizing nineteen elderly native Caribs on the Waijombo as I was returning, as well as uniting five couples in matrimony, and taking with me to Batavia four of the kind of paraphernalia that the witch doctors and priests use among the Carib tribes for their magical arts. The Amerindians place much confidence in these accessories and it is this superstition that keeps them from receiving baptism and even from going to instructions.

Among those who received baptism and matrimony and who gave over their implements is their chief, Christiaan, who received the name Augustine. Thanks be to God that I have been able to baptize their leader because the devil never stops keeping busy. The witch doctors—of which there are many—are determined not to accept baptism, not even in danger of death. They were dismayed when they heard that their leader had been baptized and all the more so because he had turned over his magical instruments. Some preceded him, others imitate his example to the point that there's well-founded hope that during the coming year almost all of the Amerindians that I can visit—by the grace of God—will receive baptism. Right now, their number is already at four hundred.

The leader, Christiaan—now Augustine—together with the rest is building a church which soon will be completed and then we will be able to impart instruction to children and adults regularly.

From these few bits of news I can give Your Reverence, you can understand that there exists great hope that all of the Amerindians, with the grace of God, will accept the faith. The Arowak Amerindians are very capable and desirous to learn, with some exceptions, and are good Christians, indeed, excellent ones. On the other hand, the Caribs (with exceptions) are in no way inclined—I'm speaking of the elders—to receive baptism and listen to the instructions. They must be visited in their own camps or houses and be instructed separately; one almost has to beg them to be instructed such that we see verified in them [the words of Jesus] "compel people to come in" [Luke 14:23].

Nevertheless, the goodness and mercy of God is great and certainly has compassion for them. Therefore we need to pray. Pray much and to teach them to pray, that is the principle. In this way we can achieve all things.

When will the Blacks of the jungle receive the grace of God? Let us hope soon. I have run into some here and there so as to be able to baptize and marry some of them, but up until now only a small number. For the most part they are very much attached to idolatry. Let us hope, nevertheless, that God will extend his compassion also to them, as well as to the other hundreds of millions who today do not yet know him, and all the more to the great number who know him but do not seek to honor him and even go to the point of denying him. Let us also hope that God in his mercy will call millions of pagans to his Church and his service. For this let us always pray.

[Give my] greetings, my Reverend Father, if possible, to your brother Louis, as well as to the Reverend Fathers, especially Father Vogels, Jansen, and Anthony.

Repeating my heartfelt thanks and asking for your blessing, I remain, Very Reverend Father, in the Hearts of Jesus and Mary,

Your Subject and Thankful Son,
P. Donders, C.Ss.R.

PS: Since the New Year will have begun before you receive this letter, I cordially greet Your Reverence. May God give you abundant grace, strength, wisdom, zeal, and perseverance in the conduct of your difficult office, for the glory of God and the good of all of us. May he grant you many years for the benefit of our Congregation and fill you with his Spirit. Let us pray to God for this intention. I also recommend to your holy prayers our poor lepers, the Amerindians, the Blacks, and myself.

I remain yours, Reverend Father, in the Hearts of Jesus and Mary,

Your humble son,
P. Donders, C.Ss.R.

14. November 14, 1873, Batavia.
To a Confrere in Holland (Father Aegidius Vogels [?]).[6]

Father Pete again writes to his old friend from his youth in Tilburg. The topics parallel those of the previous and following letters to his provincial superior.

Again, Donders reminds us that the power behind apostolic activity lies in prayer. He talks insistently about prayer and maintains that his pastoral experiences lead him back to prayer and that prayer produces abundant ministerial blessings.

It is interesting to note that Donders speaks of thirty-one years on the mission (sixteen of which were among the lepers). In this same year of 1873, Blessed Damian [Joseph de Veuster, 1840–1889] arrived at his leper colony in Molokai, Hawaii, where he will die of the disease after sixteen years of pastoral service.

J.M.J.A.T.
Batavia, November 14, 1873

Reverend Father,

I feel guilty that I have not written to you for so long. I hope to repair this as far as possible by means of this present letter. The Arowaks are doing very well, far beyond all expectation. On the Maratakka, almost all, with few exceptions, have been baptized and married, and thirty-five of them have reached first Communion.

On September 17, the thirty-first anniversary of the beginning of my apostolate here, I administered first Communion to twenty people, and on the same day, as I returned, I gave others three hours of instruction, baptized a child and seven elderly, and married a couple.

In all, among the Arowaks along the Upper Waijombo and Upper Saramacca, I have about fifty people who frequent Communion.

With the Caribs, however, there is still much lacking. Still, there we proceed little by little, despite the fact that they have tried to make my work difficult and, if possible, to block all my service. Indeed, for the past two years those so-called piaïmans or witch doctors have determined not to receive baptism nor to attend instructions, and to impede others from doing so. Therefore, they are teaching the young people magical arts. Nevertheless, these are hard to learn, since one must drink tobacco water for six weeks without being able to eat almost anything. All this is very bad for their health. They hold these magical arts in great esteem and they place full confidence in them when they are sick.

Last year, I had the good fortune of baptizing their leader, by name Christiaan. I named him Augustine. He renounced magic and voluntarily turned over his magic implements in which—to their way of thinking—[magical] forces exist. So many others followed his example that on that very day I succeeded in baptizing nineteen elderly men and women, and married five couples. Since then I have succeeded in baptizing several witch doctors. I've taken many of the magical instruments to Batavia. Here right now, I have an attic full of magical instruments!

On October 26, I solemnly blessed (with the faculty of blessing new churches), the Church of Saint Joseph. For the most part, they constructed the chapel themselves, although slowly for the reasons I mentioned above. The day before the blessing of the church, October 25, the principal magician Louis (now, at his own request, called Alphonsus), asked for holy baptism because he found himself attacked by a dangerous dysentery.

It seems that divine Providence intervened here, since dysentery has sickened mainly the witch doctors and many of them have already died. Three of these live near the church and two of them are gravely ill. One will receive baptism; I often advise the other to receive baptism and I tell him at the same time of the unhappy situation that would develop if he reached the point of death in this way. It is, alas, in vain; he did not request it.

I am aware, in truth, Reverend Father, that there is nothing better than to pray for these poor blind people. Pray much, Very Reverend Father, that God, by the intercession of his Holy Mother who also wishes to be their mother, in his goodness and mercy will have pity on all of them.

In total, there are now 432 baptized Amerindians, fifty-five married, and some fifty who take Communion. Would that this number increase quickly!

I also wrote to Very Reverend Father Provincial, just as last year. I do not doubt that His Reverence will tell you about what I wrote him.

Let us recommend each other to persevere in our holy vocation and to reach the crown of the fortunate.

In the Hearts of Jesus and Mary I remain yours, Very Reverend Father, wishing you a happy New Year,

Your servant and confrere in Christ,
P. Donders, C.Ss.R.

15. November 14, 1873, Batavia.
To the Very Reverend Johan Shaap.[7]

Donders again reports to his provincial superior about his activities. Although he continues to work among the lepers, his heart is set on the care of the nomadic Amerindians since he has another Redemptorist at the leper colony to care for its needs. His work with the Arowaks is his great consolation because of the wonderful way in which God has blessed it. His is a very personal ministry, not to large masses of people, but to small groups, one-on-one, and by seeking out the most far-flung small tribes. Here is where he feels most deeply to be a Redemptorist.

That religious life was not a bed of roses seems to be mirrored in his closing remarks about a Brother Matthew who did not seem to fit into the life of the mission.

By now it should be clear to us how all of Father Pete's life centered on two compelling beliefs: the constant, all-encompassing will of God at work in his ministry, and the need for constant prayer. Like a true lover, God was always the support of Father Pete's life and the ever-present partner of his conversations.

J.M.J.A.T.
November 14, 1873, Batavia

Very Reverend Father,

To satisfy your wishes, I write you a few words, especially about what is going on with the Amerindians.

First, about my very dear Arowak Amerindians. In September, I visited them on the Maratakka and on the Waijombo [rivers]. I no sooner arrived at the Maratakka when everyone, except for a few who were transporting wood through the jungle, was eager to learn and receive the sacraments. I thus stayed there with them for six days so I would not lose out on any instructions, which they received with extraordinary enthusiasm.

On September 17 (my thirty-first anniversary of work on this mission), I felt the greatest happiness, by the grace of God, in admitting twenty persons to first Communion. At Mass, I gave communion to twenty-two, since two of them had been admitted to Communion last year. I truly wished that Your Reverence had witnessed this solemnity and could have seen their faith and devotion. All were properly and modestly dressed. The altar was adorned; no greenery was lacking. Instead of flowers, they had arranged bird feathers, for example from crows and parrots. Three long tree trunks were set up to serve as seats and as a communion table from the Epistle side to the Gospel side. They knelt on these tree trunks at the consecration and Communion. When they approached for Communion, two of my oarsmen held the Communion cloth. Your Reverence would certainly have approved of such an Amerindian camp!

After the solemnity, we left, much moved emotionally. Following three hours of navigation, we reached the place where the wood carriers were who had not been able to attend. They stopped working and I told them I wanted to give them instruction. There were several among them who had not been baptized. Well, they washed up, put on their clothes, and came to instructions.

I taught them for two or three hours and, on that very day, I had the joy of baptizing seven adults and one child, as well as marry one couple. All this on the 17th; we worked until nightfall!

Then I also visited Nickerie, where I baptized two children, distributed Communion to five persons, among whom there was a pair that I think have not received for the last seven years.

On the way back, still on the Upper Waijombo, I gave Communion to nine Arowaks. Therefore, in all, a total of twenty-nine received first Communion on this trip.

Lastly, I visited the Carib Amerindians on the Lower Waijombo. After thirty days of travel I was back in Batavia. The number of communicants among the Arowaks is around fifty. Would that the Caribs, by God's grace, reach the same number! These people, seduced by the devil and by the infamous witch doctors, have conspired for the last two years not only to block the construction of one church among them, but to cause trouble for the missionaries to the point where they have stopped them from working.

Still, despite the opposition of the devil and the witch doctors, on October 26, with the permission of the Reverend Bishop, I blessed and solemnly inaugurated the Church of Saint Joseph, which, much to the devil's distress, the very same natives had built almost alone. God also intervened there, by punishing them, especially the witch doctors, with grave sicknesses. On this occasion, the head witch doctor, becoming very sick, asked for and received holy baptism.

So we advance little by little. The Lord, as I hope, will follow us with his help. We hope in him and pray a lot.

Between October [18]72 and October [18]73, there have been 105 Amerindians baptized. The total now reaches 432. The marriages contracted among the Amerindians add up to fifty-five.

Here is, Very Reverend Father, a short synthesis of the work among the Amerindians. I finish by recommending the natives and me to your holy prayers. On my part, I wish you a happy and successful New Year. Would that the New Year might bring the triumph of the persecuted Church and its freedom from the hands of our enemies! Let us pray to the Heart of Jesus for this intention, along with all the Church.

Repeating my wishes for all the heavenly blessings and begging your paternal blessing, Very Reverend Father, I remain in the Hearts of Jesus and Mary,

Your Reverence's devoted son in Christ,
P. Donders, C.Ss.R.

PS: Thanks be to God that Brother Matthew has left. We can get along without the Brother.

**16. January 2[–4], 1874, Batavia.
To Monsignor Johan Swinkels, Titular Bishop of Amorium,
Vicar Apostolic of Surinam.**[8]

Unfortunately, no letters from Father Pete during his first sixteen years serving the lepers at Batavia have come down to us. Therefore, we must rely on these later letters from his second sojourn to learn from him personally about his life among these exiled people. One major issue he had to face dealt with the treatment of the children of lepers. The colonial government had laid down norms and had begun to use force behind them. Here he pleads with the bishop to intervene with the authorities in favor of the children.

He also shows his concern for the education of the children and for the training of leper youngsters for employment. From the time the Redemptorists took over the work at the leper colony, Redemptorist Brothers had taken up the task of running an apprentice school there.

Again we find an insight into how the spirituality of Donders was not an "otherworldly," utopian dream, but a down-to-earth recognition of the totality of redemption, "Whatever you do to the least..."

J.M.J.A.T.
January 2, 1874, Batavia

Very Reverend Father,
 During these holidays, three of my rowers came to me to ask for more money for the job of rowing my boat because they receive nothing from the government since they are healthy and the fifty cents a day is too little for someone who has to pay his own way. I have been expecting this for a long time. Since their reasons are valid, I promised them for the future sixty-four cents a day, hoping that Your Excellency would approve this decision and be happy with it.

Note: In the boat for the city there are thirteen people, children and adults, to be examined [for leprosy]. Some of the children, eight or nine, had gone into hiding, and they had to hunt them out and take them all since the agent, M. van Meerten, is here to follow the strict norms of [illegible title] in the name of the governor. Thirteen left today by boat. The total number of adults and children has to be twenty-four or twenty-five, and five of them are minors: three little girls a few years old and two little boys. Some, nevertheless, remain hidden; still, they have to be found because the orders are strict; they are to be followed for good or ill.

One little Chinese boy named Charles was saved from death by a woman since the father, when he received the notice to send even this child to the city, wanted to kill him rather than give him up. When I found this out, I begged van Meerten to leave the child alone, because I was afraid that if he used force either the father or the parents would end up dead. At first, he said no; I protested, along with the doctor, out of fear of shedding innocent blood. He gave in. But then he received by boat new norms, even more severe and he came to read me the letter. I told him I would protest, above all for the use of violence, and the doctor said the same. Finally, the agent had the mother contacted again and permitted her to take the child to the city herself and to stay with him until the medical examination was over. If he was found to be infected, she would have to come back to Batavia by boat bringing the boy. If he was declared healthy, it would follow that the governor would allow the child to stay with the mother for two or three more years since he is still so young.

This is what happened. The mother is now traveling with the child, and the agent repeated the promise to the father in my presence. Still, can the agent keep his word and let the boy come back with this mother? I fear not. What will be the consequences when they find out that they have been deceived? Will they commit suicide? With the doctor's agreement, some of the older children will return, the ones between the ages of eight and sixteen. The older ones must go to learn a profession.

Hence, [they look on] the children as the property of the state, in a Protestant orphanage (in order to make them Protestants or

Brethren). God free us! I trust in the Good God to take these children under his protection and that Your Excellence will find the way to save them from all dangers. Let us pray for this intention. I promised their relatives and everyone to write Your Excellence in order to recommend to you these unfortunates. I add a short list. Father van Vlokhoven should know them all.

Meanwhile, carpenters came here to repair all buildings, workmen to dig and repair the drainage, and an assistant doctor is to come. A lot of expense. I don't know why; might it be that they are going to send more infected people from the city or the plantations?

Today, January 4, the octave day of [the feast of the] Holy Innocents, the little ones who were hidden go by boat to the city. Two mothers who have the youngest children are also being allowed to go with them to the city. The fathers also go along as oarsmen. The agent promised the mothers that the governor will visit them at the Government's Establishment. Then they can try to take the children back with them to Batavia after they have been examined until they are somewhat older. But will they [really] be allowed to do so? There are three girls among them, two who are twins; it would be good for all three of them if [it turns out] they are declared healthy but the mothers are not allowed to bring them back to Batavia that they could be accepted in our Providence Orphanage. I hope that divine Providence will take care of them. For the other children—ages five, six, seven, eight, nine, ten, twelve, fourteen, and sixteen, but particularly those up to age ten—I would hope that they could also go to school with the Brothers or Sisters. The other youngsters have to learn a trade. God, so I hope, will provide in everything and for all.

Here is the list of those who had to go. Those marked with a little cross are the five little ones.

[Paragraph of names omitted.]

The agent asked me to write to Your Reverence, asking you to use your influence with the governor so that these five little ones can come back to Batavia until they are six or seven years old. I add, if that does not happen, that then at least they be accepted in our orphanage.

Blessed be God! All has turned out well. The agent is happy and has written a very moving letter to the governor about these little children that he read to us. The doctor also sends Your Excellency his greetings.

I again recommend to Your Excellency all of those on the list, especially the children, and I ask for your episcopal blessing. I remain, in the Sacred Hearts of Jesus and Mary,

Your Excellency's obedient son,
P. Donders, C.Ss.Red.

17. December 29, 1874, Batavia.
To Monsignor Johan Swinkels.[9]

Father Pete's concern over the children of the lepers continues. He also notes a bit of record keeping. Catholics who wed members of other denominations must obtain a dispensation from one of the Church's laws against such a union. These are granted by the local bishop. Obviously because of the distance, Monsignor Swinkels gave delegation to Donders to grant a certain number of such dispensations; when he had done so, he renewed his request for further delegation.

Again, Donders' devotion to God's will appears as a theme.

J.M.J.A.T.
Batavia, December 29, 1874

Very Reverend Father,

As you asked me to do, I inform you that I have given the following dispensations:

December 11: Crispijn Andreas de Meer married Emelina Loods, non-Catholic, with dispensation *super illiceitate*. Witnesses were Louis de Meer and Johannes Rumaar; on the Monitor Plantation, Saramacca.

December 15: Pier Carel Jacobus Goede married Philippina Josephina Kees (of the Moravian Brethren). Witnesses were Augustinus Butheine and Nicolaas Ven, the same [place], Saramacca. With dispensation *super illiceitate*.

Philip Louis Durepee married Susanna Charlotte Grunberg (Lutheran) with dispensation *super illiceitate*. Witnesses were Augustinus [Butheine] and Nicolaas Ven, as above.

This means three dispensations of the same category (together with an earlier one, that makes four), so I still have one. It would be good if Your Reverence could give me the faculties for five more.

Yesterday (on Holy Innocents' Day) the schooner unexpectedly arrived here suddenly to bring to the city's orphanage at the Government's Establishment all the seemingly healthy children two years and older for an examination, along with the adults who seem to be healthy. Later, I will give you the numbers. It would be a good thing if Mr. Haase would be appointed director of the Government's Establishment, as there was talk of before. But will it happen?

I have a well-founded hope that things will go well with the schoolmaster for the Amerindians at Tabiti. Next week (*Deo volente* [God willing]) I will go there; I heard that I will be able to baptize some children and aged people there. So the next time, I hope to write more about this and hopefully [it will be] good news. Let's pray to God and put all our trust in him.

We wholeheartedly wish Your Reverence a happy New Year and God's best blessings.[10] Though this year starts with crosses, it cannot but contribute to our salvation and eternal happiness (if we accept and bear them with subjection to God's holy will). May the Good God give you many more years and graces so as to become a great saint. *Fiat, fiat.* [Amen, amen.] For this, we will pray.

Asking your episcopal blessing, we remain in the Sacred Hearts of Jesus and Mary,

Your Reverence's humble son,
P. Donders C.Ss.Red.

18. January 18, 1875, Batavia.
To the Very Reverend Johan Schaap, Superior in Paramaribo.[11]

Monsignor Schaap, whom we met as the provincial superior of the Dutch Province, has now completed his work in that post and has been assigned to direct the mission in Surinam. This brief letter serves merely as a polite note to his superior because an occasion has arisen for communication in a country with no postal system. The short postscript about a list of supplies provides us with a sense of the isolation Father Pete, together with the other missionaries, must have often felt in their ministry. While the list appended to this letter has been lost, we find a similar one in letter #20, page 169.

By now, we are aware how all Donders' letters, including this one, manifest his constant awareness of the presence of God in all his works.

J.M.J.A.Th.
Batavia, this 18th of January, 1875

Very Reverend Father Superior,
 Since Joseph is going to the city by boat to bring the doctor's children to you, I have a good chance to write you and to receive something or other from you. Joseph can bring back with him these things as well as those already requested.
 We want to know how it will go with the children. The schoolteacher among the Amerindians in Tabiti is performing well and is doing things just as we want. This was our only hope that things would proceed well.
 Nevertheless, I know of nothing special to tell you. I try, and I always will try with God's grace, to obey your direction so that I may live in greater unity with God now and one day to enjoy the blessed happiness of dying and possessing God forever. Amen.
 Please greet the reverend fathers and brothers, and let us always pray for one another. Sending a friendly greeting also to

Father Startz, I remain in the Most Sacred Hearts of Jesus and Mary, Very Reverend Father,

                    Your Reverence's humble child in Christ,
                                    P. Donders, C.Ss.R.

PS: In the margin, I am sending [the list] of our needs.

19. *May 3, 1875, Batavia.*
To the Very Reverend Father Peter Oomen, Superior of the Dutch Redemptorist Province. [12]

Father Oomen (1835–1910) became provincial in 1874 and held the position until 1887. Thus, he was still provincial when Father Pete died. He later went on to serve in the world-wide administration of the Redemptorist Congregation. This is the first of fifteen letters to Father Oomen that we still have, making Father Pete's correspondence with him more extensive than what remains with anyone else.

In this first letter to his new provincial superior, Father Pete gives him a quick summary of his happiness in his religious vocation and his present apostolic work.

Since we have already heard these things the provincial is hearing for the first time, we can notice a bit of the person behind the work. Notice the concern that the ministry can find permanent root. (Today, we might question this desire to change the nomadic nature of this indigenous culture; in Father Pete's time, the question did not even arise. His concern was for them to be able to know Jesus Christ.) We might also take note of how his description of facts is framed by the echoes of his entire spirituality: thanksgiving for God's graciousness.

J.M.J.A.Th.
Batavia, this 3rd of May, 1875

Very Reverend Father Provincial,
At the request of the Very Reverend Father Superior, I take the liberty of writing Your Reverence, and mentioning a thing or two.

As far as concerns me, Very Reverend Father, I can never thank the Good God enough that he would call me to our Congregation of the Most Holy Redeemer. May God give me the grace of living as a true and fervent Redemptorist and of persevering until death. Every day I beg this of the Mercy of God and of the intercession of the Most Holy Virgin Mary, our most dear Mother.

It is now about nineteen years that I have been fulfilling my ministry here in Batavia. Also for almost seven years I have been visiting the plantations on the Saramacca. I visit, catechize, administer baptism and the holy sacraments to three different tribes of Amerindians: (1) the Arowak Amerindians, and these are the best; (2) the Caribs; and (3) the Warouwi. The Warouwi are not many, and year by year their numbers decrease because they are nomadic and live disorderly lives. A great many of them, I think three quarters, are baptized and united in marriage; some are confirmed and admitted to most holy Communion. Because they are [always] on the move, it is very difficult to teach them as we should. On the Tabiti, about one hundred live together. There, with the permission of the vicar apostolic and superior, the school teacher, or better catechizer, is located to teach the children and even the adults. This has recently begun and to good advantage. Would that we could do the same here and in other places; this would be very useful, in fact, necessary, to make the good something permanent; but it is difficult to get them to live together.

God alone can take care [of all this]. Therefore, prayer is the main thing, for what could we possibly do without the help of God? Nothing. So allow me to commend myself to your prayers along with these pitiful Amerindians, as well as the Reverend Fathers and Brothers, that in his mercy, the Good God will have mercy on them and on the forest Blacks as well, who mainly still live in paganism and idolatry.

I, too, pray for you every day, Very Reverend Father, that all of us may live as true Redemptorists and in the end all enter together into the joy of God.

I ask that when you have the chance, you give my greetings to the Reverend Fathers, especially Vogels, van Rijckevorsel, Jansen, and van Mens. Reverend Father Startz, who is also writing you now [and] has already been in Batavia for almost two years.

With a friendly greeting in the Most Sacred Hearts of Jesus and Mary, Most Reverend Father, [I remain],

Your Reverence's humble son in Christ,
P. Donders, C.Ss.R.

20. June 16, 1875, Batavia.
To the Very Reverend Father Johan Schaap, Superior in Paramaribo.[13]

The Consecration to the Sacred Heart of Jesus is a devotion centered in sympathizing with the suffering Jesus in order to make reparation for all sins committed. It is seen as way of reuniting the human race to its loving Savior. Its roots go far back in the Church and became more formal in the Middle Ages. It emerged as a common practice of prayer to heal the wounds the Church suffered by the Reformation and was furthered by the visions of Saint Margaret Mary Alacoque (1647–1690). Pope Pius IX established the Feast of the Sacred Heart for the whole Church in 1856 and encouraged the devotion. One of its consequences was the growth of more frequent Communion.

The many references to people being allowed to communicate found in Father Pete's letters remind us that until the time of Pope Saint Pius X (1835–1914), because of the influence of the rigorism introduced into the Church in the 1700s by Jansenism, the reception of Communion was rare. Even among religious sisters and brothers, re-

ception more than once a week required a confessor's permission. Pious laity communicated once a month.

Devotion to the Sacred Heart is an evident part of Donders' spirituality as is obvious by his constant reference to it in the conclusion of each letter.

Very Reverend Father Superior,

This evening the public courier is moving on to the city. I use this opportunity to write you.

We received everything [you sent] in good shape; also the flour and the alcohol lamp; for these things I thank you.

Today we solemnly made our consecration to the Sacred Heart of Jesus. The church was beautifully decorated. Almost everyone received Communion. The consecration, as desired by His Holiness Pius IX, was done very solemnly. Everyone together, each holding a lit decorated candle in hand, participated in the ceremony of consecration after a solemn holy Mass with exposition of the Blessed Sacrament. It was indeed a celebration for the Batavians. The doctor and the director participated in the feast by distributing the candles. Now, we hope, the desires of the Sacred Heart and of Blessed Margarite Alacoque have been fulfilled.

Would that Jesus in his infinite mercy console his afflicted and troubled Church and be its help. May he hear all our prayers. It is certainly everyone's desire, and principally the Holy Father's, that the Church triumph and spread; may all heretics, on this feast, acknowledge the true Church and return to it! May it be so! Thanks be to God and Mary!

We are sending Your Reverence some empty chests and bottles, pictures and public papers. This time, please send large and small hosts, some nails to repair the houseboat, cheese and smoked meat, shoe polish, and, lastly, some laundry soap for the housekeeper.

Please greet the vicar apostolic and the priests and brothers [for me]. From our hearts we greet Your Reverence and pray for you.

I remain in the Most Sacred Hearts of Jesus and Mary,

Your Reverence's humble son and confrere,
P. Donders, C.Ss.R.

21. (Undated), 1875, Batavia.
To his confrere, Father Cornelis van Coll, in Paramaribo.[14]

Again we see Father Pete concerned about the leper children.

Dear Confrere,

This is an answer to the first part of Your Reverence's letter; the second part follows. The maid of the doctor, who is the grandmother of the two children, will probably come to the city soon to speak with the Fathers and Monsignor about the children. In my opinion, it would be best if they could be accepted into the orphanage. I hear from the wife of the doctor, however, that Monsanto, the father of the two children, has already had himself appointed as tutor right from the beginning. I fear this will be the case, unless the Governor through the Monsignor would be able to do something about it so that F. I., the grandmother, could be appointed tutor. If she comes to the city, Your Reverence will decide what to do.

All yours in the Most Sacred Hearts of Jesus and Mary,
P. Donders, C.Ss.R.

22. July 17, 1876, Batavia.
To the Very Reverend Peter Oomen.[15]

Father Pete makes another report to his provincial superior in Holland.

We should notice that his correspondence begins to make a subtle shift. Where his early longer letters had much to say about his apostolic work, now we see he has much less to say about that. In its place, more reflection appears about his inner life, his spirituality hidden in the outer actions.

Here he gives an account of some of his work, but he has more to say about his joy in his vocation as a Redemptorist and his trails in bringing the Gospel to the native peoples.

J.M.J.A.T.
Batavia, July 17, 1876

Very Reverend Father Provincial,

To satisfy your just request, I will recount several things. First, heartfelt thanks to Your Reverence for the very beautiful Stations of the Cross that we erected and solemnly blessed on the second of this month by faculties requested and granted by our Most Reverend Superior and Pro-Vicar Apostolic. Both you and I can rejoice that I am able to say that the faithful of Batavia make the Stations more frequently now than in the past.

I also thank you for the large and very lovely corpus of Our Lord for our cemetery. As soon as a suitable cross has been made for it, we will solemnly bless it and erect it in the cemetery.

I can never thank God enough for having called me, who am so unworthy, to our holy Congregation of the Most Holy Redeemer. May the God of Goodness and the Most Holy Virgin grant me perseverance. I pray for this intention every day. Allow me to recommend myself to your prayers that I live and die a holy Redemptorist. I pray every day for Your Reverence, especially during holy Mass.

I am doing well, thanks be to God. I can regularly visit the plantations and the Amerindians. These visits are, thanks be to God, rich in crosses and setbacks, especially among the Carib Amerindians, as well as among most Blacks on the plantations. Among the Arowak Amerindians the situation is better.

What we still have to wish for are good catechists and teachers. We hope we can enroll some. In two places, in Tabiti and Calebas, the catechists are working to great advantage. The little children are learning the catechism and prayers well, and doing the same at reading and writing. It is sad that their parents often do not show up with their children. If only there were some way we could get all of them to agree to gather in one place. Then we could surely work with greater satisfaction. Nevertheless, this is not something in the nature of the Amerindians.

Still, everything is possible for God. He will provide. He gave up his only-begotten Son for them. Jesus shed all his blood for them too. Thus, let's hope, trust, and pray a great deal for them. Saint Alphonsus, so I hope, along with the Mother of God, prays for them that they all may ultimately become good Christians and Catholics, and that the Blacks in the jungle also enjoy this same result.

We note, Your Reverence, that among the Amerindians the work proceeds slowly. We have baptized some five hundred, many of whom, especially the children, have already died. Baptizing them, however, is not enough; it is more difficult to succeed in making them live as Christians. Only God can accomplish this change. Patience and prayer must be our weapons.

I beg you to recommend me, though unworthy, in your prayers and sacrifices along with the Amerindians and Blacks. With my warm greetings, Reverend Father, I remain in the Hearts of Jesus and Mary,

Your Reverence's devoted son and brother in Christ,
P. Donders, C.Ss.R.

23. January 20, 1877, Paramaribo.
To the Very Reverend Peter Oomen.[16]

Perhaps Father Pete has less to say about his work because it is very much "more of the same"; the same peoples, the same successes, the same trials.

In this letter, his undying confidence in the God "who can do all things" is again manifest. "How necessary and effective prayer is."

Still, prayer is not enough. To this there must be added self-sacrifice for others, as well as appreciation for their customs and a preferential love for them.

J.M.J.A.T.
January 20, 1877

Very Reverend Father Provincial,
 Since I have been here for a little while, the Most Reverend Vicar Apostolic asked me to write Your Reverence.
 Since my last letter, I visited the Amerindians on the Maratakka last year in September where I baptized some older adults of the Arowaks and Warros, and so it turns out that all of them have been baptized except for one child who will receive baptism in Nickerie at the first opportunity. Half of them now receive Communion. All of them could receive holy Communion if they were sufficiently catechized.
 The people there are, thanks be to God, good people. On the other hand, the Caribs leave much to be desired. We would be tempted to stop going out to them if we were not persuaded that God is almighty and that he, in his infinite mercy, can also enlighten them with his light and move their hearts.
 I beg you to remember me in your holy prayers along with these poor Amerindians that the God of Goodness illumine them and that we can come to know them better and love them all the more.
 Now I know how necessary and effective prayer is. God asks of us penitence and sacrifice in order to gain these souls for whom Jesus willed to lay down his life and his precious blood.
 In spite of all, God in his goodness also wishes to console us from time to time. Thus, last November, in my ten-day journey along the Saramacca [to visit] the plantations and the Amerindians I succeeded in baptizing ten adults and children, marrying four couples (two of whom had lived in concubinage for the last eight years), and administering [first] Communion to thirty-nine. Thanks be to God and Mary!
 Allow me to request your fatherly blessing and to again recommend myself to your prayers so that I persevere and praise and bless God for all eternity together with these poor Amerindians.

With my sincere greetings, I remain in the Hearts of Jesus and Mary,

Your Reverence's devoted son,
P. Donders, C.Ss.R.

24. February 3, 1878, Batavia.
To Very Reverend Johan Schaap, Pro-Vicar Apostolic of Surinam.[17]

In this letter to his religious superior, Father Pete explains his efforts, at the vicar's request, to find a suitable place for conducting services on one of the plantations. During this period soon after the emancipation of the slaves, the Blacks remained as low-paid workers on the same plantations for a period of ten years.

We are not sure what the dispensation discussed was. During this time, it was a Redemptorist custom to abstain from meat on Saturdays in honor of the Blessed Virgin; perhaps there was a request for a dispensation from this. It does not sound as if the pro-vicar granted it.

J.M.J.A.T.
Batavia, February 3, 1878

Most Reverend and Illustrious Lord and Father,

Yesterday, Saturday afternoon, I arrived in Batavia. I found Reverend Father Verbeek and everyone else in good health. Father Verbeek was very happy when he saw all that I had brought back with me. He was very busy bookbinding and making rosaries. If Your Reverence has any to bind, he would gladly do so.

I was at the Catharina Sophia plantation. Director Geefke was absent. Doctor Desse who owns it was there and I had a pleasant conversation with him until Geefke returned. While there, I asked to be allowed to have religious services in the house on Friday morning and Doctor Desse accepted this and said he had nothing against it. But Geefke, after I presented your request and desire, was totally against it and said: (1) it was too soon; (2) he would come to the city next month; (3) he was very busy with the milling. He asked when I would return there. I said in March. Then it would be better and he would find out how many Catholics were on the plantation. Even the storekeeper, who was then in the city, is a Catholic.

I remained there until evening after supper. Then I took the boat to Dankbaarheid, which was nearby, and said Mass there as is the custom. Saturday morning I moved on to the Kent Plantation and after lunch returned to Batavia.

As Your Reverence asked me to do, I spoke with Father Verbeek about that Saturday dispensation and gave him the reasons about which Your Reverence wrote. Everything was in order.

From my heart, Very Reverend, I thank you for the kind and cordial reception and for all the gifts. Father Verbeek also thanks you and greets Your Excellency. I hope that, by God's goodness, your health increases and that you completely get well. Let us pray for this.

P. Donders, C.Ss.R.

25. June 8, 1880, Batavia.
To Very Reverend Pete Oomen, Provincial.[18]

As we read this letter that again briefly describes some of his work for the Maroons in the forests, we must remember they are written by a man of seventy, not a youth of twenty-five. What became of the frail, sickly weaver boy who occupied the early part of our story? This significant change of his physical being is perhaps one of the great signs of his special closeness to God.

This letter reveals Father Pete's spirituality as it manifested itself in his religious vocation when he speaks about his own vocation and about that of his provincial superior as Donders congratulates him of the feast day of his patron saint.

J.M.J.A.T.
Batavia, June 8, 1880

Very Reverend Father Provincial,

The great feast of your patron, the apostle Saint Peter, is drawing near. I offer you my cordial good wishes then. May the God of Goodness, through the intercession of Saint Peter, grant you many graces and help so that you may govern all of us, your sons, in a way that [helps us] persevere in our holy vocation and reach that perfection that God wants of us, and at the same time, after we have procured the glory of God on earth by sanctifying ourselves and by working for the salvation of a multitude of souls, we can praise God in heaven for all eternity. This is what I wish for you, Very Reverend Father Provincial. May the God of all that is good give you wisdom, courage, and grace through the intercession of the most holy Virgin Mary, Our Mother, and your patron, Saint Peter.

As far as I am concerned, Very Reverend Father, day by day I see more clearly the great good fortune that was given me in being called to our holy Congregation of the Most Holy Redeemer. Every day we thank God, but this happiness is so great that that I can never thank him enough. May he help us to remain faithful unto death so that, after our passing, in union with our Father Saint Alphonsus, we can thank God and his holy Mother Mary forever. Let us pray for this intention.

I remember Your Reverence in my daily prayers and holy sacrifices [of the Mass]. Please allow me to commend myself and the poor Amerindians to your prayers. I continue to visit, as always, the indigenous people, the plantations and the Blacks on the small holdings. During my last trip among the Blacks I received the greatest satisfaction in distributing sixty-eight Communions and baptizing eight children. The Amerindians are just too widely dispersed; sometimes they are here, sometimes there, almost always moving about. Very many of them are already baptized, close to six or seven hundred. But many of them have already died, especially the children.

I hope and pray that, because God is all-powerful and all-merciful, we can still work with greater success for their salvation. May God himself be merciful to them!

Repeating my prayers and wishes, and asking your fatherly blessing, with my profound greeting,

I remain, Very Reverend Father, in the Hearts of Jesus and Mary,

> Your Reverence's faithful servant and son in Christ,
> P. Donders, C.Ss.R.

26. August 1, 1880, Batavia.
|To the Very Reverend Father Cornelis van Coll, Pro-Vicar Apostolic of Surinam (during the absence of Father Schaap).[19]

The next three letters (#26, #27, #28) show Father Pete dealing with the day-to-day demands of life in the leprosarium at Batavia. We might notice, amid all these banal matters, that he shows neither scrupulousness nor presumption. He does what needs to be done, even if he must make on-the-spot decisions that must be reported to his superior. Yet the reporting is clear and unapologetic. He does what he has to do.

This attitude is probably an outflow of his trust in God and his humility in being willing to make mistakes, knowing that wisdom lies in prudence, not in correctness.

Batavia, August 1, 1880

Very Reverend Father,

Herein Your Reverence will find last month's account for July together with the report of the [Mass] intentions celebrated. All of us, Reverend Father van der Kamp, Brother Frans,[20] and I congratulate Your Reverence wholeheartedly on your temporary appointment to replace Monsignor. We will pray for you to the Good God who imposed this great burden and duty on you, [asking] that he help you to bear them and to fulfill the obligations to his greater honor and for the salvation of your soul and of all who are entrusted to your care.

As usual, I report those married with a dispensation: on July 30, on the plantation on the Lower Saramacca, Frans Denner was joined in marriage to Juliana with a dispensation *super illiceitate* in a mixed marriage. The witnesses were Paulus Liber and Frederik Filon.

I was at the Catharina Sophia [Plantation] and met Mr. Cohen and his wife. They would like to marry in church but preferred to wait until they come to the city, where they will go in six weeks. They had had some upset that day, I think with their housekeeper, and they were not in a good mood to do it right away; that's what they told me. Since I heard that the woman had already received the sacraments in the city, I agreed that they wait until they go to the city.

Monsignor wrote me before he left that he would not be opposed to my traveling to the Maratakka since I heard the Amerindians had come back from the Corantÿn where they had stayed for a couple of years. I thought that in place of going to the city I would do better making the other journey during the upcoming high tide since Father van de Kamp is still here.

Then later on, I can come to the city *[here some words are illegible]*. I will undertake that journey if God wills, since Your Reverence left it up to me whether to go up to the city now or not. By then, Father van der Kamp will probably be in North America. Your Reverence will be so kind as to send money for that long journey of three to four weeks.

Recommending myself to your prayers, I remain with best regards in the Sacred Hearts of Jesus and Mary,

Your humble servant and most devoted confrere,
P. Donders C.SS.R.

27. August 16, 1880, Batavia.
To the Very Reverend Father Cornelis van Coll.[21]

J.M.J.A.T.
Batavia, August 16, 1880

Very Reverend Father,

I thank you for your information regarding the journey to the Maratakka and I agree completely with your Reverence. I will postpone that journey until the Good God will allow it and another Father will be able to come to Batavia; the will of God be done in everything. Mr. Roseveld sent a tombstone, mortar and cement. Mr. Hogerhuis forwarded the stones, mortar, and cement to the director to erect a monument on the grave of the late Antoon Roseveld in the cemetery [in Paramaribo]. They have already started working on it. Thus far, I gave them permission to do so, but I told the director that I would write you about it because in the city of Paramaribo, there is payment due for that kind of a monument.

So, would you be so kind, Reverend Father, to tell me if and how much has to be paid for it?

The outside of the church has just been painted.

Brother Frans is well.

Thanks be to God, Father Startz recovered but this [illness] can come back. God alone knows what is best. His holy will be done. Otherwise, everything is as usual. Cordial regards from Brother Frans and me.

In the Hearts of Jesus and Mary,

Your Reverence's humble servant
and most devoted confrere,
P. Donders C.Ss.R.

28. August 24, 1880, Batavia.
To the Very Reverend Father Cornelis van Coll.[22]

J.M.J.A.T.
Batavia, August 24 1880

Very Reverend Father,
   Many thanks for your much appreciated letters and for offering me the faculty to give dispensations when I need to do so. I still have several dispenses left from the Monsignor so that at the moment I don't need them. If necessary, I will inform you in time.
   Another question. Four or five weeks ago we had to take the Stations of the Cross in the church down, and it will take another two or three weeks before everything is ready and dry. Thus, it will take almost two months before it can be put up again. Isn't it necessary, in order to gain the indulgences and favors, to reerect the Stations again canonically and bless the paintings and crosses anew? If it is necessary to do this again, I then request the faculties, etc.
   Here everything else is as usual.
   Let us pray a great deal for one another.
   With best regards in the Sacred Hearts of Jesus and Mary,

Your humble servant and loving confrere,
P. Donders, C.Ss.R.

29. September 14, 1880, Batavia.
To the Very Reverend Father Cornelis van Coll.[23]

Another letter dealing with pastoral problems. As we will see in the next letter (#30), some serious problem had arisen with Father Pete's helper, Joseph, that would prove to be a great concern for Father Pete. Again, this letter witnesses to his calm and trust in God.

J.M.J.A.T.
Batavia, September 14, 1880

Very Reverend Father,

Sunday morning at a quarter to eight, we arrived here and found everything quiet. I wanted to visit the plantation Catharina Sophia as we agreed. But the water was so low that it was not possible to reach the landing site. Later, I will do my best to settle that affair if I can. I intend (God willing), if there is no obstacle, to begin my long retreat, next Sunday evening, the 19th. Please pray for me that I may do it well; I too will pray for your Reverence.

The big question has been decided but not yet carried out. Joseph will tell you better than I can write. The director has behaved firmly and helped me well. May the Good God reward him. When I have finished my retreat, I will tell you more.

With kind regards, I remain in the Sacred Hearts of Jesus and Mary,

Your Reverence's humble servant and confrere,
P. Donders C.Ss.R.

30. October 1, 1880, Batavia. To the Very Reverend Father Cornelis van Coll.[24]

> *Donders' missionary work and his personal spirituality, as for all of us, had to face the concrete problems of daily life, which many times do not allow these efforts to succeed. In this letter, he describes such a case that he ultimately had to give up on because it involved his assistant, Joseph, which meant that Donders was not accepted as an impartial arbiter of the argument.*
>
> *Father Pete sees his way through this problem by prayer. Still, behind that prayer lies his absolute confidence in God. He realized that he had made a wrong decision earlier and needed to change his mind. Without a great humility, he might have resisted such a decision, but his*

trust in God no matter what lay behind all his prayer and apostolic work.

J.M.J.A.T.
Batavia, October 1, 1880

Very Reverend Father,
   I am enclosing the accounts for the past month along with the intentions of the Masses celebrated, and also a package for Father Odenhoven.
   The problem between the two women and the men, etc., is not over. During my retreat, they were more or less at peace, but yesterday they started at it again, now violently, as Joseph reported to me last night. He then told me that he wanted to move his wife, Leentje, to the city to live there and that he too wanted to leave Batavia later. But then Wilhelmina would have to be removed from Batavia; if not, the whole matter will get worse. What to do? I left things to God and Mary.
   I wanted to consult the director, but he has such a great fear of the people that he did not want to get mixed up in the affair for fear of creating rivalries. He thought that both sides should be put aside and that I should act.
   What better could I do than to ask God and Mary about what I should do? For this reason I prayed the rosary in church with hope and confidence that Mary, the good Mother of Perpetual Help, would give me advice. And see, it now came to me clearly what I should do and how to save myself from the terrible Wilhelmina clan.
   Joseph told me yesterday that the matter should have been straightened out a long time ago and the "trobbis kaba" [troubles finished] if he would have been working for a doctor or a director, because then the case would have been taken to the regional judge, and so forth, and that he was not happy that I had rejected [this approach]. While I was praying, the idea came to me that it would be better to make Joseph happy since the regional judge could decide and I could keep out of the decision. It could prove to be nothing. There had not been a poisoning; discussions, yes, but no injury or anything else to deserve punishment, and so on.

I went to find Joseph to tell him that I could not decide this affair because they had no faith in me and, since they would not reconcile for the good, I had thought that the regional judge is the one who must decide. Joseph was so happy with this that he immediately canceled his move to the city and thanked me. He personally brought the matter to the judge and made sure that I was left out of all these questions. Now I hope the Good God and Mary can put the best conclusion to this sad affair. Thus they have all they want, that is, both sides.

Please pray a Hail Mary for this intention. Joseph will see to it, as far as he can, that this letter and package make it to the city.

My best wishes to all the Fathers, etc. I remain in the Hearts of Jesus and Mary,

Your servant and loving confrere,
P. Donders, C.Ss.R.

31. November 14, 1880, Batavia.
To the Very Reverend Father Cornelis van Coll.[25]

These next three letters (#31, #32, #33) are brief notes about ordinary matters. Still, in them we can see the type of life that Father Pete had to live as he remained the only priest and Redemptorist among the lepers in the isolated colony in Batavia.

J.M.J.A.T.
Batavia, November 14, 1880

Very Reverend Father,

Enclosed I send you the account for the month October. I already gave you the intentions celebrated when I was in the city on October 25.

I was at the Kent Plantation to baptize a child and there I found the newlywed people. It seems that Kato Kerstens wanted to ask for the dispensation, even though they themselves had already asked for it. If it had to be refused since the husband, a Protestant, does not agree the children are to be baptized in the Catholic Church, then Father Romme has to know that. They are here at the plantation only temporarily and will come back to the city.

Cornelia, the housekeeper, asks Brother Frans to send the planks for her coffin that he promised.

Pray please for Batavia since it becomes worse and worse; I mean in religious matters and let us pray mutually for one another that we may be save. With kind regards for all the Fathers and Brothers, I remain in the Hearts of Jesus and Mary,

Your Reverence's humble servant and confrere,
P. Donders, C.Ss.R.

PS: Could you be so kind as to ask Brother Pius to send hosts if they have not yet been sent.[26]

32. December 12, 1880, Batavia.
To the Very Reverend Father Cornelis van Coll.[27]

J.M.J.A.T.
Batavia, December 12, 1880

Very Reverend Father,

Since Joseph is going to the city in a corial with his brother, I take this good opportunity to send the boxes for hosts. Your Reverence asked me recently which issues of the *Volks-missionaris* [the periodical, *The People's Missionary*] were missing. To this I answer the fifth and tenth issue. I would appreciate it if you could send me these two.

Could you be so kind as to arrange that, on the last day of this year, the patron and the exercise of a virtue is drawn for me and to please send these to me when it suits you because, since I am all alone, this is not so easy.[28]

In my next letter, I will send you the names of the members of the living rosary.

Could you be so kind, Very Reverend, as to let me know if the bishop arrived and to congratulate him on my behalf for the time being on (1) his episcopal consecration and (2) his safe return.

Here everything is the same.

I wish Your Reverence and the Fathers and Brothers a Blessed Christmas and New Year, along with God's good blessings. That is what we will pray for.

With my kind regards and recommending myself and the Batavians to your prayer I remain in the Hearts of Jesus and Mary,

Your Reverence's humble servant and confrere,
P. Donders, C.Ss.R.

33. January 2, 1881, Batavia.
To the Very Reverend Father Cornelis van Coll.[29]

J.M.J.A.T.
Batavia, January 2, 1881

Very Reverend Father,

Herein you receive the list of the [persons] baptized and married last year in Batavia, on the plantations, and [among] the Amerindians: sixty-six baptized, fifteen couples married. Along with it is the account of the month of last December with a surplus of two cents, also the report of the intentions celebrated in the month of December.

I also send the names of the members of the Living Rosary of Batavia to be united with [those of] the city of Paramaribo, as you wished.

NB: Be so kind, Very Reverend Father, as to tell Brother Frans that the Batavia ferry is leaving here tomorrow for the city to take [some] sick people; [this is] a good chance to send the planks for the director back with the ferry. As they agreed with one another earlier.

When you receive this letter, the bishop with the two Fathers[30]

and the Brother[31] will probably have arrived. Then, give the bishop and his companions my cordial greetings and congratulate all of them as I asked you to do earlier. Be so kind, as well, as to ask Monsignor for his episcopal blessing for me.

Also, if Monsignor agrees, I will come to the city soon. Your Reverence will be so kind as to let me know at the first opportunity, whether His Lordship approves. Afterward, we can discuss some things orally.

Let us pray a great deal for one another.

Greeting you kindly, I remain in the Hearts of Jesus and Mary,

Your Reverence's humble servant
and most devoted confrere,
P. Donders C.Ss.R.

34. June 28, 1881, Batavia.
To the Very Reverend Father Peter Oomen, Provincial Superior.[32]

Father Pete is now seventy-two years old and for the last nine months has been the only priest at Batavia. He still continues his voyages to the plantations and to the interior seeking the most abandoned. He still feels the presence of God in his good health and his ability to continue his missionary work despite his lack of companionship.

He mentions his request to the bishop for two priests to preach a mission in Batavia, thus giving the lepers the freedom to unburden their souls to someone who is not constantly dealing with them in so many daily matters. Thus, they will not be ashamed to say what they believe they must.

J.M.J.A.T.
June 28, 1881, Batavia
Very Reverend Father Provincial,

Yesterday, by God's goodness, I finished my [annual] retreat. Oh, how Good God is to all who seek him. Every day I understand better what a great joy it is to be called to the Congregation of the Most Holy Redeemer. May God and Mary, his holy Mother, grant me perseverance in my holy vocation and in continually striving for perfection so as to receive some day the promised crown.

As Your Reverence knows, I am alone here for the work, but I am happy. I use the time to visit the plantations and the Amerindians, particularly since God makes himself especially present with his help and gives me very good health. Thanks and praise for everything!

This year we have again received a great favor: the Jubilee. I hope that, through the goodness of God, this will be for the good of the salvation of souls in Batavia. Because of this, I have asked the bishop to send later, when the mission in Paramaribo is finished, two priests to preach a holy mission here as well and take care of all the confessions. I will not hear any confessions so that all may be free to confess. God wants all, especially the hardened, to sincerely convert.

Allow me, Very Reverend Father, to recommend to your prayers these poor and unfortunate [people]. Every day I remember this in my prayers and sacrifices. Let us remember one another that we may be saved and become saints.

My cordial greeting, Very Reverend Father, and begging your paternal blessing, I remain in the Hearts of Jesus and Mary,

Your Reverence's servant and son in Christ,
P. Donders, C.Ss.R.

35. July (?), 1881, Batavia.
To the Very Reverend Father Cornelis van Coll.[33]

The letters to the bishop and to Father van Coll mentioned in this letter have not come down to us, nor has the list he mentions.

Reverend Father,

I was surprised not to receive a letter or the things I requested but I [now] understand: my letter was addressed to the bishop and I now learn he remains in quarantine and Your Reverence did not open the letter. Could you please send the three items in the attached list as soon as possible?

I send two boxes, if Rups has room for them with him: (1) with oranges, (2) with old newspapers, books and two or three boxes. And some parrot feathers for the Sisters.

How disappointing for the Monsignor and Bor[r]et[34] to have to pass twenty-one days [quarantined] on the ship.[35] What else can be done than to respect God's holy will and submit oneself to its dispositions? Let's pray for them and for ourselves.

With kind regards to all Fathers and Brothers, Reverend Father, I remain in the Hearts of Jesus and Mary,

Your Reverence's humble servant
and most devoted confrere,
P. Donders, C.Ss.R.

36. August 8 [and 17], 1882, Batavia.
To the Very Reverend Father Peter Oomen, then in Surinam for a canonical visitation.[36]

The next three letters (#36, #37, and #38), written on the occasion of an official visit of the provincial superior to the mission in Surinam, are primarily formal in nature. The first and second are a greeting to Father Oomen on his arrival and a farewell on his departure. They show Father Pete's reverence for his religious superior. The third is a request for assistance to a group of benefactors in Holland; this letter manifests his concern for the material needs of the mission.

J.M.J.A.T.
Batavia, August 8, 1882

Very Reverend Father Provincial,
Thank God for your safe arrival in the colony. I give you heartfelt congratulations on your happy and peaceful arrival. I hope that the Good God will bless your effort and work so that the hoped-for purpose of your visit will be attained for the greater glory of God, for the good and well-being of us all, for your solace and reward, and for the benefit of our Congregation.

This is what we pray to the Good God for. Brother John reverently greets you, as I also do. Begging your blessing, I remain in the Most Sacred Hearts of Jesus and Mary, Very Reverend Father,

Your Reverence's obedient servant and son,
P. Donders, C.Ss.R.

[On a separate leaflet:]
Very Reverend Father Provincial,
The number of baptized Amerindians so far is 664
Batavia Institute, September 17, 1882

37. September 24 (with a postscript of September 25), 1882, Batavia. To the Very Reverend Father Peter Oomen.[37]

J.M.J.A.T.
Batavia, 24 September 1882

Very Reverend Father Provincial,
As you requested, I am sending you the open letter along with a list of things for the ladies of the Beneficent Sodality. When you receive this letter, the time for you to leave will be near. When it arrives, Very Reverend and Best Father Provincial, may the Good God guide you, take care of you, and bring you safely into

the company of your children [confreres]. May your angel protect you. For this I and the lepers pray.

Please remember to send me, if it is possible before your departure, the *Private Confession to God Alone* of Saint Bonaventure, copied by the late Reverend Father Bernard.

Please remember your promise to send a small pump-organ especially for drawing the Amerindians into the church. May the Good God bring about their conversion! I also hope to obtain the ten-volume series of the books of saints' lives. For all of these I am most grateful.

Please accept at this moment, Very Reverend Father, my sincerest thanks. May the Good God reward you a thousand times over!

Meanwhile, we pray, and persevere in praying, for Your Reverence. Goodbye until [we meet in] heaven. Let us pray for each other, that we may see each other there in happiness.

I now remain in the Most Sacred Hearts of Jesus and Mary, Very Reverend Father,

> Your Reverence's obedient servant and son in Christ,
> P. Donders, C.Ss.R.

PS: As I promised you, I will write you twice a year.

Today, the 25th, I received your precious letter, together with a beautiful picture in honor of my fortieth year of residence in the Colony. The greatest thanks, Very Reverend Father, for your kindness.

As you ask, I will pray for Lemmens. Oh, if the Good God is merciful to me and allows me to see and love him after death, then I will certainly remember the Congregation and Your Reverence and will pray for you.

Furthermore, Very Reverend Father, I bid you a safe journey and the precious blessings of God. Please cordially greet everyone I know in the homeland. P. Cornelia would also like a picture as a souvenir. She would be most grateful for it if you can send one even after your departure. Excuse me if I am being troublesome.

38. September 24, 1882, Batavia.
To the Ladies of the Blessed Sacrament, at Tilburg.[38]

J.M.J.A.T.
Batavia, 24 September 1882

Most Honorable Ladies,
   I have heard how charitable and diligent you are in providing necessities for the Lord's house that the religious services may be conducted everywhere with suitable splendor and solemnity. Most certainly this excellent work of charity is for the honor and glory of the Good God whom so many others offend. May the Good God be a hundredfold reward for you.
   Confident in your charity and beneficence, I, the parish priest of the Batavia Institute that cares for lepers, take the liberty of presenting this enclosed list to you most noble ladies. If you could succeed in the task, most pleasing to God, of providing the needs mentioned in this list, you would place me and our poor lepers under great obligation to you and we would always pray for you out of gratitude.

Your servant,
P. Donders, C.Ss.R., Parish Priest

39. September 25, 1882, Batavia.
To his confrere Father Willem Luijben, at Paramaribo.[39]

This amusing little note is difficult to explain since we do not know the circumstances. Were these wakes disturbing the settlement? Were they occasions of drunkenness or other difficulties? Did they seem superstitious to Father Pete? Oh, the trials of a pastor!

Very Reverend Father Luijben,
   The old lady, Anna Wiebers, who has lived here for some time with her daughter, the wife of Joseph Serret, left for the city. Why? Guess if you can! As Joseph and Leentje told me (when she

left, I did not see her or speak with her). Guess! [It was] because, when someone died, I forbade the men and women to gather in the home of the deceased and to sing, etc., and spend the whole night there. Thus she went to the city so as not to miss this pleasure since they can enjoy it there, it seems. Who could ever expect that of an old woman?

Greeting you kindly I remain in the Sacred Hearts of Jesus and Mary,

Your most devoted confrere,
P. Donders, C.Ss.R.

CHAPTER FIVE

PARAMARIBO AGAIN

40. January 20, 1883, Paramaribo.
To the Governor of Surinam.[1]

Here we have the letter Father Pete wrote, at the bishop's request, asking the governor for the pension due him as a citizen of the colony. It is about this pension that his friend, Father de Beer, must have teased him in a letter of the following year, because we find Father Pete protesting in Letter #46 that he did not ask for the pension because he wanted to retire and lead a life of ease!

To His Excellency the Governor of the Colony Surinam,
    With due respect, I, P. Donders, a Roman Catholic priest of the second class, living at Batavia and staying temporarily at Paramaribo, inform you that he has asked His Lordship Monsignor J. H. Schaap, Vicar Apostolic of Surinam, for honorable discharge from his ministry. As seen in the attached letter, this was granted him from March first.
    In a resolution of December 23, 1862, he was acknowledged as a clergyman of the second class and in that quality he received, from the first of January, 1863, an annual stipend of 1500 guilders.
    Born October 27, 1809, he reached the age of seventy-four and therefore, by virtue of the abovementioned document, has fulfilled the term of office required by law.
    Therefore, he addresses Your Excellency, asking respectfully

that you grant him a pension corresponding to a twenty-year term of office.

> Respectfully yours,
> P. Donders.
> Paramaribo, January 20, 1883

41. March 28, 1883, Paramaribo.
To the Very Reverend Father Oomen.[2]

This letter was written a year after the visit of Father Oomen to Surinam when Father Pete celebrated his forty years in the mission. The civil government had also granted Father Pete at the age of seventy-four a pension of 600 florins.

Since the provincial superior's visit, Father Pete had been transferred to the Capital and had now been there for a month and a half. The letter shows his happiness at the opportunity to again live in a community.

J.M.J.A.T.
Paramaribo, March 28, 1883

Very Reverend Father Provincial,

God, who governs all things well, has chosen to move me to another place and to grant me the benefit of community life. God so disposed the circumstances that the bishop decided it was imperative that, due to Father Verbeek's ill health in Coronie, Father Romme should go there. Then, since there is so much work, the bishop determined that Father van Blokhoven should go to Batavia for a time.

My Very Reverend Father, how happy community life makes me! And moreover, how much there is to do here! Knowing the desires of the Reverend Bishop, I asked His Excellency that, if it pleased him and God, he would give me the pleasure of living here in the community. And he willingly did so, as you see. Still, if God disposes otherwise, I am open to go and live anywhere that you or the Reverend Bishop choose to send me.

During Eastertide, we have much to do and the bishop is very satisfied. Thanks to God all goes well, even though the devil works against us by means of the Brethren. They do everything they can to draw lukewarm Catholics in. And they accept everyone, even those who live evil lives, for baptism and what they call "The Great Good,"[3] in a way that they have totally changed their practice. Still, we hope that the God of Goodness will open their eyes so that they see their error. On our part, we make efforts to bring back those who leave.

I have now been here six weeks, but we are so pressed by work that I still cannot visit either the Amerindians or the plantations.

"How very good and pleasant it is when kindred live together in unity! [Psalm 133:1]. I have experienced this and I give thanks to God for having arranged it so.

I pray for Your Reverence every day, Very Reverend Father. Remember me, I beg, that I may be a true Redemptorist and persevere in my vocation because this is what I desire above everything else.

With a hearty greeting and abiding in the Sacred Hearts of Jesus and Mary, I remain,

Your Reverence's obedient servant
and son in Jesus Christ,
P. Donders, C.Ss.R.

42. October 8, 1883, Paramaribo.
To the Very Reverend Peter Oomen.[4]

Again Father Pete expresses his joy at living with his confreres and no longer being alone. He feels himself a living part of the Congregation, identified with the common plans proposed by the superiors, and hopes to persevere with the help of God. More than a letter, this seems like a spontaneous outburst of spirit!

J.M.J.A.T.
Paramaribo, October 8, 1883

Very Reverend Father Provincial,

It is time, both from duty and promise, to write Your Reverence. First of all, I thank you wholeheartedly for your very precious and encouraging letter of May 1.

Every day I experience more and more the great gift of having been called to our Congregation and to be able to live as a brother in community, as the Scriptures say: "How very good and pleasant it is when kindred live together in unity!"

How Good God is to the one who surrenders himself to him and submits completely to his holy will, the one that discovers his will in the will of superiors, and who for this reason happily obeys in everything and gives himself to it. How consoling it is to be able to think: I am doing what God wants me to do!

How admirably God arranges everything! It is he who gave me the desire to do great work in bringing about his glory through the salvation of the souls redeemed at great price. He gives me the strength and health that I need to work here. Moreover, [he gives me] a wide region in which to work, whether here in the city or on the plantations or with the native people, etc., and to do so with great success, thanks be to God.

I had great satisfaction in reading in your letter that Your Reverence happily prays that we may receive from God the grace to convert sinners and unbelievers, because without grace we can do nothing. With grace, however, as Saint Paul says, we can do all things. As I promised you, I think of Your Reverence every day and I will always remember you.

I greet you with all my heart and ask your paternal blessing as I remain in the Hearts of Jesus and Mary,

Your Reverence's sure servant and son,
P. Donders, C.Ss.R.

PS: Please give my greetings to the Reverend Father Jansen, Father Antonius, Father van Mens, Father Startz, etc.

Chapter Six

Coronie

43. December 21, 1883, Coronie.
To the Very Reverend Father Peter Oomen.[1]

Due to Father Stassen's illness while he was assisting Father Romme, Donders had to move from Paramaribo to Coronie. Besides the parish, chapels on two plantations, the confraternities and schools, Romme and Donders had to care for the nearby villages. Finally, this move brought together the two fellow novices of the past, the first men to enter the Redemptorist Congregation in Surinam.

It would be hard not to smile at the joy we find in this letter that seems to burst freely from his heart.

J.M.J.A.T.
Coronie, Maryshoop
December 21, 1883

Very Reverend Father Provincial,
    It has pleased divine Providence to move me to another place, Coronie, to work here for the salvation of souls. Here again there is much to do for the conversion of so many sinners. Since God in his goodness has granted me health and strength for the task, for which I can never give thanks enough, I hope with his help to use them for his greater glory and for the salvation of souls redeemed by his precious blood.

Oh, what great comfort it is to think: I am here to do the will of God! O holy will of God!

I cannot succeed in thanking the Good God enough for his grace and for the call to the Congregation. May he himself give me perseverance. I hope for this by the mercy of God and the intercession of Mary, the Mother of God and our mother. How sad it is that Father van Mens, who lived so long in the Congregation, gifted with so many talents and after working so hard, has not persevered! Let us recommend one another that we may remain in our holy vocation and be saved.

I take this opportunity to wish Your Reverend a Merry Christmas, and that prosperity, health, and many graces be granted you by the Child Jesus. I also hope you have a happy New Year filled with the greatest of the Lord's blessings. May the Lord grant you many years of life as well, for his greater glory and the salvation of us all. I pray for this intention every day. May Your Reverence please remember me as well.

I am using the occasion of the good Father Romme's sending you his letter to write this one as well. The two co-novices are finally living in the same house.

With my tender greeting and asking your paternal blessing, I remain in the Hearts of Jesus and Mary,

Your Reverence's servant and son,
P. Donders, C.Ss.R.

44. March 3, 1884, Coronie.
To the charitable society that provides sacred vessels and vestments for poor churches at Tilburg.[2]

As we saw in letter #38, in September 1882, Father Pete, as the parish priest in Batavia, wrote to this Association of the Blessed Sacrament. His request received a positive response while he was in Coronie, and the bishop asked Donders to send his personal thanks, since the gift was meant for him and for the lepers in Batavia.

While the letter offers his thanks, Father Pete does not hesitate to ask for more: this time in the form of prayer, especially before the holy Eucharist. Beginning with this letter, we can notice the more frequent appearances that thoughts of eternity make in his correspondence.

J.M.J.A.T.
Coronie, March 3, 1884

Most Distinguished President,
I have received from Monsignor, our beloved bishop, the most comforting letter telling me that the branch of the Association at Tilburg that helps poor churches with furnishings has sent to our foundation in Batavia on the Coppename River a precious quantity of altar furnishings and decorations. The bishop and reverend confreres say that they received these wonderful gifts due to me personally. They tell me that the people of Tilburg think of Batavia because Father Donders is there. I can hardly believe this. It is almost forty-two years since I left Tilburg. Who can remember the poor young priest of those days? Nevertheless, I want to believe it because my superior has stated it.

By this letter, it is my task to express to you, Most Distinguished Lady President and all the ladies of the Association, my sincere and profound recognition of your precious remembrances. Oh, be sure that I will pray for the Association and for all of you to our loving Mother Mary and to the Sacred Heart of the Good Jesus to grant you and your assistants here his grace and blessing, and later, heavenly glory.

I add a word of good advice, which I ask you to accept from an old man of seventy-five. Among all the tasks that you as associates, lovers of the Lord, can achieve, none should be more appreciated, none more worthy of greater fervor and fidelity, than visits to Jesus in the Blessed Sacrament. It is worthwhile to remain there and pray, thank, and beg for all material and spiritual needs.

If you pray there, most worthy benefactors, also remember me, an old man, and beg that our Lord, in life, in death, and ever afterward, will be generous and merciful in his judgment.

The bishop says to tell the ladies that it was good that they did not know that Father Donders no longer lives in Batavia; otherwise their gift would not have been so generous. In truth, the undersigned no longer lives in Batavia. After having resided there for a period of twenty-six years in the leprosarium, the bishop asked me to enjoy the blessing of common life with my confreres, something I lived deprived of for many years.

Once more, most distinguished ladies, I thank you. May Jesus and Mary bless you, in whose hearts I remain,

Your thankful and humble servant,
P. Donders, of the Congregation of the Most Holy Redeemer

45. April 16, 1884, Coronie.
To his nephew, Michiel van der Brekel.[3]

This is the only letter to a family member that has come down to us, although this one alludes to another letter sent earlier to the same nephew. Donders thanks him for the prayers that his relatives say for him. Since the nephew mentioned to him the poverty in which he was living, Donders answers by explaining the three dimensions of Christian poverty: identification with Christ the poor man, manifestation of love for God, and the chance for complete confidence in divine Providence. This is the way he experiences it himself since he has taken the vow of poverty.

He also mentions his many activities in Coronie.

J.M.J.A.T.
Coronie, April 16, 1884

My Dearest Nephew,

I received your letter of January 20 with the greatest joy, where I learned that you, along with your children and grandchildren who number forty-two, are all praying for me. I offer you heartfelt thanks for these prayers. I ask that you persevere in them as I pray daily for all of you, especially at the altar during the holy sacrifice of the Mass. Let us pray for one another that we all reach salvation and we can be united forever around God.

I appreciate your bodily weakness from age and poverty. Take comfort knowing that our Savior willingly and for love of us became poor and died in the greatest poverty. He said himself: "Blessed are the poor in spirit, for theirs is the kingdom of heaven" [Matthew 5:3]. Undergo your precarious situation with patience out of love for God and you will ultimately be rich in heaven.

I am happy to be poor by the religious profession by which I own nothing and can dispose of nothing as I wrote you before.

Put all your confidence in the God of Goodness who said: "Strive first for the kingdom of God and his righteousness, and all these things will be given to you as well" [Matthew 6:33]. And it was not in vain that he taught us to pray, "Give us this day our daily bread" [Matthew 6:11].

I am now working in Coronie, near the seacoast, where we two priests exercise our ministry in three churches. Our parish extends four and a half hours [to reach its border]. Every Sunday we take turns in Burnside, two and a half hours away from our house, with the celebration of Mass, preaching, confessions, and catechism. There is enough work, but, by God's goodness that gives me strength and health, I work with gusto for the salvation of souls.

Pray for me that the God of Goodness grant me the grace of perseverance and a holy death. Let us recommend one another that we may be saved. Let us love God who deserves all our love and who is offended and ignored by so many people.

I greet you with love, dear nephew, along with your children and grandchildren. To you all, I wish the Lord's peace and I remain in the Hearts of Jesus and Mary,

The one who loves you,
P. Donders, C.Ss.R.

46. April 16, 1884, Coronie.
To the Very Reverend Antoon de Beer, at Tilburg.[4]

Father de Beer was the superior general of the Brothers of the Tilburg Institute. Father Pete thanks him for his interest in the mission in Surinam. This is one of the few remaining letters of Father Pete that was not directed to one of his confreres or superiors. It is interesting to see that it does not differ in attitude or style from these other letters, showing that the thoughts and sentiments expressed in them were not just "put on" to impress his superiors.

J.M.J.A.T.
Coronie, April 16, 1884

Very Reverend and Distinguished Friend,

Thank you with all my heart for your very kind letter of January 26. Thank you as well from my heart for your interest and work for my sake and that of our mission. May the God of Goodness repay you a hundredfold now and later. As you wish and request, I will pray for Your Reverence that God grant you abundant graces in carrying out all your duties for the greater glory [of God] and the salvation of your soul and of all those confided to your care, and that Your Reverence receive an eternal reward when you have completed your work. I ask these graces for you especially during holy Mass. I also beg you to keep me in mind in your prayers.

The real reason I requested and received a pension was at the request and insistence of the bishop, and was not so I could put aside my duty and work since, by God's goodness, I can still work well even though I am almost seventy-five years old.

I never succeed in thanking God enough that he gives me health and strength to work for the salvation of souls. After working fourteen years in the city of Paramaribo and on the plantations, I was sent to the Batavia leprosarium on the Coppename River where I remained for a period of twenty-six years. Finally,

I find myself in Coronie on the seacoast. There are two priests here, along with two brothers who labor in the school.

Our parish here includes three churches. The first is about four and a half hours away from the last. Our house stands about half way and is called Mary's Hope, formerly a plantation. Every Sunday one of us, either Father Romme or I, travel to the Burnside Plantation, about two and a half hours from our house to celebrate a high Mass, preach, hear confessions, catechize, etc. We return home in the evening by carriage because of the long distance. The third church is on the Welgelegen Plantation, about two hours distant from our house; it is there that we carry on most of our weekday work.

As you can see, I didn't take out a pension so I could rest up and sit around, but in order to work for the salvation of souls redeemed at so great a cost, as long as God gives me strength and health.

Let us recommend each other [to God] and keep up our prayers for our salvation.

With my kindest greeting and a thankful heart, I remain in the Hearts of Jesus and Mary,

> Your Reverence's servant and friend,
> P. Donders, C.Ss.R.

PS: Please do me the favor of giving my greetings to the president and other members of the Society of the Most Blessed Sacrament, and thank them once again for the things they sent to the church in Batavia.

47. June 29, 1884, Coronie.
To the Very Reverend Father Peter Oomen.[5]

> *Father Oomen had recently been reappointed to his position of provincial superior in Holland and would hold that responsibility until 1887. Fathers Donders and Romme write him from Coronie to congratulate him and to beg God's blessings on him and on his work of promoting the holiness of the Congregation.*

J.M.J.A.T.
Coronie, June 29, 1884

Very Reverend Father Provincial,

First of all, my congratulations for having been reappointed provincial. And we congratulate ourselves for this decision by the rector major, or better, for the choice and holy will of God. May the God of Goodness grant you his choice graces so that you may be able to bear the burden imposed upon you for his greater glory, and for our salvation and perfection. I never cease praying every day for this intention.

I am as well as ever and I cannot thank God enough for this favor. I hope to use my strength and health, with God's help, for his greater glory and the salvation of souls.

Oh, how happy I feel to see myself as a son of the Congregation and in being able to know and fulfill the will of God! May he help me to respond to such great graces to persevere in my holy vocation, and to reach eternal salvation by the merits of our Most Holy Redeemer. I beg you to recommend me in your prayers.

The beautiful, precious items sent us from Tilburg have just reached us. I wrote them a thank-you letter.

The bishop administered the sacrament of confirmation here to eighty-three persons, counting both children and older persons. He was very happy. He also ordered the construction of a new cemetery on a piece of land belonging to the church that will be very helpful for the faithful and for us.

I don't know what else to write you. Very Reverend Father Romme is also writing Your Reverence and will perhaps recount other things.

With my affectionate greetings and begging your fatherly blessing, I remain in the Hearts of Jesus and Mary,

Your Reverence's true servant and son,
P. Donders, C.Ss.R.

48. October 3, 1884, Coronie.
To his confrere, Father Antoon Hengst, in Holland.[6]

Father Hengst (1815–1886) was professed a Redemptorist in 1844, after five years as a diocesan priest. He was rector of the community in Wittem, Holland and, from 1877 to 1886, served as provincial consultor.

This is obviously a note written to console Father Hengst, a past benefactor of Batavia, in a time of illness, which Donders had just learned about.

J.M.J.A.T.
Coronie, October 3, 1884

Very Reverend Father Antoon,
 In the bishop's last letter that we received a short time ago, he mentioned that your health had taken a downturn, especially recently.
 I deeply sympathize with you as a brother. I will never forget your great generosity toward my lepers in Batavia in sending a pump-organ some time ago. Actually, I am not very good at playing it, and for many years I was without an assistant so I was not able to use it during holy Mass, but only during exposition of the Most Blessed Sacrament. Still, both for these poor people, as well as for me, it proved a great delight.
 Moreover, I heard from the bishop's own lips that you have become, in many ways, an outstanding benefactor of the mission. Because of this, I pray often for you and will pray even more often from now on.
 This is because the mission of Surinam is so dear to me. You may know, Father Antoon, that I have served here in this mission for a period of forty-three years and in all that time I never left it. Nor do I want to. The Good Jesus grant me the grace to die here.
 I always enjoy good health and can fulfill all duties, even to celebrate Holy Mass, etc., in Burnside, two and a half hours from Mary's Hope. This is a precious grace that perhaps I have received by virtue of your sufferings.

I am old (I am about seventy-five). So death cannot be too far away. Therefore I hope that Your Reverence will pray for me that my end may be happy.

In the Hearts of Jesus and Mary, I remain, Very Reverend Father Antoon,

> Your humble servant and confrere,
> P. Donders, C.Ss.R.

49. October 29, 1884, Coronie.
To Very Reverend Peter Oomen.[7]

This year, Father Pete took his annual ten days of retreat in two five-day stretches over two weeks. He tells us he spent his time seeking to place himself in complete union with the saving plan of God, so he thought less about the past and more about the days that remained for him to complete his journey to his desired goal. His old age was not filled with anxieties or regrets but with gratitude.

J.M.J.A.T.
Coronie, October 29, 1884

Very Reverend Father Provincial,

Again it is the time I should and have promised to write you. I made my annual retreat with the Very Reverend Father Romme. Thanks be to God! We made it over two weeks, five days each week so we would be free on Saturday and Sunday for confessions and for celebrating the sacred rites and preach as usual both here and in Burnside.

I treated the spiritual exercises, thanks be to God, as if they were the last days of my life, even though by God's goodness I still feel strong and well, despite having celebrated my seventy-fifth anniversary of birth and baptism. [Everyone] at the time wished me another twenty-five years of life and told me I ought to be able to survive all those years. Still, I cannot forget the warning our Redeemer gave to everyone: "Be prepared" [see

Matthew 24:42]. Everything as God wishes it. May the holy and adorable will of God be done in all things. May the God of Goodness give me the grace of perseverance in his love and in my holy vocation.

We have presided over many marriages this year, most of the couples having lived in concubinage for many years; others may yet follow them as well. Thanks be to God and Mary!

Our new cemetery is almost finished and will soon be blessed. The Very Reverend Father Romme is also writing you; I am sure he will tell you many other things.

I pray every day for Your Reverence, that the Lord watch over you and give you the grace and the blessings needed to fulfill his holy will and that you may afterward, as a reward, reach the heavenly kingdom. I ask you to keep me in mind in your prayers. Begging you fatherly blessing, with my dearest greetings, I remain in the Hearts of Jesus and Mary,

Your Reverence's true servant and son in Jesus Christ,
P. Donders, C.Ss.R.

50. August 18, 1885, Coronie.
To Very Reverend Father Peter Oomen.[8]

The apostolic life is not two parts, mission and consecration, artificially joined. Apostolate and spirituality form together a unified whole. Father Pete's extraordinary activity was always hand in hand with continuous prayer. He understood well that to truly participate in the Son's love for the Father and for human beings had to produce a spirit of contemplation.

J.M.J.A.T.
Coronie, August 18, 1885

Very Reverend Father Provincial,

I find the greatest pleasure in wishing Your Reverence well on the completion of twenty-five years of priesthood. I offer you my congratulations and with you, Reverend Jubilarian, I thank God for the grace and the privileges that he has granted you in abundance over this period of twenty-five years. May this God give you many years more of his precious grace and rich blessings so that you may employ them for his greater glory in your own salvation as well and in that of the souls confided to you and for the good of the whole Congregation. I moreover hope that at the end of your journey [you receive] the crown of perseverance and eternal joy and well-being in the company of our holy father Alphonsus. Every day I will pray the God of Goodness to grant you all this in abundance together with the precious gift of perseverance.

I am still in good health, thanks be to God, and am still strong. I can fulfill all my duties for the salvation of souls.

The conversion of sinners moves along little by little. Lately many have married and prepared for their first Communion who had lived for years in concubinage.

God is truly good and merciful to poor sinners. Recently I catechized a sixty-year-old woman who after a long life of sin approached holy Communion for the first time. She showed great fervor in learning doctrine and now every morning at 6:00 AM after more than an hour's trek she arrives at church and has done so for the past two months. May God grant her perseverance!

How unhappy and worthy of compassion are sinners! Let us pray to the God of Goodness to illumine and convert them. What a worthwhile remedy for this is the apostolate of prayer!

Are we, all of us, confreres of this apostolate? It would give me much joy to know it to be so. Let us pray for each other that we may persevere and be saved.

Once again, Father Jubilarian, I wish you every type of good and blessing, but not without first asking your father blessing, as I remain in the Hearts of Jesus and Mary,

Your Reverence's true servant and son,
P. Donders, C.Ss.R.

Chapter Seven

Batavia Again

51. March 10, 1886, Batavia.
To his confrere, Brother Alphonsus (Antoon Koenen),
at Paramaribo.[1]

At the age of seventy-seven, Father Pete returned to his beloved Batavia. This will be his final appointment. The Apostle to the Lepers had to spend his last days among his dear lepers. No one, least of all Father Pete, expected this to happen when he left in 1883. But this good fortune was a consequence of his membership in a religious congregation of missionaries, for the sickness of a confrere or the needs of the apostolate often demand the availability of a person to go elsewhere.

J.M.J.A.T.
Batavia, March 10, 1886

Reverend Brother Alphonsus,

Many thanks for your letter of January 18. I had to wait a long time before I could answer. I thank you also for your gift. I will try to fulfill your request and that of the schoolchildren. I will pass the various bits of news on to Reverend Father Romme.

Yesterday I received a letter from Monsignor in which he asked me to come to the city soon and to get a room ready for a Father who wishes to stay here for a while for a change of climate and to learn Pidgin English. Therefore, this evening I will make the trip. Please inform Father Romme.

Pray please a great deal for me. I will pray also for you. Greeting you kindly, I remain in the Sacred Hearts of Jesus and Mary,

Your Reverence's affectionate confrere,
P. Donders, C.Ss.R.

52. July 20, 1886, Batavia.
To Very Reverend Father Peter Oomen.[2]

Despite his age, Father Pete again seeks to renew the apostolate he considered his most important work, the conversion of the Blacks of the forest. Some of the tribes began to inhabit a location "close" to Batavia ("only" two or three hours away by boat!) and this would permit him to reach them.

He also comments on the Extraordinary Jubilee Year proclaimed for 1886 by Pope Leo XIII's encyclical "Quod Auctoritate" (December 22, 1885). The pope was deeply involved in the political turmoil in Europe at the end of the nineteenth century. So he proclaimed this time of special prayer for all Catholics to renew their public life so that states and nations might be led in an atmosphere of holiness.

> ...a State is what the lives of the people make it... so, unless the individual citizens lead good lives, the State cannot keep in the path of virtue, and without offending. Civil government and those things which constitute the public life of a country come into existence and perish by the act of men; and men almost always succeed in stamping the image of their opinions and their lives upon their public institutions.

J.M.J.A.T.
Batavia, July 20, 1886

Very Reverend Father Provincial,
 Your Reverence knows that for some time I have again found myself in Batavia, my first residence. God has willed it thus; may his holy will be done.
 I have wanted to write Your Reverence for a while, but I have put it off because I wanted to be able to give you some comforting news.
 Your Reverence will have already been told that, with permission [text is unclear], I have initiated an attempt among the Blacks of the forest who are building their houses near the Coppename River, a two- or three-hour journey from here by river and have bought some land to cultivate for their own sustenance. They came from the Upper Saramacca. One part of them has already set up their homes. Others are soon to follow, and luckily their numbers should swell from eighty to three hundred or more. A few of them are already baptized by the Moravian Brethren, but these, because of the great distance, have not visited them to give instruction. I cannot write much about them because I have only been there twice; but I hope that I may soon tell you more.
 I recommend myself and the others, among all else, to your holy prayers and sacrifices so that God in his mercy may give them the grace of true faith and that I can work fruitfully among them.
 Reverend Father Jan [Bakker] is beginning to feel ill and has gone down a great deal. He writes to you himself about this.
 Reverend Father Timmermans, who was staying here for several months to learn the Pidgin English language, etc., has moved on to Coronie.
 I received the bishop's letter about the jubilee proclaimed by His Holiness Leo XIII. I will announce it to the people this coming Sunday. I hope it produces good results. May God grant that here and in other places the faithful follow the fatherly advice of His Holiness and reap its fruits.

How much progress evil is making! What will happen to this society? I hope that the God of Goodness hears the prayers of true Christians and society becomes Christian.

Very Reverend Father, how happy are we whom the God of Goodness has called in his mercy out of the corrupt world into his service in the Congregation! Certainly we can never give the thanks we owe to God for if we persevere in our vocation we can also hope, as our father Saint Alphonsus says, to reach eternal happiness. May the Good God grant us perseverance. Let us pray for it without ceasing.

As I promised Your Reverence, I keep you in mind in my prayers and sacrifices. Likewise, I recommend myself to your prayers along with all those who have been confided to my care, along with the Amerindians and the Blacks.

With my tender greetings and asking for your paternal blessing, I remain in the Hearts of Jesus and Mary,

Your Reverence's servant and son in Christ,
P. Donders, C.Ss.R.

53. December 16, 1886, Batavia.
To Very Reverend Father Peter Oomen.[3]

This is Father Pete's last letter that has come down to us. It was written a month before his death and two months after his seventy-seventh birthday. He still feels strong. He does not mention, however, that just at this time he had to confide to Father Jan Bakker, his companion, that he had begun to feel pain and difficulty in urinating. He remains happy and thankful to God. He manifests his satisfaction at having made a nineteen-day apostolic journey to the natives on the Maratakka River whom he had not visited for almost seven years.

Absent are all the details of his labors of his early letters; in these last letters, these activities are mentioned in a few broad strokes. What is important now is perseverance.

After all these years, even now at the age of seventy-seven, he has retained the same hope, vigor, and trust in God that he had when he stepped off the boat in Paramaribo at the age of thirty-three—no, his hope is deeper, his vigor is more lively, and his trust, even more profound.

J.M.J.A.T.
Batavia, December 16, 1886

Very Reverend Father Provincial,
   This year is reaching its end and, by God's goodness, we will be beginning another year. Therefore, Very Reverend Father, I cannot do less than wish you a happy New Year. May the God of Goodness grant you many more years, as I hope and wish.
   The great God, who out of love for us chose to be born a child and to become our Savior, that dear Jesus, grant you, my Reverend Father, health and strength, his holy love and precious graces so that at least for many more years you will guide us and lead us to heaven.
   Every day, Reverend Father, I will pray for you so that these wishes of mine may be realized and that all of us reach eternal salvation. Oh, when will the day arrive when we will enjoy this great, this supreme, fortune as we persevere unto the end in our holy vocation? It is for this perseverance that we pray daily.
   I cannot tell you many relevant things, Your Reverence. I am still healthy and strong. This past October, with the most illustrious bishop's approval, I have visited the Amerindians on the Maratakka. Seven years had passed since the last time I visited them. I baptized seven children and two aged women among them, and performed the matrimony of one couple.
   The number of these natives has greatly diminished, to the point that in three different places, in Maratakka and on the Nickerie River, I only found forty of them. Several had gone to visit their relatives on the Corentin River in the English territory [British Guyana] and many remained there. I do not know if they will return.
   After a journey of nineteen days, I returned to Batavia safe

and sound, thanks to God. Things are going poorly with regard to the Blacks who live in the jungle. But let us have patience and trust in God who is all-powerful and rich in mercy. I ask you to remember them in your prayers along with me. Our setbacks and crosses come from God as well, and without the cross nothing goes as it should.

Once more, Very Reverend Father, I wish you God's special blessings. Seeking your fatherly blessing, with my affectionate greetings, I remain in the Hearts of Jesus and Mary,

Your Reverence's humble servant in Christ,
P. Donders, C.Ss.R.

CHAPTER EIGHT

AUTOBIOGRAPHICAL AND OTHER WRITINGS

Four other written documents have come down to us from Donders, two autobiographies, an "Account of Conscience," and entries in the chronicles of Batavia. These are translated here.

Donders was accepted as a Redemptorist novice on July 24, 1866. On the following November 1, he received the habit and his novitiate officially began. On June 24, 1867, he made his profession. It is a requirement in the Redemptorist novitiate that the novice write an autobiography or curriculum vitae of his vocation up to that time. No such document, however, is known to have existed in Father Pete's case and so the presumption is that, for whatever reason, the task was overlooked. Only seven years later does such a work appear (October 13, 1874), due to the request of one of his superiors (perhaps the superior in Paramaribo at the time, Father Schaap).

To this was added an "Account of Conscience," a more intimate statement of one's state of spiritual awareness.

1. First Autobiography (October 13, 1874)[1]

J.M.J.A.T.
A.M.D.G. and B.V.M.

I was born in Tilburg in 1809. God was pleased to awaken in me when I was very young, from the age of five or six, an ardent desire to enter the priestly state to work for the salvation of souls who are so dear to him. By the marvelous dispositions of Providence (when I lacked the necessary means to take up the studies and was already twenty-two years old), I came to obtain the means to accomplish it in an extraordinary manner, or better, a miraculous manner. The first instrument that Providence made use of was the venerable parish priest of Tilburg, W. van de Ven, who managed to have me accepted as an employee of the minor seminary of S. Michiels-Gestel (due to the fact that at the time all young men had to enlist in the army because of the revolution and so there were no servants at the seminary). For six months, if I am not mistaken, I was the only servant; this is how it was until another arrived and I could begin the first year of secondary (school). When the time of study and classes was over, I went to help the other employees. It was by this routine that I completed the seminary curriculum of the minor seminary at S. Michiels-Gestel.

In the meantime, I received from the rector of the major seminary, Philip van de Ven, the *Annals of the Propaganda of the Faith*, which I read. From this reading there was born in me the desire to work for the salvation of souls in America or elsewhere.

At this time and later, I felt no special desire for religious life, but only to become a priest and work for the salvation of souls. Nevertheless, out of obedience to the Very Reverend President [of the seminary], I visited the Jesuits in Belgium, but the provincial superior, considering my age and maturity (I was then twenty-six), let me know that I was not meant for their order.

The president then advised me to go to the Redemptorists of Saint-Trond [Belgium], and if not admitted there, to the Franciscans. The rector [of the minor seminary], H. Smits, gave me a letter of recommendation that I had requested. I went with that to Saint-Trond, stayed there for a few days and received a scapular of the four confraternities from the rector who sent me with another postulant to the provincial superior in Liege [rather the Visitor, Father Frederik von Held], who is still alive. Again, he judged, after consulting with Father Bernard [Hafkenscheid] (because I did not know how to speak French and the provincial did not have command of Dutch), that I was not called to the Redemptorist community.

I then went to the Franciscans. They were suspicious, and with reason, for the letter of recommendation had been opened. They did not want to receive me immediately, but rather asked me to begin philosophy and to come back in a year if the inclination remained. I returned home on foot. I recommended myself to divine Providence, "Lord, what do you want me to do?" At this, God consoled me as if I had attained the greatest success.

I entered the major seminary at Herlaar to begin philosophy. Father G. van Someren, then a professor there and my special benefactor, was of the same mind. Providence had chosen him, along with Very Reverend Pastor W. van de Ven, to be the instruments to lead me to my destiny. Providence arranged all that I needed. Much later I came to understand that I had been granted a scholarship for those five years of study in the major seminary. The parish priest of Tilburg, W. van de Ven, took it upon himself to obtain for me the title for sacred orders.

Now a priest, and even long before (when the Prefect of the Mission of Surinam, J. Grooff, visited the seminary three years before I came to Surinam), I cherished a burning desire that grew every day to travel to Surinam as a missionary.

Finally the happy day arrived that I received from the Bishop of Curium the notice that the boat for Surinam was ready to depart and would be weighing anchor within eight days. I said goodbye to the reverend Fathers who acted as the agents of Providence and lavished their care upon me. I also took leave of my mother and my brother. Then I left alone. So, with all my bonds severed, I placed myself entirely in the hands of God. Oh, from then on I have experienced how Good God is and how he busies himself with those who trust in him and leave all for his sake. Even more than a hundredfold he has bestowed on me, for whether on the ship or in Surinam, I have found fathers and mothers who have poured their care upon me. And the God of Goodness has done even more. He gave me an ardent desire to work for the salvation of souls, and here I have found satisfaction for this desire for he has granted me an abundance of work for the past fourteen years in Paramaribo. In trials he has given me acceptance and patience.

And finally, this most kind and marvelous providence has led me to the Congregation of the Most Holy Redeemer. On June 24, [1867], the feast of John the Baptist, I had the inexpressible joy of uniting myself with God and the Congregation forever by means of the three vows. May the most gracious God, through the merits of his Son, Jesus Christ, grant me the grace of perseverance, something I ask for every day and which I hope to always request. I hope to succeed through the intercession of the Most Holy Virgin Mary. Amen.

October 13, 1874
P. Donders, C.Ss.R.

2. The Account of Conscience[2]

These paragraphs are responses to a list of questions, which we have included at the beginning in brackets although they are not in Donder's text. They are probably a set of questions asked of all novices or students at the time.

[1. Is your spirit peaceful or troubled and why?]
[2. Are you attentive in prayer or dry?]
[3. Does the practice of virtue trouble you? Which virtues?]
[4. Do you have an aversion to the common exercises and the ministries in the monastery?]
[5. Are you content in your vocation?]
[6. What desire do you feel to make progress in the virtues?]

[7. Do you feel antipathy against anyone or attracted to anyone?]
[8. Do you need anything material?]
[9. How is your health?]
[10. Do you feel hindered by temptations and how do you handle them?]

Since an account of conscience is one of the most important things...I pray and beseech the God of Goodness to deign to help and illumine me. Come, Holy Spirit, and send a ray of your light from heaven.

1. Whether my spirit is peaceful or troubled, I answer: peaceful. The whole time I have belonged to the Congregation, there has not been a day, not even an hour, in which I have not been very happy with my holy vocation and with common life, except for a few trails and temptations that, with God's grace, I have overcome.
2. Whether in prayer I have been attentive or dry, I have to say: from time to time, attentive and fervent; still often dry. The best that I can do when this happens to me is to humble myself before God, since without his grace I cannot have a single good thought or, as you counseled me, to meditate on the Way of the Cross, above all during evening meditation.
3. As far as virtues are concerned: I have a great desire to gain them all. Especially the most profound humility, meekness, submission to the will of God and to suffer for the love of Jesus who suffered so much for me. It seems to me that I have good will, but the works I do worry me. Still, what would these virtues mean if they have not been tested? I pray for this, Very Reverend Father, that you help and test me in this.
4. Community exercises produce great comfort in me because they are done out of obedience.
5. As before: I remain happy with my vocation right from the first day until today.
6. For all, but above all for obedience, for fulfilling the holy

will of God, and for suffering and being held in low esteem out of love for Jesus.
7. I do not believe that I have any aversion toward anyone, nor do I have any awareness of loving another excessively. What I hope for is that everyone becomes holy.
8. It has been taken care of.
9. Out of God's goodness, I am in very good health.
10. At times I have temptations against the holy virtue of chastity during my prayers, especially during the recitation of the Breviary. As far as I can tell, I get rid of them by God's grace and I pray. Also at times, but rarely, I am bothered by thoughts of pride; with God's grace, I am able to cast them out immediately.

For the rest, Very Reverend Father, I do not know what else to tell you. I hope that Your Reverence questions me and teaches me, because if it is possible and your occupations allow, I would like to go to confession to Your Reverence next Friday or Saturday so that you may have the chance to know me better that way. Please tell me, then, what day and time seems best to do so.

I remain Your Reverence's obedient son in the Sacred Hearts of Jesus and Mary.

P. Donders, C.Ss.R.

3. *Second Autobiography (August 13, 1897)*[3]

Again, it is not clear why and for whom Donders wrote this second autobiography, but it helps us to see what events stood out as pivotal in his mind when thinking of his spiritual journey.

J.M.J.A.T.
A.M.D.G. and B.V.M.

To satisfy the wishes of Your Very Reverence, I am trying as best I can to describe the guidance of divine Providence from my early youth up to today. The Good God, to whom I cannot be sufficiently grateful, preserved me from many dangers to which my salvation might have been exposed. He gave me the grace to pray often and a sure, although still imperfect, love and devotion to his Mother Mary, to whom after God I ascribe my vocation to both the priestly and religious states of life.

Even as a child I had a strong desire to someday become a priest and, although humanly speaking it seemed impossible because my parents were poor, I kept believing that some day I would be a priest. When I was eighteen, I had to submit to the military service lottery, and I drew a low number. Even here the Good God helped me. How? Since at the time I did not seem to possess a strong constitution and I appeared outwardly unhealthy, I was given a year's postponement by a doctor's advice. This was stretched out for five years until I was declared exempt from military service by the special providence of God. My profession was first as a thread-spinner and then I learned to weave textiles, which I did right up to the day I left for the minor seminary at S. Michiels-Gestel, first as a servant, since [the seminary] had no others; then later, I would take up studies.

But how did this happen for me? Again, through the good providence of God that ordains all things toward our salvation. When I was about twenty-two, during the octave of Pentecost I wrote a letter to my parish priest and confessor (Very Reverend Father W. van de Ven, who is still alive today), in which I expressed my desire for priesthood along with the reasons that led me to do so and that brought about this desire. Very Reverend Father spoke with the rector of the minor seminary, H. Smits. How marvelous is God's providence! At the time, there was a lack of servants in the seminary, because all the young men had been called up for military service and so it was agreed that I would be accepted into the seminary as a servant. The late Father Vogels who was then the assistant pastor in Tilburg came to my home and brought me the good news.

Later, after the half-year that I served as a servant, another servant was hired and then I could attend class and help the servants the rest of the time. This is the way it was for four or five years in the minor seminary as I dedicated myself to the studies. During this period, the rector of the major seminary, [Father] van der Ven gave me the *Annals [of the Propagation of the Faith]* to read. This reading raised a desire in me to become a missionary to work for the conversion of unbelievers when I was a priest.

Meanwhile, the president of the major seminary wanted me to go to the provincial of the Jesuits at Ghent to present myself as a postulant; but the Jesuit provincial decided that I did not have a vocation to their order because I was already twenty-six years old. Thus, I set off again the next day early in the morning. When I had gotten home, the president wanted me to go again, this time to the Redemptorist Fathers at S. Truijen; he said these did almost the same [missionary activity as the Jesuits]. I obeyed. I asked the regent for a letter of recommendation which he gave me. The president added, "If these do not accept you, there are monasteries of other orders in S. Truijen where you should ask whether they will accept you." This I did.

The rector of the Redemptorists sent me along with another candidate to the provincial superior in Liege who at the time was Very Reverend Father de Held.[4] That was the first time that I saw (the late) Father Bernard [Hafkenscheid] and spoke with him.[5] Not accepted here either, I went out of obedience to the Franciscan Fathers in S. Truijen, who, not convinced of my vocation, advised me to take up the philosophy studies and then, after a year, come back if I was so inclined.

So again, with nothing accomplished, I returned but I had the comfort of knowing I had obeyed the president and had acted as he had recommended. The Good God, who willed all of this, consoled me along the way and I obtained the firm trust that someday I would be a priest and a missionary. "Thank God, who consoles us in all our troubles." Returning home again, I brought a letter from the guardian of the Franciscans back from S. Truijen.

At this point it was established in my mind that I was no longer to think of the Franciscans because that was certainly not my vocation, and so with the others I took up philosophy and later theology. Thanks be to God, these studies were more successful than learning Latin during the study of the humanities, etc. Since the professors knew that I wanted to be a missionary and at the time everyone was going to North America, Professor G. van Someren, who is now the dean and parish priest in Eindhoven, said that our Dutch colonies were in great need of priests and it was only fair that we give preference to our own colony. If I was not very averse to going to Surinam, I could then speak with the prefect of the Surinam Mission, J. Grooff, who was to visit the seminary in a few days.

He indeed came and we agreed I should go there as soon as possible, with the proviso that I first complete my theological studies and be admitted to the priesthood. This was decided in 1839 at the major seminary in the town of Haaren. Two years later, in 1841, by the goodness and mercy of God, I was ordained a priest. There was, however, no chance of leaving by ship before 1842 in a boat belonging to Mr. Rothuis of Amsterdam. Before leaving Holland, I spent three weeks as an assistant at the parish in the town of Warmond.

Finally, on August 1 we went to sea and on September 16 or 17 we arrived safely in Paramaribo. A few weeks after my arrival, Prefect Grooff took me with him to the leprosarium in Batavia where we stayed for several weeks. On the feast of All Saints we returned again to Paramaribo.

Reverend Fathers Jansen and Kempkes lived in the city [Paramaribo] but shortly afterward, Reverend Father Kempkes left for Batavia. Reverend Father Schepers was building a church in Coronie. Meanwhile, there came from Rome the appointment of His Excellency Father Grooff as a bishop, i.p.i.[6] and vicar apostolic in the [Dutch] East Indies. Before he could leave, His Excellency and Reverend Father Janssen came down with the dysentery that was raging and many—among them, even Reverend Father Janssen—were brought to their graves. I was the only healthy one among all of these sick people. The Good God gave me the health, strength, and courage to care for the sick and to baptize unbelievers. Scarcely out of his sickbed, His Excellency had to leave for his episcopal consecration and then to go to the East Indies.

Meanwhile, Reverend Father Kempkes had to leave Batavia and take the place at Coronie of Reverend Father Schepers who had to come to Paramaribo as pro-vicar. Thus, there were two of us in Paramaribo, but this left no one in Batavia. From time to time, the pro-vicar took care of it himself for four weeks, and so then I was alone and on Sundays I had to binate, lead the public prayers, etc., and take care of the sick, teach the children, etc. Toward the end of 1843, Reverend Father Heinink came from Europe to our assistance and quickly took up the duties in Batavia. In 1844, Reverend Father Meurkens came from Europe.

When His Excellency Bishop Grooff was expelled from the East Indies, he returned to Paramaribo as Apostolic Visitor [1847]. In 1849 Reverend Father Heinink died in Batavia where later [1851] his role was taken by Reverend Father Magné. In 1852, His Excellency Bishop Grooff died.

In 1851, yellow fever (*gele koorts*) struck Paramaribo especially among the foreign-born and in a short time sent many to their graves. I went to the military hospital twice a day and finally I caught the fever. It was four weeks before I got my health back and could resume my various labors and duties.

After the death of Bishop Grooff, Most Reverend Father G. Schepers was named bishop, i.p.i., and vicar apostolic and therefore had to go to Holland to be consecrated. Reverend Father Kempkes was then in Coronie and Reverend Father Magné in Batavia, and thus it was for two years that I and Reverend Father Meurkens were in Paramaribo and in charge of the plantations. His Excellency Bishop Schepers brought Reverend Father Swinkels back with him and so our numbers increased. In the meantime, we were awaiting some religious sisters and I was given charge of Batavia, where I remained alone for ten years, until it pleased God that Reverend Father Meurkens, who had been named pro-vicar at the death of His Excellency Bishop Grooff in 1863, had to leave for Europe because of ill health. The Reverend Redemptorist Fathers were then given the Mission of Surinam and His Excellency Bishop J. B. Swinkels, bishop, i.p.i., came to Paramaribo in 1866 with two priests and one brother.

It was the desire of *Propaganda Fidei* and of His Holiness Pope Pius IX that all of us secular priests not leave the mission but remain. I used the occasion of my first trip from Batavia to the city to request His Excellency to admit me to the Congregation because I had for a long time, especially after I had read the life of our holy Father Alphonsus Mary written by Reverend Father Bossers, desired to become a Redemptorist if it please the Good God to give me such a vocation. I prayed to the Good God and the Blessed Virgin Mary to know God's holy will. And the Good God heard my prayers.

In spite of my age (fifty-seven), I was admitted by the rector major, and after an eight-month novitiate, I professed vows in 1867 on the feast of Saint John the Baptist. And now I am happy over the mercy of the Good God. Only one thing remains: to live as a perfect Redemptorist and to persevere in this vocation unto death. May the Good God grant me this through the intercession of his holy Mother and our holy Father Alphonsus!

After I had resided about ten months in the city of Paramaribo, His Excellency sent me again to Batavia so that I might work there with the two Fathers. Then it pleased divine Providence to offer the Indians, who up to that time had been neglected, the chance to know and love him. In 1868, I began this work first in the area of the Tabiti River, then on the Upper Saramacca, Waijombo, and Maratakka rivers, as well as for the Arowak and Warros Indians, and for the Caribs.

Unfortunately, the outcome did not match the hopes, except for the Arowaks, among whom evangelization moved along gradually, but the lack of sufficient instruction does not allow the extent that could be otherwise reached. The number of baptized is near six hundred, counting both children and adults. Among the Carib Indians, because there are a very great number of children and almost all are baptized, there was an attempt with a schoolteacher, but it failed. Drunkenness and immorality, etc., blocks their conversion. But God is omnipotent; Mary, the Refuge of Sinners, is their mother as well. Therefore: pray, trust in God and his holy Mother, do penance, for the saints say that from the day of Christ's death "souls have been redeemed by his blood."

May I be able, by the sacrifice of my life, to bring it about that all know and love God as he deserves. Still, may God's holy will be done in all things. The holy will of God and perfect obedience always and in all things are my consolation, and I hope that they will be my solace in the hour of my death. Amen.

> The Leprosarium of Batavia
> August 13, 1879, the Feast of the Blessed Virgin Mary,
> under the title of the Refuge of Sinners,
> P. Donders, C.Ss.R.

4. From the Batavia Chronicles (May 1868)

The Redemptorists generally keep ongoing chronicles of their various provinces, missions, and regions. Donders seems to have been given this task in May 1868. The following portion, translated by Reverend Samuel Boland, C.Ss.R., is from this entry and gives us another look at the work of Father Pete from his own hand.[7]

May 1868
The Indians

The Indians are the original inhabitants of Surinam. They used to be quite numerous, but through their misuse of alcohol and their very disorderly lives they have dwindled very much. There are three tribes, each with its own language, very different from those of the others: the Caribs, the Arowaks, and the Warros.

Through association with the Negroes and Coloreds, most of them speak and understand Pidgin English, with the exception of the women, children, and old men of the Caribs. They all used to be pagans, but I have not found among them any idolatry in the proper sense of the word.

They have magicians or witch doctors, whom they call Paije—doctors, or Padjassi—great doctors. They have no word to mean God: the word Tamvesie in their language also means grandfather. They believe vaguely that there is some sort of life above. In the history of Surinam we learn that in the past some ministers of the Moravian Brethren began to preach to the Arowaks in Nickerie, but they did not continue. Some French priests, too, from Manna in Cayenne baptized many children, so Bishop Grooff said, near the river Marowijne. Since, however, the Indians are nomads, wandering about the whole region, nothing can be done with them unless they are properly instructed.

I attempted this several times in the past, when I was working among the lepers here in Batavia, but without success. Now that we have two Fathers here, I thought I should try another way, for it is truly a matter of sorrow that these poor people, redeemed just like ourselves by the precious Blood of Jesus Christ, should live and die under the power of the devil. I, therefore, wrote to ask the bishop to allow me by way of experiment to seek out and instruct them in their own houses and encampments. The bishop agreed and readily commended the work. Really, of the Indians and of some of the Negroes it can be said in these parts: *Compelle intrare*, as Jesus said in the Gospel.

My first visit was to the river Tibiti, ten or twelve hours from Batavia. The babies there have been baptized and the older children and adults are being instructed for holy baptism (Caribs).

At the river called the Wayombo again almost all the children (Caribs) were baptized and the rest are under instruction. This is a slow procedure. The Our Father and so on must be repeated hundreds of times for them before they can keep anything in their memories, but as always there are exceptions.

On the Upper Saramacca, twenty-five hours from Batavia in the opposite direction, there are many Arowaks, more civilized, better clothed, and with a better knowledge of Pidgin English. I baptized not only the children but the adults as well, married them and gave some of them Communion.

Seven hours further on there are Caribs, who at first refused, but now give hope that they can be taught. The biggest difficulty in their regard is to get them together, because they live a distance of some hours from the river, so that many streams have to be traveled in a canoe, which is a hollowed out tree trunk. If we could bring all the Indians together, at least each tribe, and if we had enough Fathers for two to stay with the Caribs, then with God's help, without which we can do nothing, we could make something out of them.

First, one has to win their confidence, because they are suspicious, especially the so-called witch doctors or magicians. I have seen the way these *Piajmans,* or witch doctors, behave. In the beginning they tried to tell the rest that I was going to take away all their children after I baptized them. When that did not happen, they said the children would all die; and once that was seen to be false, several of them agreed that the children be baptized.

One Indian said to me that if one could not be saved without baptism, he preferred not to be baptized so as not to be separated from his ancestors. I asked him to come with me to the church (a hut consisting of four or five poles and a roof of branches) where I was to celebrate Mass. He promised and came along. After Mass he said to his wife: "Let us have our baby baptized." I thanked God and did it at once.

An Indian woman was very ill, and I thought she could live only a few days since she was unable to eat. The witch doctor or magician was worn out with practicing his arts. He would suck on a hand or an arm, blow tobacco smoke on it and suck on it again. He would go through this process of sucking, breathing tobacco, and sucking and then stand up and breathe out the evil spirit into his hands. I asked him if the woman would get well, and he answered he had no idea, since he had not been a magician for long. I asked the woman if she preferred to be baptized, and she agreed. I did what I could to teach her the most necessary truths and dispose her as well as I could to contrition, and then, telling her to have nothing more to do with these foolish practices, baptized her. To my amazement the woman did not die. She got better, but fell back into her old ways. I think she is still alive, though this happened five months ago.

The Caribs are almost naked, but are learning modesty, and some of them are getting themselves clothes. I am constantly urging the rest to buy clothes. When they work cutting timber or sarsaparilla wood they can get money or clothes; but they prefer to buy alcohol. The Coloreds and some Europeans provide them with spirits for their own material gain.

The Arowaks and Warros are better clothed, more civilized than and not as much given to alcohol as the Caribs.

The Caribs—Their Way of Life—Houses—Clothing

These people live in the bush, generally preferring the higher ground. They live by hunting and fishing and they grow cassava, bananas, and the like.

They use bows and arrows. Some, many of them in fact, have guns. They work for the Europeans and the Coloreds, cutting sarsaparilla wood and clearing land, being paid in alcoholic drink (rum), tobacco, and clothes. Generally speaking, they do not live long on account of the abuse of alcohol; and for this they blame the Europeans and others through whom they get the liquor (gin and rum).

When these cannot be obtained, they make an alcoholic drink they call *tapana* or *wokoe* from the ripe cassava (*Iatropha*). They also have a reddish-colored drink they call *kasve* and another that is black and called *pajewaroe*. There are some exceptions, persons who reach a fairly advanced age.

Their Houses

Their houses or huts are open to the air at both ends and can not be locked. Furniture consists of hammocks, bows and arrows, guns, and fish hooks. The women make the hammocks from cotton, and with a certain type of clay mixed with bark of a tree they make pitchers and dishes of various sizes. They also work in the field and do the cooking, so that they work much harder than the men.

Ordinarily, they are practically naked, with large knives in their belts. Now, as a result of our urging, they are starting to buy clothes for themselves. They are at home in the water: everyone can swim: men, women, and children. They use canoes made by hollowing out tree trunks.

Their Religion

Last century ministers of the Moravian Brethren began to evangelize the Arowaks, but had to give up. Some little children were baptized in various places by Bishop Grooff and the early priests. If they survived beyond the age of seven, there was no provision for further care of them. Many people near the river Marowijne were also baptized by French priests from Cayenne.

We have begun now to visit and teach them in the places where they live; and it is necessary to keep this up if we want to have any hope for them. It would be good if we could bring them together; but that is not possible, because they live by hunting and fishing, which means that they cannot be restricted to a particular place. They now live scattered about in small groups: in many cases just a few families live together. By God's goodness, though, we are not losing heart that if we win their confidence and God gives his help, without which we can do nothing, we shall overcome every difficulty. By now I have reached the point when nearly all of the children have been baptized.

The Arowaks

These are better clothed, work well, understand and speak Pidgin English better than the Caribs; but they are few in numbers and they, too, are scattered about the country. Among them not only the children but also the adults have been baptized. Some, too, have been married and admitted to first Communion.

I have occasionally seen some Warros, and I have baptized a few of their children. These people are fewer in number. Perhaps at some later time I shall be in a position to write more about them. These three tribes have languages that are different one from the other.

PART III

Blessed Peter Donders: His Spirituality

CHAPTER ONE

THE MISSIONARY SPIRIT OF PETER DONDERS

FABRICIANO FERRERO, C.Ss.R.

I. For the Latin American Church

Peter Donders is the symbol of a place (Surinam) and of a historical period (1842–1887) that, at first sight, could seem to show little serious prophetic witness. His beatification, however, implies ecclesiastical recognition of the missionary activities achieved by the groups of priests and religious such as he. He is the humble apostle of Surinam, in which the Church was gradually born in a population made up mostly of slaves. Therefore, he is called to represent all those prophetic personalities and serve as a link between the glorious saints and heroes at the origins of the Church of Latin America and its impressive contemporary martyrology.

At least that is the way that one of his first Spanish biographers saw him:

> This edifying life ought to offer us Americans much greater interest because, on the one hand, the arena in which this holy missionary sacrificed his daily life on the altars of charity through forty-five long years was Dutch Guyana, an integral part of our South American continent, and, furthermore, this new Peter Claver (to whom this holy apostle of South America can be compared) not

only lived in our lands but in our own days, since he died only two years ago.[1]

Still, our Blessed Peter is not a flamboyant person. He indeed belongs among the quiet and simple missionaries who, with their heroic virtues and their human limitations, went about building the Christian communities of Latin America. His is not some unique role that impresses us today, but he stands out as an authentic representative of so many men and women who gave the best of themselves to build up the Church of God on the "outskirts of Catholicism." His biography brings pure torture for anyone who wishes to follow the classical lines of writing history because it is difficult to find anything extraordinary in his personality or in his lowly work. [He was hidden] in the anonymity of a colony along side others building Christian communities out of simple and radical fidelity to the Gospel in everyday life in the backwaters of the world, of society, and of the Church. Figures like Donders merit little attention. In them, what is extraordinary lies in the perfection and heroicity of ordinary life, in "perpetually doing all things well," as his most authoritative biographer, J. Kronenburg, puts it.

Because of all this, his presence in the Latin American Church and our reference to this fact in order to understand better his role…

> is not a metaphor or a simple allegory. Before all else, it is a vivid and profoundly moving example that continuously becomes richer in the context of life (with its pain, struggle, hope, death, and resurrection) in our Christian communities along the breadth and width of our continent. Therefore, an approach…is only possible out of the faith and life of the poor of the earth, out of hunger, persecution, torture, fear, exile… From this perspective his words and his testimony regain their truly extraordinary dimension, namely, that of the radical call of the Gospel that transforms [Donders] into "Good News" for us."[2]

Almost all of Donders' biographers try to give us an image of him according to the missionary ideals emanating from the principles of that century. To discover his role in the Latin American Church, however, we will try to work out of the attitude that the Medallín and Puebla documents presume. Therefore, we begin with these suppositions:

- Peter Donders incarnates the figure of nineteenth-century missionaries who chose to conduct their priestly or religious activity in the Catholic missions of the colonies, dedicating themselves totally to the evangelization of the most lowly and needy.
- His priestly and religious vocation is, at one and the same time, essentially missionary. "Apostolic Missionary" and "Redemptorist Missionary" will become his two outstanding titles.
- This missionary vocation stems from the cry of the "outskirts of Catholicism" and demands an exodus from the center of Christianity toward the slums of the cities and toward the outlands, as a profound presence in the world of the poor.
- In Peter Donders, this [missionary] vocation shows an absolutely clear development. First, amid a vague restlessness to become a priest, he hears the call of America. "This reading [of the *Annals of the Propagation of the Faith*] raised a desire in me to become a missionary to work for the conversion of unbelievers when I was a priest."[3] To respond to this, he seeks to become a religious. When he got nowhere, he opted for Surinam and completed his preparation for priesthood. He leaves for Dutch Guyana as an Apostolic Missionary and never returned.
- In the midst of his missionary activity, he meets one of the religious communities he had sought in Holland and becomes a Redemptorist.
- His pastoral activity is laid out in a series of steps that we can distinguish, taking into account his progressive movement toward the "outskirts."

II. The Apostolic Missionary (1848–1866)

The archives of the Diocese of Paramaribo preserve two documents dated April 14, 1842. One is the decree of the Sacred Congregation of the Propagation of the Faith declaring Donders to be an "Apostolic Missionary." The other is the certificate with special faculties that were usually granted on such an occasion.[4] Both documents are marked with the proper seals and signatures. So it was that, from 1842 to 1866, Donders signs all of his letters with the title "Apostolic Missionary."

III. The Birth of a Missionary Vocation (1831–1841)

The mystique of the apostolic missionary in the history of the missions dates from the very beginning of the ecclesial turmoil that culminated in the [establishment of the] Congregation for the Propagation of the Faith and of many missionary institutes.

The period stretching from 1815 to 1926 produced an incredible missionary rebirth in the Catholic Church. Christian vitality, which presupposed the interior renewal of the Church [at the roots of the Restoration Period] and the political unrest that culminated in the International African Conference of 1876 and the Conference of Berlin in 1885, gave rise as well to a new missionary movement. When we add to this the great scientific and technological discoveries with their influence on missionary travels, we have a much more complete explanation of an ecclesiastical phenomenon that reached almost to our own days.

There was another determining factor: the influence of the European social revolution. It was, in fact, the recognition of the dignity of the worker that led as well to the recognition of the dignity of the poorest and most needy people of the world. Every person, no matter how humble, has some inviolable rights. It is, then, not strange that there would be ever more forceful talk against slavery, talk that increased into a social movement and that, together with explorers, colonizers, merchants, adventurers, and scientists, would include men and women missionaries who joined to their supernatural concern for evangelization a humanitarian desire to end such suffering. Thus, in mission territories, there began to spring up schools, hospitals, dispensaries, leprosaria, etc., with a new orientation.

The ideology that supported this tendency appears to have been influenced strongly by personalities as distinct as Rousseau, de Maistre, Chateaubriand, as well as by popular literature about the missions (such as the *Annals of the Propagation of the Faith*). It is to these different sources that the interest, sympathy, and compassion for the "uncivilized" peoples owed their beginning and the greater recognition they gained. Perhaps we could say today that it was a romanticized, idyllic vision of the pagan world and of missionary activity. Nevertheless, it certainly occasioned many vocational calls, such as those of Blessed Donders and of his confrere, Saint John Nepomucene Neumann.

In the two autobiographical accounts of his life (1874 and 1879), Donders distinguishes clearly three separate calls: his priestly vocation, his missionary vocation, and his religious vocation. He believed he felt an incipient call to the priesthood from his earliest childhood, from the age of five or six. His missionary vocation, on the other hand, was added to the priestly vocation at a precise moment and with very exact motivations.

a. From the Call of North America to the Cry of Surinam

His first missionary call arose during his years in the minor seminary from the picture that impressed him through his reading about the people in America. "From this reading there was born in me the desire to work for the salvation of souls in America or else where."[5] This is why his superiors sent him to try to find a place among the religious congregations dedicated to the missionary apostolate. He was refused by all. And he admits, "At this time and later, I felt no special desire for religious life, but only to become a priest and work for the salvation of souls."[6]

Since he could not become a religious missionary, his seminary's superiors finally accepted the fact that he could become a diocesan priest. We have seen how he discovered his call to Surinam while in the major seminary (see pp. 30–32).

We can deduce the kind of image that Monsignor Grooff painted from the role that the bishop himself played in the history of that mission. We realize what it meant to Donders from the way he wrote about the decision he made at that time, phrasing it in terms almost like those of a civil document, indicating time and place: "This was decided in 1839 at the major seminary in the town of Haaren."[7]

b. Missionary Priest

From that moment until the end of his seminary days three years later, he waited anxiously for the day he could leave for Surinam. We can feel his happiness many years later as he recalled that day in his first curriculum vitae:

> Finally the happy day arrived that I received from the bishop the notice that the boat for Surinam was ready to depart and would be weighing anchor within eight days. I said goodbye to the reverend Fathers who acted as the agents of Providence and lavished their care upon me. I also took leave of my mother and my brother. Then I left alone. So, with all my bonds severed, I placed myself entirely in the hands of God.[8]

Those words reflect the missionary spirit that inspired his whole life and broke out in the missionary restlessness that in a few years would be capsulated in the title he gloried in: Apostolic Missionary.

IV. The Evolution of His Missionary Spirit

This missionary restlessness underwent a series of progressive steps or levels. Let us look at them.

a. The Sense of a Calling

The fact that Donders experienced this desire for missionary work not as wanderlust or an urge for excitement in new places is apparent in his constant attribution of this sense as due to God's work. We only select examples from the beginning and end of his missionary life.

> It is true that not everyone can work as a missionary in this vineyard; indeed, it is the Lord who must call them for this.[9]

> How admirably God arranges everything! It is he who gave me the desire to do great work in bringing about his glory through the salvation of the souls redeemed at great price. He gives me the strength and health that I need to work here.[10]

b. The Decision and Promptness of Response

The clarity of his call demanded a prompt and decisive response. This is visible in his curricula vitae. But the quality is most evident in his letter after his arrival in Surinam:

> The following morning, while I was in church, I unexpectedly received notice that the boat would leave immediately. I left the church—since it was God who was calling me—without being able to celebrate the holy sacrifice. I grabbed my breviary and left, abandoning myself into the hands of his divine providence to which I recommended myself.[11]

It required a complete departure from all ordinary human goals, as the same letter testifies:

> I often thought of my travel companions with the greatest sympathy, as they try to do everything possible to pile up a temporal treasure but who have no care for God and their eternal happiness. This proved to be a motive that urged me to sacrifice myself for God and for the salvation of souls as much as these poor souls were doing for what would bring them unhappiness both in time and in eternity.[12]

c. An "Exodus" Spirit

The response presupposed an heroic dependence on God to follow Christ and seek his kingdom. Almost every one of his writings states explicitly or implicitly the phrase, "For the Glory of God and the salvation of souls." His most quoted Scripture passages are from chapter 19 of Matthew's Gospel, where we find the invitation of Christ to leave all and follow him. This was not just a passing phase. It is verse 29 that gives him the understanding of his whole life:

> I can say, Reverend Father, that I reached the destiny to which the Lord called me and "his right hand upholds me." "Blessed be the God and Father of our Lord Jesus Christ, the Father of mercies and the God of all consolation" (2 Corinthians 1:3). I see the promise already fulfilled that our Sanctifier gave us in the gospel, "Everyone who has left...brothers or sisters or father or mother..., for my name's sake, will receive a hundredfold" (Matthew 19:29). I have abandoned parents in the spiritual life, my true friends at the seminary and elsewhere; but the One whose promises never fail has returned them to me.[13]

To understand the biblical inspiration of this attitude we must read it in its context and through the eyes of Donder's humility. Then we can grasp the interpretation given them by Donders:

- like the apostles (apostolic missionary),
- they left all things (missionary exodus),
- to follow Christ (disciple of Christ),
- who gave his precious blood for the salvation of souls, including those who live in darkness and the shadow of death, such as lepers, the poor, and slaves (*kenosis*, emptying of Christ),
- for the honor and glory of God (the building of the kingdom)

- for this reason, as for Christ, they will be exalted (apostolic hope)
- therefore, just as did Christ and the apostles, he placed his confidence in the "Good God," or "God of Goodness," as he often phrased it, who is the "Father of Mercy, in his "Fatherly Providence."

d. Consciousness of the Mission

This merciful love of God is not something to be sealed hermetically within one's own feelings. God called him to work for his honor and glory (Reign of God) and for the salvation of souls (conversion and freedom), for those for whom Christ spilled his precious blood. The Providence that guided him to the priesthood is one and the same with that which led him to be a missionary. This was not done, however, for a global or general purpose. Peter Donders sensed himself to be sent to the concrete reality of Surinam to work for the most abandoned. This was to be the field of his endeavor, "our mission," as he said from the beginning.

This is what led to the immense joy he felt when he arrived here:

> I can say, Reverend Father, that I reached the destiny to which the Lord called me and "his right hand upholds me."[14]

Together with this joy we discover as well a very clear awareness of the task being assigned him and of the means he must use to accomplish it. He mentions how he was struck by the first sermon he heard after his arrival in Paramaribo given by Monsignor Grooff: "The Most Reverend Prefect preached on the text, "Go out and preach, etc." (Matthew 28:19). During it, he exhorted me to help him and his assistants, in his words, to carry the iron cross."[15]

e. His Sense of Being Incarnate

This mission was not just a place. It was a Christian community and these were real human beings. Like all great missionaries,

Donders was impressed from the start by the people who received him and he began to identify himself ever more with the problems and difficulties of those he was called to evangelize.

The comments about this aspect of the missionary life he has left us in the letters are rich and abundant. We will limit ourselves to pointing out some of the most characteristic examples that appear in the letter he wrote in November 1842 (see p. 104).

- Admiration and surprise in the face of this new reality: "I cannot hold back sharing a few words about this place with you since I am now so wonderfully delighted with everything here."
- Emotion and compassion: "When I saw these poor lepers drawing close, Reverend Father, I could not hold back my tears."
- Personal excitement over the new reality: "I have to admit to Your Reverence that this ceremony deeply impressed me the first time it took place. Imagine if you can this scene..."
- Gradual identification with the most lowly: lepers, slaves, natives, etc., with whom he shared all things, for whom he prayed as he would for himself, and for those that are close to death. He was convinced that Surinam was his true "homeland."

f. Moral Indignation and Prophetic Stance

His incarnation in the place of his destiny brought about an increase in Donders' missionary spirit, widening it out into an ethical indignation that is characteristic of the great missionaries of the Latin American Church. This concrete reality of Surinam as Donders comprehended it and lived it, caused the prophetic dimension to unfold in him, which completed the missionary sensitivities that had made him leave Europe in the first place.

In effect, ethical indignation blooms spontaneously in a believer who is incarnated into the world of the poor as it did in Jesus of Nazareth and tends to manifest itself in prophetic denunciation of evil.

The contradictions in this reality are seen intuitively in a wise and judicious understanding that we could call sacramental, because it intuits the symbols of the fundamental character present in events, namely, the presence of oppression and the urgency of liberation. In this faith, many Christians arrive at an understanding that such a situation contradicts the historical designs of God and see that poverty constitutes a social sin that God does not wish. This demands an urgent change to help brothers and sisters and to lead all into obedience to God. This perception usually expresses itself in the language of prophetic denunciation and with a vocal demand for change, as an expression of ethical indignation. Moreover, it embodies itself in the practice of totally committed love....The situation cannot continue this way; it demands an alteration of the social relations and the bestowal of greater power on dominated groups, so that there are new, less oppressive structures.[16]

[The prophets of Israel] did not limit themselves to strongly denouncing society's sin without proclaiming God's reaction to this sin. This reaction of God can be summed up in three proclamations: the announcement of punishment, the demand for conversion, and the word of consolation.[17]

The most explicit testimony to this apostolic attitude in Donders is found in his letter of 1846 (see pp. 127–128) that could very well be included in anthologies of the Church's prophetic witness in Latin America. In order not to weaken its original force, we direct you to his own words. Here we will only point out the aspects that seem most significant to us.

- *A prophetic vision of the reality of Surinam*, above all in regard to the slaves. It is true that at first he was struck by the sight of the lepers in Batavia. Nevertheless, he states that he does not see in them the ultimate tragedy of the colony.

What he sees as crying out to the heaven is slavery and the various forms of exploitation and injustice.
- *Denunciation of those responsible.* When he speaks of the Amerindians, he alludes to the difficulties they suffer arising from their way of life: nomadism, language. In other cases, especially when he speaks of the slaves, it is very clear whom he sees as responsible.
- *Prophetic reaction.* Donders' spirituality allows him to discover the hand of God in natural calamities themselves. In his letter of 1843, he points to the fact that the plague has brought many to seek the grace of baptism. In later letters he points out similar trials as warnings of worse chastisements for sin.
- *Hope of Liberation:* All of this is united to a sense of the mercy of universal redemption, the ultimate reason for his missionary evangelization. He therefore points to the concrete means of this freedom such as the bulls of Pope Gregory XVI as well as the abolition of slavery in North America.
- *The Impossibility of an Authentic Evangelization Without a Prior Liberation.* This is what reinforces his hope. For Donders, the greatest obstacle missionary evangelization encounters in Surinam arises out of the structures of injustice and slavery. "From all this, Your Reverence may gain an idea of the many difficulties we must contend with, and see that Faith and morality cannot advance quickly until the traffic in slavery and the plantation-system are totally suppressed, as in North America, where they deal with free persons."[18]

V. The Pastoral Action of an Apostolic Missionary

Missionary spirit embodies itself in the action of evangelization by means of a complex of pastoral activities. To understand this, it is necessary to take into account the purpose for which the missionary undertakes this work, the message to be proclaimed, those to whom it is directed, and the means to be used.

a. The Objectives of Missionary Evangelization

Donders' thought on this can be summarized in a few expressions that appear often in his letters:

- "[To] illumine with the light of Faith those who still lie in darkness and in the shadow of death"; seek "the conversion of so many unbelievers and so many indifferent Christians"; "so they know and love the Good God"; "to bring it about that all know and love God as he deserves."[19]
- To bring it about that "they recognize him as their creator and serve him with sincerity" out of freedom by offering him "honor and glory" and "by living a Christian life."[20]
- To seek "the conversion of souls for whom Jesus Christ gave his life."[21]
- To struggle against impiety by the only weapons that work: "the cross and confidence in God."[22]

The encyclical *Evangelii nuntiandi* (nn. 8–9) sums up this very objective in two expressions: "the Reign of God" and "liberating salvation." These apply perfectly to Donders' style.

b. Content of Message

We can try to organize a list of the main thoughts that formed the substance of Donders' preaching and teaching by means of a few quotations.

- God is Love and Mercy: "Truly, God is good and merciful toward poor sinners."[23]
- The Incarnation of our Lord, Jesus Christ: His remark about the difference between his preaching and that of the Brethren: "These persons, who after a great many years of instruction and who many times have participated in the Lord's supper, understand nothing of the mystery of the incarnation of Jesus Christ, etc."[24]
- The redemption of souls "for whom Jesus chose to give his life and precious blood."[25]

- Christian life, that is indeed God's work, and that, little by little, needs to be brought to reality among the new communities in Surinam.[26]

c. Preferred Audience

Donders did not exclude anyone from his pastoral ministry. Nevertheless, there is an evident preference in his life for the world of the marginalized and abandoned. There were the socially marginalized: the slaves and lepers. There were those abandoned in the city: the poor and sick. There were those who were geographically isolated: the Amerindians and Maroons. His entire ministry was one of reaching out to those on the outskirts. The measure of their distance from society and care was often expressed in "hours of travel" needed to reach them. There were three distinct arenas for his work:

Paramaribo (1842–1856): The first fourteen years of Donders' sojourn in Surinam were spent in the capital city. As was explained in Part One, Chapter VII, Surinam's population was under 60,000, about 7,000 of whom were Catholic, both slave and free, living in the capital; another 5,000 or so Catholics lived in other parts of the colony. From the time that Monsignor Grooff left shortly after Donders' arrival, there were never more than four priests in the entire colony during this period: Schepers, Kempkes, Heinink, and Donders. This usually meant that only two priests cared for the entire city of Paramaribo.[27]

The situation in the colony was never ideal for religious ministry. A few years after this period, in 1880, the bishop described the most rampant abuses:

> ...indifference, slavery to the fleshly passions, superstition. Moreover, sloth and instability of the kind that they are able to change the norms of life and religion as often as they change their clothes....Not the least of the causes of these evils is the same type of disordered lives of almost all the Europeans, including those in the highest places.[28]

Donders' letter of June 5, 1843 (see p. 114) tells us his first works were those of instructing children and adults in the catechism as well as attending the confessional. There was also the soldier's garrison to care for, Batavia's lepers, and some plantations. There was the dysentery and yellow fever epidemics that made Donders the doctor and nurse of his confreres and the consolation-giver of the city as he cared for the sick and dying, and buried the dead. We also cannot forget the beggars and homeless who found him a support and advocate.

Donders obviously did not spend his time loitering in the "high" society of the city. All the reports we have placed him amid the sick, needy, despised, and outcast.

The Batavia Leprosarium (1856–1866): Perhaps the summation of his involvement with the lepers lies in his letter of November 13, 1842 (see p. 104): "When I saw these poor lepers drawing close, I could not hold back my tears." Unfortunately, we have no correspondence from this period. We have only the letters he wrote when he returned to Batavia in 1885, but they are enough to show us how completely he entered into their lives. What we know of his commitment and actions come mainly from the recollections of those who testified at his beatification process. On his part, his letters mention little of the day-to-day life amid this terrible disease. It seems that he came to see this life as "ordinary," as something he lived through, expecting and desiring nothing else. These were his "dear lepers" "for whom Christ shed his blood as well as for us." This was "his place," ordained by Providence.

He saw this community of suffering, not as an evil to avoid, but as the chosen arena in which it was his task to uncover for its members the hidden care of God for the little ones. While others banished these people from their lives, he chose to be the symbol, the sacrament, if you will, of the God who did not leave them orphans. His choice (or better, his realization of God's choice for him) could not be better expressed than in his words of that November 1842 letter.

Yet, how good is God and what great care his paternal providence gives! For many, this disease is their unique path to reach eternal happiness. Here many have learned to know and adore the one true God whom they otherwise never would have known and adored. Here many find the most beautiful occasion to do penance for their sins by putting up with their infirmity, pains, and miseries until they reach eternal happiness in this way. Furthermore, they have a father, the Most Reverend Prefect, who not only consoles their hearts but who also takes care of them bodily, sharing with them the pious alms from Holland and other places that have been given him.[29]

What Donders saw as "extraordinary" during his first stay at Batavia was his realization of the even greater spiritual needs of the slaves on the plantations.

The Plantations (1842–1866): The plantations were agricultural establishments, privately or governmentally owned, that exploited the work of slaves. They were operated by the owners or by overseers. The pitiful state of these human beings, as we know, passed through two equally depressing stages in Donders' day. First, there was the period of actual slavery when they were indeed property, treated no better than animals. Then followed the period after their emancipation in 1863, when as "free" people, most continued to work as meagerly paid laborers on the same plantations while others were thrown on their own resources and began to live without homes or in the barest shelters in the city. Donders' letters have told us of the evils of both periods (see pp. 128, 146–147).

Dealing with the former slaves who left the plantations for the city, Donders acted as already explained for all the poor of Paramaribo. His missionary activity with those who lived on the plantations shows us more aspects of the type of people he tried most desperately to help.

We recall that the apostolate to the plantation slaves began long before Donders arrival in Surinam. At first, Catholic priests were allowed on the plantations, but around 1829 the prefect apostolic, Bishop Groof, was forbidden to visit them further. Gradually, the prohibition fell away but it was not until 1863, when slavery was abolished, that completely free access was available. Donders did manager to gradually work his way into more and more plantations in the years leading up to the emancipation. After that, dealing with the former slaves became more difficult because they were dispersed more widely in the colony,

Donders' pastoral activity on the plantations is extremely interesting. First of all, he tried to overcome the difficulties placed in his path by the owners and overseers, "making them see the advantages that the preaching of the Gospel could bring them."[30] To overcome this, he tried to unite to his zeal for the salvation of souls a more humane treatment [of them]…[and so] little by little, the administrators became less opposed and in the end, more than a few of them began to consider it an honor to be able to give some aid to a missionary who was so venerated everywhere"[31] He was thus able to gradually increase the number of visits, something that was very important to increase the slaves' trust "since they had never before seen a Catholic priest and had no knowledge of Christ the Redeemer."[32] Witnesses at the process of beatification often mentioned his biweekly visits to the plantations when he had access to them, and how he tried to draw to the parish house those who had come to live in the city.[33]

From the testimony, we can list some of the activities of a strictly evangelical missionary type that he employed:[34]

- Visits to the fields where the slaves worked to gather them and speak with them, outside in a shed or in the open air.
- Activities with these groups such as drilling them by repetition of the fundamental truths of the Faith so that they can memorize them; presenting a form of Christian life they can follow; extirpation of pagan practices (he strove to collect the superstitious or idolatrous objects they brought with them); formalization of marriages; celebration of the Eucharist; administration of the sacraments; developmental instruction.

- Visits to their habitations.
- Efforts to arrange a community and catechetical organization for the periods when no missionary could be present.

VI. The Redemptorist Missionary (1866–1887)

Donders believed that the high point of God's providential action in his life was his religious vocation to the Congregation of the Most Holy Redeemer, precisely in Surinam, where he had been led as an apostolic missionary. As he said shortly after his profession, "How admirable is his Providence! At fifty-eight, he has accepted me as a religious, right here in Surinam and in Paramaribo! I cannot express to you, my Reverend Friend, the joy and satisfaction I feel."

1. Genesis of His Religious Vocation

In 1879, when Donders was asked to write his (second) curriculum vitae about the origins of his religious vocation, we seem to find two basic motives: the figure of Saint Alphonsus Maria de Liguori and the event of the confiding of the mission in Surinam to the Redemptorists. We could say that he discovered a coincidence of his ideals with those of Alphonsus and with the work of the Institute. Therefore, when the Congregation arrived in Surinam to take over the mission to which he had consecrated his life as an apostolic missionary, it was logical that he would desire to incorporate himself into the community. In that way he could now live in common with others the missionary charism that had inspired his whole life. "Peter Donders was a Redemptorist before he entered the congregation." The "Apostolic Missionary" already had the missionary charism that belonged to the group founded by Saint Alphonsus. Donders expresses all this very simply in his Second Autobiography (see p. 225).

This change, the most profound in his life, took place without any great trauma: "The change from a diocesan priest to a religious happened with no difficulty. Thanks be to God! Everything is working together for my good."[35] This communion of charisms allowed him to live within the Congregation the very spirit that had enlivened him as an Apostolic Missionary. It is from this union that arise the peacefulness of spirit, the happiness, and the enthusiasm he reflects in his account of conscience of 1874 and in his later correspondence.

2. Religious Vocation and Missionary Spirit

The reinvigoration that appeared in the life of Peter Donders after 1867 arises from his total identification with the apostolic Redemptorist Community. In his correspondence from that period of his life we sense how the Congregation and all it stood for became his own. He saw his apostolate strengthened by the arrival in the mission of Surinam of missionary personnel which until then he had begged for unsuccessfully and he felt himself fully incorporated into this new group. At the same time, thanks to the dynamism of the Congregation, he felt that the Catholic Church of Surinam could hold its own against the Protestants and the Moravian Brethren, its great antagonists, even in the field of education.

Because of all this, it is worthwhile noting how, after his incorporation into the religious group, he was strengthened in the very aspects that were most significant in his missionary charism. Let us enumerate some:

- The experience of submission to the will of God, now lived by means of religious obedience and common life.
- The significance of prayer and confidence in the God of Goodness and in his paternal providence, which little by little was transformed into his experience of life and into a means of the apostolate.
- The sense of [reaching out to those on] the margins as service and sacrificial surrender, because "From the day of Christ's death, 'souls have been redeemed by his blood.'"[36] In his heart it was the most abandoned who occupied a special place: the lepers of Batavia, the slaves of the plantations, the Blacks of the forest, the nomadic Amerindians. "Jesus Christ spilled his precious blood as much for them as for us"; these, too, just as we, are children of our Good Mother Mary.[37] It is not

strange that he was so willing to sacrifice his life so that they could "know and love God as he deserves."[38]
- The reality of fraternal communion: Donders felt himself loved, esteemed, welcomed, strengthened on all sides. Starting with his religious profession, the references to his "vocation" and his happiness in common life are constant.
- His missionary and redemptive sense: as his life went on, his love and identification with the Amerindians grew to the extent that he felt a sort of failure in his apostolate to them. He loved them, he lived their isolation, and understood that he had to be slow in the process of Christian transformation. Anyone who would stay among them would feel anxious to evangelize and would ponder how, despite being redeemed, they still lived in darkness and the shadow of death.

In this context it is significant that his entrance into the Congregation coincides with the beginnings of his going in search of the indigenous people in order to help them to know and love the Good God. Now he is no longer alone as he was before. The presence of the apostolic community allows him to go beyond the borders of Batavia and even further. His letter of May 29, 1869, contains all of the freshness of a new missionary movement as soon as he is professed as a religious (see p. 137). In it we discover what Donders supposed the union of religious missionary vocations would be. This latter, not only did not suffer any loss, but was reinforced by all the energy of an apostolic community consecrated to Christ the Redeemer for the evangelization of the most abandoned. Donders provides us with historical testimony to the harmony between apostolic mission and religious life.

His autobiographical remarks of this period also call our attention to the spontaneous expression of the community and evangelizing dimension of his life. Without any doubt, it was the common life which had been created in the mission and in which he was so happy to share that had contributed to this. The means for transforming it were the traditional ones of religious life: his account of conscience, his written correspondence with his superiors, his presence in the Redemptorist community, permissions and information on apostolic activities, etc.

3. Apostolic Activity as a Redemptorist Missionary

At first sight, nothing seems to have changed in Donders' apostolic activity. His work in Paramaribo and in Batavia seems the same as before. In spite of all this, his missionary vocation urges him toward a new field of labor, that of the world of forests and jungles in order to bring the Good News to the indigenous people. This will become his specific apostolate of this period.

a. Among the Aboriginal People of Surinam

After Donders had spent about ten months in Paramaribo, the bishop again sent him to work in Batavia with two confreres. This allowed him the freedom to pursue a work he considered more pressing: bringing the Gospel to the Amerindians and Maroons of the jungle.

> Now, however, I am no longer alone as I was before, but rather I am with another priest. Therefore, I have more time to visit the plantations and to instruct the Blacks. It has been a year now that, with the permission and at the urging of the apostolic vicar, I have been occupying myself with the natives, the first settlers of this colony, in order to teach them to know and love God.[39]

A message he sent to his friend Gerard van Someren clearly shows Donders' personal attitude at the beginning of this new apostolate:

> Your Reverence certainly understands that we're dealing with a task that develops very slowly. With the Good God's grace, however, without whom we can do nothing, I hope to succeed in gaining all of them for God. Jesus Christ spilled his precious blood as much for them as for us....

> May the Good God, in his infinite mercy, bring it about that there be a total conversion among them. Let us pray that there will be only one flock and one shepherd. Let us also pray a great deal for each other. With prayer we can obtain everything.
>
> Permit me to recommend to your prayers and sacrifices our Congregation, myself, and the poor native people, that the God of Goodness and our dear Mother Mary, who is also their mother, illumine and comfort them to take up and bear joyfully this gentle yoke of Jesus so that they may participate with us in the joys of heaven.[40]

b. In Coronie (1883–1885)

After his apostolate in Batavia with the lepers and the Amerindian peoples, Father Donders hoped to end his days in the community at Paramaribo, where he arrived on February 7, 1883. He expresses this hope in a letter to his provincial:

> My Very Reverend Father, how happy community life makes me! And moreover, how much there is to do here! Knowing the desires of the Reverend Bishop, I asked His Excellency that, if it pleased him and God, he would give me the pleasure of living here in the community. And he willingly did so, as you see. Still, if God disposes otherwise, I am open to go and live anywhere that you or the Reverend Bishop choose to send me.[41]

But his presence at Paramaribo did not last long. The sickness of Father Stassen in Coronie required that Donders be sent to take his place. This would be a new step in his Redemptorist life and his apostolic activity. His state of mind is reflected in these lines of a letter to the provincial written in December 1883:

> It has pleased Divine Providence to move me to another place, Coronie, to work here for the salvation of souls. Here again there is much to do for the conversion of so

many sinners. Since God in his goodness has granted me health and strength for the task, for which I can never give thanks enough, I hope with his help to use them for his greater glory and for the salvation of souls redeemed by his precious blood.[42]

His pastoral attitude at this time is described in various letters of 1884. Let us look at one passage in a letter written to his nephew:

> There is enough work, but, by God's goodness that gives me strength and health, I work with gusto for the salvation of souls.[43]

c. In Batavia to the End

The only way that the "Apostle of the Lepers" could fittingly end his days was in Batavia. Perhaps neither he nor anyone else expected this after his departure in 1883. It was the result of his joining an apostolic community, because the sickness of a confrere and the needs of a ministry confided to it frequently demand of its members a willingness to move to a new location just as Donders experienced at the end of his life.

His apostolate toward the community at Batavia was as it always had been: dedication to the lepers, and unflagging journeys to evangelize the Blacks and aboriginal groups. These words from the report of Monsignor Schaap to the Holy See sum this up perfectly:

> [Father Donders] has, since 1855 dedicated himself to the poor people afflicted with leprosy in Batavia, becoming their servant by making himself "all things to all people." From this place of residence he usually makes journeys to the plantations in the neighborhood and into the deepest jungles. The continuous rejection by the Amerindians is unable to quench the spirit of this strong man even in the least.[44]

For a witness to the apostolic activity Donders performed for Batavia in the last year of his life, we need only look at a paragraph he wrote about himself a few months before his death. They are deeply moving when read if we keep in mind his age and his earlier letters of 1842–1846. This is the culminating moment of pastoral zeal in an apostolic missionary become a Redemptorist missionary.

> Your Reverence will have already been told that, with permission *[text is unclear]*, I have initiated an attempt among the Blacks of the forest who are building their houses near the Coppename River, a two or three hour journey from here by river and have bought some land to cultivate for their own sustenance….I cannot write much about them because I have only been there twice; but I hope that I may soon tell you more.[45]

The situation did not change and the failure seemed to become all the more evident. A month before his death he wrote again:

> After a journey of nineteen days, I returned to Batavia safe and sound, thanks to God. Things are going poorly with regard to the Blacks who live in the jungle. But let us have patience and trust in God who is all-powerful and rich in mercy. I ask you to remember them in your prayers along with me. Our setbacks and crosses come from God as well, and without the cross nothing goes as it should.[46]

Conclusion

At the end of these pages the words of Father Didier come to mind, words that he spoke two years after the death of our Blessed Peter.

> May they rest in peace on American soil, these venerable ashes of this new and grand apostle of our young continent. The grateful lepers of the fortunate city of Batavia spread abundant tears upon the cold stones of his lonely sepulcher. His memory, as that of the Just, will live forever. The present generation, and those to come, will pronounce his blessed name with profound veneration, especially in these South American lands, his adopted country and the fortunate arena of his apostolic combats and glorious triumphs. His confreres, the sons of the great Alphonsus, particularly those called as he was to cultivate this young South American vineyard of the Lord, will find in his shining example, not only the path they ought to follow, but also a strong stimulus to become imitators of his rare virtue and evangelical zeal. Thus, by imitating him, they may procure the eternal salvation of countless souls and come at last to share with him the eternal joys and unspeakable delights in the Land of the Fortunate."[47]

Despite the time-bound language in which these words were written, they allow us to discover an image of Blessed Peter Donders that is perfectly suited to the Church of our day.

In the face of the overwhelming task of the evangelization of Latin America, Peter Donders, the apostle of Surinam, is one of the apostolic missionaries who laid the first stones of the Church of God in this continent, bringing the Good News to communities of its lepers, Amerindian peoples and Blacks scattered among its rivers and forests.

Chapter Two

The Spirituality of Father Peter Donders

Ignaz Dekkers

I. Introduction

For many reasons, it is not easy to describe Father Peter Donders' spirituality. First of all, "spirituality" itself is not very clear term. It comes from "*spiritus*," that is, "spirit." We speak of people's spirit, that is, their interior or spiritual makeup with its own proper characteristics. In religious literature, it signifies the personal way that one lives out the Gospel. In this sense, we can speak of a "Franciscan spirituality." As a serious Christian, Saint Francis of Assisi sought to live the Gospel, but he did so in his own unique style. What intrigued and fascinated him was one precise aspect of the Gospel: the poverty of Christ, "The Poor Man of God." Thus, Francis' whole life remained marked, impregnated, and colored by this fundamental ideal. Francis truly had a special spirituality, a peculiar form of living the Gospel which focused on the poor Christ.

Thus we must raise a similar question with respect to Donders: what was his spirituality? This question presupposes another: did Father Peter Donders have his own way of living the Gospel, of following Christ and loving the Lord? This chapter consists of two parts: his Christian life, first considered as a whole, and then analyzed in some more specific aspects.

II. An Overall View

It is obvious that to understand the personality of Father Peter Donders properly, we must situate him in the context of his time. He lived in the nineteenth century (1809–1887). In him, we encounter characteristics of his time. Therefore, we are not surprised, for example, that his spirituality was not particularly biblical, liturgical, ecclesial, or ecumenical. These characterize today's spirituality. To tell the truth, his spirituality was "traditional" in the best sense of the term, that is, profoundly and solidly Christian and apostolic.

Donders was, without a doubt, a man of profound faith, one who was deeply religious. Numerous aspects of his life make this evident, as one can see by simply scanning his biography. It is said of Blessed Pope John XXIII that he conversed with God's saints as familiarly as he did with the simple people of his native town, Sotto il Monte. Although Donders did not have the vibrant, jovial, and expansive look of Blessed Pope John, his familiarity with God's world and his saints was very much like the pope's, namely, intimate and habitual.

He was certainly not a great theologian. His theological study, as was the custom of the time, was done through the manuals of the period. He was not an intellectual and his education was noticeably limited. Indeed, when would he have found time for specialized theological studies, since his missionary work and care of souls totally devoured every moment of every day? He did not develop a systematic spirituality, and still less did he write one. Nonetheless, he usually knew how to extract the marrow and juice from what he read, not so much intellectually as wholeheartedly and personally.

Pete, or Father Pete ("Peerke," his Dutch nickname), as he was usually called, lived as a Christian. That statement can seem simple and almost trivial. It is true that as we peruse the story of his life, we do not encounter many achievements that strike us as outstanding. His life had none of the adventures of a Saint Francis Xavier. Father Pete just lived an ordinary life. Nonetheless, be careful not to be trapped by the sound of that word *ordinary*.

Indeed ordinary, that is to say, humble, modest, discreet, unnoticed; but with such substance! The more one reads of what he did, the more one becomes convinced of his greatness. He lived the Gospel of Jesus Christ in a singularly constant and purposeful manner, up to the point of heroism. This was not an occasional matter, happening every now and then, or in some particularly urgent need. No, it was a constant affair, every day, every moment throughout his whole life. Thus, it is not surprising that when he was still alive, people called him a "saint." Even when he was a seminarian, his companions had already given him this title, without realizing all that it meant. Later, in his ministry, however, when he was called a "saint," it was because one saw in his way of living something eminently Christian, something of a true disciple of Christ. God knows that Father Pete gave his whole self and wore himself out on behalf of the people confided to him. Still, it is not enough to say that he was a totally dedicated missionary. We must also indicate the source of his missionary zeal, namely, that his whole being was profoundly united to God.

In him both interior and exterior formed one single unity. What does this mean? Saint Thomas speaks of three states of life: the contemplative, the active, and the mixed or apostolic. In this last named, contemplation and action form an organic unity. Contemplation leads to action; action leads back to contemplation. This is exactly Donders' case. The statement that all of his being was profoundly united to God does not mean that we are trying to speak of a mystical life that closed him into an interior world. Is such a type of mystical life even imaginable? For Father Pete, to be united to God and to consecrate oneself totally to the proclamation of the Good News was one and the same. He was 100 percent missionary. We can say without exaggeration that for Father Pete, "It is zeal for your house that has consumed me" (Psalm 69:9). What he did for "souls," as he expressed it, that is, for his brothers and sisters, is difficult to recount. We who live in the twenty-first century and who have no idea of the primitive and difficult situation in which he had to live and work, cannot exactly imagine what his service involved. If he had not enjoyed robust health, he would quickly have found his grave among the other young missionaries buried around the cathedral of Paramaribo.

It often happens that the apostolic fire which devours persons leads them to live a life on their own; it turns them in into "holy hermits." Instead, during the last twenty years of his life, Father Pete lived his Christian life in a religious congregation. It was in this group that he followed the Gospel of Jesus Christ, involved himself apostolically, and lived out all that made his life truly missionary. This fact is worthy of note. For many years, he had been a diocesan priest and worked alone in the leprosarium at Batavia. Then he entered the Redemptorist Congregation. From that point on, he lived as a religious in a community, giving himself totally to it with the same dedication as he had always lived from his youth.

We would search in vain for extraordinary elements in Father Pete's spirituality. Those who know Donders only by what they read about him would find his life to look rather monotonous. One would be tempted to say, is that all there is? However, one must draw near and try to live with this man as he really existed, with his gifts and his limitations, seeking to place oneself in his company and follow his activities. As one works to unravel the thread of his history, one cannot avoid being fascinated. Fascinated by what one discovers in the serene firmness and the placid "obstinacy" with which this simple son of a weaver passionately engaged himself in his ideal. Father Pete stretched himself to his limit in the duty and love burning in his heart. He was not a fanatic, for the Lord for whom he lived and to whom he committed himself is Goodness and Peace. It is this goodness and peace that sustained him to the point of seeking to communicate these gifts to others, especially to those so easily forgotten, the little ones and the poor. And there were thousands of these in Surinam.

In these conditions, can one not say that he was a true Redemptorist in spirit long before he entered the Congregation founded by Saint Alphonsus? To bring the Gospel to the poor—the ideal of Alphonsus—how wonderfully Father Pete accomplished this! Certainly he did it by means of his missionary work, but even more profoundly, by the exemplary manner in which he strove to incarnate the spirit of Jesus in all his being.

III. Facets of His Spirituality

We have already underlined the fact that Father Pete does not belong in the realm of the extraordinary, and even less in that of the original. His spirituality was one that followed the old adage, "Virtue lies in the middle," not on the extremes. It was the virtue of the plain and simple Christian life lived, however, in its fullness. Let us now note some outstanding aspects of his spirituality, and not be surprised if they are qualities that belong to the essence of any Christian and evangelical life. Ultimately, to be a saint the way Father Peter Donders was does not demand particular gifts, special favors, or extraordinary talents. Instead, it requires a limitless generosity.

1. *Father Pete, the Disciple of Jesus*

a. The Spirit of Faith

Many knew Jesus. Many saw him and participated in some way in his life. Still, there were relatively few who became his disciples. Why? Because very few discovered what he was: the presence of God among human beings. Those who discovered this began to believe in him. This same pattern of the Gospel applies totally to Father Pete: he was a person who believed, a man of faith. We are not dealing here with one facet among many others. No, his faith is the heart beating within him, the air in his lungs, the light in his eyes, the strength of his hands and of his whole being, the blood running and boiling throughout his body. Where did this faith come from? What does it mean for him? How did it work in him?

This faith was rooted in his past. He was born in Tilburg (Netherlands) in 1809, in a profoundly religious environment into which dechristianization had yet to penetrate. So he breathed, right from his infancy, Catholic air. One could say that faith rocked his cradle. In the case of some saints, one speaks of a sudden conversion, of an interior shock of spiritual illumination, of an irresistible invasion of the grace of God. Saint Augustine is the classic example. In Father Pete, we find nothing of this kind. Nowhere do we find that his faith passed through a period of crisis, through some eclipse or discouragement. For him it is evident—he himself is the evidence—that his life was rooted in another life as its origin and that gave him an orientation toward God as an end. This conviction sustained him at every moment of his life. The Letter to the Hebrews (11:27) says that Moses "persevered as though he saw him who is invisible." Father Pete's life differed, without a doubt, from that of Moses. Nevertheless, in a simple way, hidden from the sight of others, did he not also see the invisible? A secret and mysterious force impelled him to consecrate himself to this "invisible something" manifested in Christ Jesus and then to seek to reveal it to his brothers and sisters. For example, we know that from the age of five or six, he dreamed of becoming a priest.[1]

b. A Life of Prayer

Whoever has discovered that the living God is to be recognized as a Father naturally desires to speak with him. There is nothing strange in the fact that Father Pete was a man of prayer and that he enjoyed prolonging it as a profound, heart to heart intimacy with God. It is said of Saint Francis of Assisi that he not only prayed a great deal, but that he "became prayer." This is also clear in a less spectacular way in Father Pete. All who knew him could not avoid being struck by his permanent interior attitude of prayer. He always and ever turned to prayer! Father Kronenburg wrote that from the time he worked as a weaver, "God drew the youngster in an irresistible manner and filled his spirit and his heart all day long."[2] Father Pete always remained known for this. Speaking of his time as a seminarian, a student noted on this point, "I believe that he always lived in the presence of God."[3]

During the period he worked in Batavia, one already found him at prayer by 6:00 AM. His day was composed of prayer, visits to the sick, and work in the garden.[4] "Even after a very busy day, his night was not always dedicated to the necessary rest. He was sometimes seen very late in the night, kneeling before the large cross in the cemetery."[5] Father Startz testifies, "Prayer was his food, the breath of his soul; he prayed without ceasing."[6] Father Pete did not think of prayer as a duty, but rather as a need, a moment to take a deep breath. There he encountered the best of himself and from there he drew new strength of spirit.

c. Eucharistic and Marian Devotion

The Blessed Sacrament held a privileged place in his spiritual life. He spent long hours in the church. There his spirit more easily raised itself to God; there he experienced more intensely the presence of the Lord who never abandoned him. Some of his contemporaries said, "It is difficult to form an idea of his devotion to the Blessed Sacrament. He taught us by his example to also practice this great devotion. He spent almost all of his free time before the tabernacle."[7] With the permission of his religious superior, he rose every night to spend a long time before the Blessed Sacrament. Donders himself explains his visits to the Eucharistic Jesus, "It is good to remain before the Blessed Sacrament; to pray, thank, and plead for all our spiritual and temporal needs."[8]

At the center of his devotion to the Blessed Sacrament was the sacrifice of the Mass, although in a manner somewhat different from ours. His epoch was less liturgical. At that time, the Mass was viewed more as an act of piety than as a community celebration, but people's interior ardor for it was no less than ours. "When he drew near to the altar to celebrate Mass," says Norbertus Donders, a neighbor, "I was profoundly impressed by the expression on his face. It shone in an unspeakable mix of seriousness, veneration, desire, and joy. Also noteworthy was his recollection during the Mass."[9]

"Near the cross of Jesus [was] his mother" (John 19:25). Whoever thinks of the son cannot forget the mother. Just as Christians of all times have understood this and their piety bore its seal, so also did Father Pete's. "In his sermons, he never omitted saying something about the Holy Virgin."[10] One notices that from his time as a seminarian, he developed a great devotion to Mary.[11]

To her he attributed, after God, his priestly vocation and later his religious life.[12]

d. Contemplation and Action

When we call Father Pete contemplative—"A contemplative in action"—we are not exaggerating. He was not someone who simply prayed a great deal. Prayer formed a part of his very self; it had ingrained itself into the depths of his being. Just as with Jesus himself, and with Mary who "treasured all these words and pondered them in her heart" (Luke 2:19), Father Pete lived permanently "before the face of God."

He was not content merely to believe in God as Father. This conviction influenced his life on an everyday basis and gave a special hue to his manner of thinking, of feeling, of working, and of being. For many, what counts most is what one can see, perceive, or touch. All the rest, even the very reality of God, pales before the things we see and becomes more or less unreal. With Father Pete, it was the opposite. The things of this visible world were for him an image, a reflection, of the profound and higher reality to which he knew they belonged. There are many examples of this in his life. We will cite only a few. He desired to be a priest. When he approached the Franciscans, he was refused. "I returned home on foot. I recommended myself to divine providence, 'Lord, what do you want me to do?' At this, God consoled me as if I had attained the greatest success."[13] In everything that happened to him, he sought and recognized the hand of God. He recounts how in his journey to Surinam, I experienced "how good God is and how he busies himself with those who trust in him and leave all for his sake. Even more than a hundredfold he has bestowed on me, for whether on the ship or in Surinam, I have found fathers and mothers who have poured their care upon me."[14]

e. Filial Confidence

His confidence in God was one with his faith. Speaking of the difficulties which he encountered in his mission among the indigenous peoples, he wrote, "Drunkenness and immorality, etc., block their conversion. But God is omnipotent; Mary, the Refuge of Sinners, is their mother as well."[15]

He had full confidence in God's plans for him. He abandoned himself totally to God, even if he did not know where God's plans would take him. "Still, may God's holy will be done in all things. The holy will of God and perfect obedience always and in all things are my consolation."[16]

In the face of everything that happened, his reaction was, "This was the plan of divine providence."[17] This attitude accompanied him to the very end of his life. In 1855, he returned to the leprosarium in Batavia. Then, as always, the same living and fervent faith in divine Providence gave life to everything, that faith that had illuminated him right from childhood. He wrote to his provincial, "Your Reverence knows that for some time I have again found myself in Batavia, my first residence. God has willed it thus; may his holy will be done!"[18]

f. Witness to the Fullness of Redemption

Up to this point, we have shown where the source of Father Pete's spirituality lay: his life of prayer and contemplation, the rooting of his entire being in God, and his profound union with God. It was here that he went to drink as from an invisible fountain of light and strength. To be near to God did not mean for him, in any way, to shut himself up into a closed world. On the contrary, he wished to communicate, share, and proclaim the goodness of God. Could the abundance of his heart have no voice? This was the reason that he sought to be a priest and it was also for this that he traveled to Surinam. This did not take place without great difficulties. Still, he did not back away in the face of problems. Behind his tranquil serenity and his gentleness, lay strength in the full sense of the word, not a physical strength but a moral force. He never cringed before the sacrifices of a missionary life, but followed his road with tenacity, obstinacy, perseverance. On July 18, 1880, Bishop Schaap wrote, "From the year 1856, Donders served the poor lepers in Batavia, truly making himself 'all things for all people.' From this post, he undertook veritable expeditions to reach the inhabitants of all the plantations in the area. He penetrated into the most inaccessible jungles. Not even the obstinate rejection by the Amerindians forced this truly strong man to retreat."[19]

2. Father Pete, the Missionary in Surinam

a. Apostolic Zeal

Very few people have committed themselves as strongly as Father Pete did to the Lord and his kingdom. On October 30, 1884, Father Romme, his companion, wrote, "Last Monday, we very quietly celebrated the seventy-fifth birthday of our holy Father Donders. Reverend Father always remains the same man of God, full of zeal. No task is too great for him, no privation too burdensome, when there is the possibility of doing something for the glory of God and for the salvation of souls....Thus, not a day passes without his going to visit the sick and the invalids in the neighborhood."[20] This zeal for the Lord and for souls goes back a long way. As a youngster, he taught catechism to the children of his area.[21]

Bishop Schepers used to say when he spoke about Donders' apostolic zeal, "If I had two priests like Father Donders, I would not need the rest."[22] In regard to a period when Donders was in the city, Father Van Coll stated, "Our house is surrounded every day by the poor and the sick. At other times, even the most inconvenient, [Donders] goes to the barrios furthest away in order to bring help and comfort."[23] We could add many other such testimonies. We will give only one, taken from the newspaper, *De Tijd*, "He indefatigably preoccupied himself with and took great pains on behalf of the sick, both in the hospital and wherever he could be of service. His ardent and charitable zeal brought the esteem and admiration of the whole colony [Surinam], not only of Catholics, but even of the members of other faiths."[24]

b. With the Lepers and Slaves

The Good News must bring salvation to the whole person, body and spirit. Therefore, it was to the whole human being that Father Pete consecrated his care and on whom he lavished his love.

The long years he passed among the lepers are silent but eloquent testimony of this. The reality of his life among them, only God knows. Kronenburg recounts, "Father Donders lived and worked among the lepers for a period of twenty-six years, ten as a diocesan priest and then sixteen as a Redemptorist. Twenty-six years! So easy to say and so much easier to read. And those first ten were lived alone, with no companions!"[25] It was during this time that he truly became all things to all people." An aged military man who was in Surinam until 1870 says, "You will not find two people in the world who would do what Father Donders did for the lepers."[26]

He also knew firsthand another misery: slavery. In an age when such words were not well received, he did not hesitate to protest, "Woe, woe to Surinam on that great day of judgment!! Woe, woe, indeed, a thousand woes to the Europeans, owners of the slaves on the plantations, to the administrators, to the directors, to the foremen (who have authority over the slaves)!!! Damned are those who enrich themselves with the sweat and blood of these unfortunate people who have no one to defend them except God!"[27]

c. His Style of Life

A characteristic that particularly marks Father Pete in this context is his simplicity, his humility without affectation. He was a stranger to all ostentation. He went his way calmly and with conviction, very conscious of his duties and responsibilities. He did what he had to do with valor and dedication, as if these were simply normal. This is the way he was in the seminary at S. Michiels-Gestel.[28] A colleague of his testified, "He was extremely humble and always willing to help. Moreover, he had a gentle spirit." "His piety consisted in nothing extravagant or singular; he never appeared strange or bizarre."[29] Someone remembered that while he was parish vicar at Warmond for a while, "He was a pastor without pretensions; he never made a fuss."[30]

In him, this humility and simplicity were paired with joviality and happiness. He was spontaneous and laughed lightheartedly with others. His words were full of gentleness and benevolence.

His whole exterior reflected tranquility of spirit and happiness. This is the judgment of his fellow students. One of them declared, "I can testify that I never met anyone so amiable, so exceptionally gentle."[31] The Prefect Apostolic, Monsignor Grooff, remarked, "Reverend Donders always presents himself as content and jovial."[32] When he became a Redemptorist, his confreres were impressed by the way he always acted with so much charity. He loved them heart and soul. Modest and lovable, happy and easygoing during recreation, freely joining in jokes and quips, he knew how to accept teasing; that is the way they described him. Father Startz, who lived with him in Maastricht, notes, "Father Donders was very hard on himself but with others he showed sympathy and affability, full of love and kindness. He was charity itself."[33]

3. Father Pete, the Redemptorist

a. A Delayed Vocation?

We recall that Father Pete entered the Congregation of the Most Holy Redeemer at the age of fifty-seven and spent the last twenty years of his life as a Redemptorist. The ease he felt in this dramatic change seems due to the fact that his life-goal was the same as the Congregation's founder, Saint Alphonsus Liguori: "to bring Good News to the poor." Pete and Alphonsus were two of a kind; they were men of deep and personal faith. Both were captivated and fascinated by Christ, so they were unremitting in their total commitment to God's kingdom. Both saw that their particular vocation was a call to the most "abandoned," those who had no one who cared enough to bring the Good News of Christ to them.

In Donders' life, one can frequently speak of religious obedience. For him, this phrase signified "to listen": to listen to others, to listen to God.

As a religious, he received God's calls mainly through the religious community and the superiors entrusted with its guidance. This is how Father Pete understood it and how he lived it. This obedience, this fundamental openness to listen, reached great heights in him. For him it was the concrete way to seek the will of God, to find it and live it.

The will of God had already long been the magnetic pole of his life. He now found this will manifest in a particular way in religious obedience. He sought God in everything and placed all of his happiness in obedience. His provincial superior, Father Oomen, declared, "Wherever obedience sent him, there he always found his greatest happiness."[34] We, who read these sentences at the beginning of the twenty-first century, must dig behind the words in order to arrive at the marrow of their meaning. Father Pete sought to serve the reign of God and to consecrate all of his efforts to it. In order to do so in a sure and complete manner, he did not wish to rely merely upon his own impressions or point of view, and so he entered a religious community. There he sought his destiny, his future, and the concrete way of working for the reign of God. "The will of God and perfect obedience always and in all things are my consolation, and I hope that they will be my solace in the hour of my death. Amen."[35]

b. A Community of Goods

These details about obedience touch on a fundamental point of his life and of his concrete participation in religious life. Even more so, after he had lived for such a long time with his own independence. To join a religious community is to share what one is and what one has. *What he was*: Father Pete participated through religious obedience by taking on the obligations and activities of the community, both inside and outside the monastery. *What he had*: he shared in the poverty and the moderate use of goods of the community. In everything, he was perfectly apostolic. What interested him was to consecrate himself to the service of the kingdom of God; all the rest remained subordinate to this objective. He used material goods *"tantum quantum,"* according to the Ignatian expression, that is to say, insofar as they were necessary or useful for the kingdom of God.

Father Pete contented himself with little and he knew how to bear valiantly the privations and sacrifices of a missionary life. Perhaps it would be more exact to say that his interior fire was so lively that the major part of these burdens lost their weight and became light. "[Love] bears all things" (1 Corinthians 13:7).

c. A Community of Life

Can we say that he behaved in ways that called attention to himself? No. His life is extraordinary, but it did not contain anything extravagant or strange. He understood that no one is alone in the world; we need one another and we must mutually support and share with one another. Donders was not a "Lone Ranger" or a great pioneer laying new paths. He felt better in a place where he had others with him, even though he had passed so many years completely alone in the leprosarium at Batavia. With his confreres, as we have seen, he was pleasant and happy to be with them. They said that he was a gentle person, but there is something more in him than just an agreeable character. He experienced happiness when he could give happiness to others. He was able to "put up with" a great deal although to do so was no easier for him than it is for anyone else.[36]

His personal acts of piety were not a burden that he placed on others' shoulders. His presence did not create a dreary atmosphere. His exactness was not bothersome to anyone. His mortification made him tolerant and accessible to others. He absolutely avoided everything that could call attention to himself and be troublesome to others.[37] Therefore, there is reason enough to say we do not see anything extraordinary in him, provided we add that he simply did the ordinary good extraordinarily well. His missionary commitment was more than just good; it was outstanding, even heroic, when we consider the strength of spirit and character needed to do all that he did, and to do it in a brutal tropical climate.

Father Pete knew that there is no Christian life without difficulties and sufferings. He said yes to it, not as something inevitable, but because in it he discovered the traces and beckoning of his heavenly Father. He followed Christ even when the journey took him through Gethsemane and Calvary. He continually repeated, "May the holy and adorable will of God be done in all things."[38] Even when his work among the native peoples seemed to be getting nowhere, may the holy will of God be done.

d. Faithful to the End

A final characteristic, one that is like the basic thread woven throughout the whole cloth: his fidelity. He was not a man of the spectacular, the grandiose, or the miraculous. "The one who endures to the end will be saved," says Jesus (Matthew 24:13). Just as with human life, the Christian life is not realized all at once. Both lives are a chain of small things. Father Pete's life provides us with an eloquent proof: seventy-seven long years; forty-five on the mission in Surinam; twenty-six of them with the lepers. Years of total commitment, patience, availability, prayer. Such fidelity in simplicity and love for the poor is indeed the fidelity of a saint.

IV. Conclusion: The Apostolic Man

We have tried to give a glimpse into the spirituality of Father Pete. Without a doubt, spirituality is a formidable word for a simple man who led a simple life. We cannot say that he created a special spiritual system or even an original one, but that he had his own particular spiritual countenance. To paint his portrait, this face of Father Donders, in a way that speaks and interprets him to a person of our day, it is necessary to reorient the literary genres and the language of the nineteenth century. To us, Father Pete's simple language, which was also that of his contemporaries who were apostles rather than great literary people, may seem weak, almost trivial, like a canned soup, prepackaged and without zest, poorly prepared or overly strong. Nevertheless, behind this simplicity, these rather pale appearances, one can recognize the face of the real man, a true Christian, a solid religious whose name was Father Peter Donders.

Is there a way to sum up this life in a few words? I can think of no better way than to call it "The Apostolic Life" in the fullest sense of the term. It is not a life that only abounds with apostolic activity, but a life in which the entire process that created the apostles unfolds, and allows a person to be fascinated by Jesus Christ even to the point of giving oneself totally to him, and in testifying to him even unto death. It is being aflame with a fire that shines and continuously gains new luster in profound and personal contact with God, the hearth of love.

Father Pete's spirituality is simply a life in Christ fully lived according to the Gospel. In him one finds all of the elements of an apostolic life: a call by God, our Father, in Jesus Christ; a response to this call in faith; a spiritual life centered on the Eucharist and nourished by prayer; and openness and fidelity to the will of God and to his plan of love.

In this portrait, one characteristic stands out: Father Pete's unlimited confidence in God. He passed through so many adverse circumstances in his life. For example, his journey toward the priesthood seemed at one point completely ended. But he knew that God, in spite of everything, was leading him where he would. This confidence impregnated his whole spiritual life and all of his apostolic undertakings. Around this confidence are clustered other noteworthy characteristics:

1. *The Source of this Confidence.* It lay in the unshakable faith that Father Pete had, even to the point of identifying faith and confidence. God was his Father and would never desert him.
2. *The Plans of God.* Father Pete was sure that God had plans for him, wise and loving plans. His task was to enter into these plans, to be attentive to the "holy will of God."
3. *Grounding in Prayer.* His uninterrupted dialogue with the Lord underpinned this confidence. This is how he cleared his path. This was the way he gained a better view of what God wanted of him. At the same time, he better appreciated all that was asked of him in abnegation, generosity, suffering, pain, and above all, love.

A final word. Father Pete's spirituality is that of a person of profound faith and great simplicity, whom the Lord called to the apostolate. The sentence from Saint Paul, "It is no longer I who live, but it is Christ who lives in me" (Galatians 2:20), sums up very well what Blessed Peter Donders was from beginning to end. Christ lived through this modest missionary apostle, someone almost unnoticed but someone, who by this very simplicity, can challenge, entice, and inspire us today.

Notes

PART I: BLESSED PETER DONDERS: A STORY OF HIS LIFE

I. Small Beginnings
1. John Baptist Kronenburg, C.Ss.R., *An Apostle to the Lepers*, English translation from the French Version of Léon Roelandts, C.Ss.R. by John Carr, C.Ss.R. (London and Edinburge: Sands & Company, 1930), pp. 5–6.
2. *Idem.*, 5.
3. *Idem.*, 9.
4. *Idem.*, 11.
5. *Idem.*, 9.

II. The Poor Young Weaver
1. Second Autobiography, Part II, Chapter Eight, p. 221 below.
2. *Ibid.*, 13.
3. *Ibid.*, 7.
4. *Ibid.*, 7.
5. Nicola Ferrante, "I processi cononici del P. Donders," SD, 391.
6. Kronenburg, 144.
7. *Ibid.*, 9–10.

III. The Priest Who Could Not Be
1. Second Autobiography, Part II, Chapter Eight, p. 221 below.
2. Kronenburg, 4.
3. *Ibid.*, 9.
4. *Ibid.*, 7.
5. *Ibid.*, p. 8.
6. Second Autobiography, Part II, Chapter Eight, p. 221 below.
7. *Ibid.*
8. First Autobiography, Part II, Chapter Eight, p. 216 below.
9. *Ibid.*
10. Kronenburg, 14.

11. *Ibid.*, p. 15.
12. Letter #10, Part II, Chapter Four, p. 141 below.
13. Kronenburg, 15.

IV. Servant or Student?
1. Kronenburg, 21.
2. *Ibid.*
3. See Samuel J. Boland, "P. Donders as His Contemporary Saw Him," SD, 235.
4. See Denkelman–Londoño, "Desde los pobres de America," *Espiritu Redentorista: La vida espiritual del Beato Pedro Donders*, Vol. 9 (Rome: Comisión de Espiritualidad C.Ss.R., 1996), 18.
5. Kronenburg, 27.
6. See Boland, 235.
7. Father Engelbert Odenhoven (1842–1915) was professed on October 19, 1863, and ordained a priest on December 12, 1867. He went to Surinam in 1868.
8. *Ibid.*
9. Kronenburg, 23.
10. *Ibid.*, 25.

V. The Unwanted Religious
1. First Autobiography; see Part II, Chapter Eight, p. 216 below.
2. Second Autobiography, see Part II, Chapter Eight, p. 222 below.
3. First Autobiography; see Part II, Chapter Eight, p. 217 below.
4. Second Autobiography, see Part II, Chapter Eight, p. 222 below.

VI. A Call From Over the Sea
1. Kronenburg, 31–32.
2. *Ibid.*, 31.
3. Ferrante, 392–396.
4. Second Autobiography, see Part II, Chapter Eight, p. 222 below.
5. Kronenburg, 32–33.
6. Second Autobiography, see Part II, Chapter Eight, p. 223 below. Bishop James Grooff became Prefect Apostolic of Surinam in 1827 at the age of twenty-seven.
7. *Ibid.*
8. Kronenburg, 38.
9. *Ibid.*, 38–39.
10. Second Autobiography, see Part II, Chapter Eight, p. 223 below.

VII. Will He Ever Get There?

1. Kronenburg, 40–41.
2. Ibid., 41.
3. Ibid., 42
4. Ibid.
5. The term *Amerindians* is the current term used to indicate the peoples who inhabited the territory of Surinam since the times before the arrival of Europeans and Africans. Donders uses the term common in his day of "Indians."
6. Kronenburg, 36.
7. Johan Janssen (1803–1843) arrived in Surinam in 1834. His untimely death is recounted below on p. 42.

VIII. Surinam, at Last

1. Kronenburg, 46.
2. Bishop Gerard Schepers was born on August 18, 1798, in Germany near Holland. He was ordained in 1829 and arrived in Paramaribo March 1, 1830, and spent the rest of his life there. He died on November 27, 1863.
3. Ibid., 58–59.
4. Ibid., 59.
5. Ibid., 60.

IX. Two Hurricanes in Paramaribo

1. Kronenburg, 61.
2. Father Johan Baptist Romme (1832–1889) arrived in Surinam on February 8, 1864, as a secular priest (he had been ordained on May 17, 1856) and followed Donders into the Redemptorist Congregation in 1867.
3. Ibid., 69.
4. Ibid.
5. Ibid., 70.
6. Ibid., 67.
7. Ibid., 76.

X. Plantations of the Spirit

1. Kronenburg, 88–89.
2. Ibid., 82.
3. Ibid., 85.
4. Ibid., 84.

XI. At Home in Batavia
1. Kronenburg, 92–93.
2. *Ibid.*, 101.
3. *Ibid.*
4. *Ibid.*, 104.
5. *Ibid.*
6. *Ibid.*, 104–105.
7. *Ibid.*, 106.

XII. The Late Vocation
1. All of these three men died within six years of arrival. Brother Lambert (Lambertus J. Swinkels) died of yellow fever on August 6, 1866, at the age of forty-nine. Father van Roij died in 1871 and Father van der Aa in 1872. Another Redemptorist priest, Father Gerardus p. Baptist arrived in the colony on November 24, 1866, and died three weeks later on December 11, also of yellow fever.
2. Arnold Swinkels was born in 1824 and arrived in Surinam in 1854. He left when the Redemptorists arrived in the colony. He was no relation of Father Johan and Brother Lambertus Swinkels.
3. Kronenburg, 112.
4. Kronenburg, 114.
5. *Ibid.*, 114–115.
6. *Ibid.*, 119.
7. *Ibid.*, 124.

XIII. Back in Batavia
1. Father Gerard Verbeek was born February 14, 1820, ordained December 20, 1845, and professed as a Redemptorist on October 15, 1860.
2. Kronenburg, 133–134.
3. *Ibid.*, 140.
4. *Ibid.*, 135.
5. *Ibid.*, 137.
6. Kronenburg, 152.
7. *Ibid.*, 146.
8. *Ibid.*, 155–156.

XIV. Back to the Jungles
1. Kronenburg, 188–189.
2. *Ibid.*, 195–196.
3. *Ibid.*, 224–225.
4. *Ibid.*, 198.
5. *Ibid.*, 227.

XVI. The Way of the Cross to Paramaribo
1. Kronenburg, 244.
2. *Ibid.*, 244.
3. *Ibid.*, 245.
4. *Ibid.*, 246.
5. *Ibid.*
6. *Ibid.*
7. *Ibid.*, 249.
8. *Ibid.*, 251–252.
9. *Ibid.*, 257.

XVII. All Things Work Together
1. Father Jan Bakker was born on February 25, 1833, and professed as a brother on September 11, 1860. He went to Surinam in 1867 and was later ordained a priest on August 26, 1883. He is usually called "Father" in letters.
2. Kronenburg, 259.
3. *Ibid.*
4. *Ibid.*, 263.
5. *Ibid.*
6. *Ibid.*, 264.
7. *Ibid.*, 265–266.
8. *Ibid.*, 266.
9. *Ibid.*, 266–267.
10. Boland, 256
11. *Ibid.*, 255.

XVIII. Rest in Peace?
1. Most of the information in this chapter is taken from Ferrante, 363–409.

PART II: BLESSED PETER DONDERS: HIS LETTERS AND WRITINGS

Chapter One: The Writings of Blessed Peter Donders
1. Published in leaflet form for insertion in breviaries.
2. The Spanish texts are found in *Espiritualidad Redentorista: La vida espiritual del Beato Pedro Donders,* Vol. 9 (Rome: Comisión de Espiritualidad CSsR, 1996), pp. 46–122.
3. Father Dekkers compared the English translations to the edited letters in the sources cited in the text. He also translated from the Dutch any

sections of the letters that were omitted in the editions used by the present translator.

Chapter Two: Holland

1. Ed. in PDR, 10, pp. 4–6, n. 1.
Bishop Henri den Dubbelden was the Vicar Apostolic of 's-Hertogenbosch. During this time of civil turmoil in the Low Countries, Holland did not have residential bishops. Donders was under his authority as a diocesan priest.
2. Gerardus Hoes, who was parish priest there since 1826, was ordained in 1815 and died May 26, 1844. He was a dedicated man but had poor health and limited capabilities.
3. At that time, people did not go very frequently to confession, so the confessional in such a small parish will not have been very busy.

Chapter Three: Paramaribo

1. Ed. in PDR, 10, pp. 6–14, n. 2.
2. Ed. in PDR, 10, pp. 15–17, n. 3.
3. Ed. in PDR, 10, pp. 17–19, n. 4.
4. Ed. in PDR, 10, pp. 19–24, n. 5.
5. Ed. in PDR, 10, pp. 24–30, n. 6.
6. Ed. in PDR, 10, pp. 30–31, n. 7. Bp. Swinkels (1810–1875) became a Redemptorist in 1845.
7. This address, "Frater" means "Brother" in Latin.
8. Ed. in PDR, 11, pp. 34–35, n. 8.
9. Ed. in PDR, 11, pp. 35–36, n. 9.
10. The language is today called "Sranan," and is described as an English-based Creole.

Chapter Four: Batavia

1. Ed. in PDR, 11, pp. 36–38, n. 10.
2. Adrianus Bossers was born on September 23, 1825, and became a Redemptorist on October 28, 1849. He had already been ordained in 1848. He arrived in Surinam on May 12, 1867, and stayed until his death on December 9, 1898. He wrote one of the most important histories of this country.
3. Ed. in PDR, 11, pp. 38–40, n. 11. John Henry Schaap (1823–1889) was a medical student in Leyden who felt called to the Redemptorists during a retreat preached at the University. He was professed in 1845 and ordained five years later. A distinguished orator, he was named provincial superior in 1868. He later became superior of the mission in Paramaribo and ultimately a bishop and pro-vicar of the mission. He died in the colony March 19, 1889.
4. Ed. in PDR, 11, pp. 40–43, n. 12.

5. Ed. in PDR, 11, pp. 43–45, n. 13.
6. Ed. in PDR, 11, pp. 45–46, n. 14.
7. Ed. in PDR, 11, pp. 46–48, n. 15.
8. Ed. in SD, pp. 137–140, n. 1.
9. Ed. in SD, pp. 140–141, n. 2.
10. Donders speaks in the plural to include Father Engelbert Startz (1837–1887) who came to Surinam in 1872 and assisted him in Batavia from 1873–1876; Startz returned to Holland in 1881.
11. Ed. in PDR, 11, pp. 48–49, n. 16.
12. Ed. in PDR, 11, pp. 49–50, n. 17. Peter Oomen was professed as a Redemptorist on October 10, 1857, and ordained on October 22, 1860. He later (1894–1900) served as procurator general of the Congregation in Rome.
13. Ed. in PDR, 11, pp. 50–51, n. 18.
14. Ed. in SD, p. 142, n. 3. Father van Coll (1842–1922) went to Surinam as a student in 1871 and was ordained there that year.
15. Ed. in PDR, 11, pp. 51–52, n. 19.
16. Ed. in PDR, 11, pp. 52–53, n. 20.
17. Ed. in PDR, 11, p. 53, n. 21.
18. Ed. in PDR, 11, p. 54, n. 22.
19. Ed. in PDR, 11, p. 55, n. 23.
20. Brother Frans (Frans Jozef Harmes; 1835–1894) went to Surinam in 1873.
21. Ed. in SD, pp. 142–143, n. 4.
22. Ed. in SD, p. 144, n. 5.
23. Ed. in SD, p. 145, n. 6.
24. Ed. in SD, pp. 146–147, n. 7.
25. Ed. in SD, pp. 147–148, n. 8.
26. Brother Pius (Jozef Timmerman; 1841–1913) arrived in Surinam in 1876.
27. Ed. in PDR, 11, pp. 56–57, n. 25.
28. Father Pete is referring to an old custom among Redemptorists that on New Year's Eve, each member of the community drew the name of a saint whom he would consider a special patron for the New Year. He also drew some special ascetical activity to perform, such as a daily prayer for a particular intention, abstaining from dessert once a week, and so on.
29. Ed. in SD, pp. 148–149, n. 9.
30. These two priests were Father Willem de Weerd (1849–1896) who worked in Surinam until his death and Charles Warren Currier who left the mission in 1882 and went to the United States where he left the Congregation in 1891.
31. This was Gerard van Tooren who was a candidate and was professed on February 2, 1882, at Paramaribo, where he remained until he was ordained on December 30, 1883.

32. Ed. in PDR, 11, pp. 57–58, n. 27.
33. Ed. in SD, pp. 150–151, n. 10.
34. Arnold Borret (Donders misspells his name) (1848–1888) was a lawyer who worked as a clerk in the justice office at Paramaribo. In 1882 he entered the Redemptorist novitiate and was professed on February 2, 1883, and ordained a priest on February 11.
35. The bishop and Mr. Borret had boarded a ship in Coronie on the way to Paramaribo. The ship, however, docked at Demerara where an epidemic was raging before proceeding to the capital and was thus forced to wait in quarantine for three weeks.
36. Ed. in PDR, 11, pp. 58–59, n. 28.
37. Ed. in PDR, 11, pp. 59–60, n. 29.
38. Ed. in PDR, 11, p. 60, n. 30.
39. Ed. in PDR, 11, pp. 60–61, n. 31.

Chapter Five: Paramaribo Again

1. Ed. in SD, pp. 151–152, n. 11.
2. Ed. in PDR, 11, pp. 61–62, n. 33.
3. This is the name used by the sect for its version of the Eucharist.
4. Ed. in PDR, 11, pp. 62–63, n. 34.

Chapter Six: Coronie

1. Ed. in PDR, 11, pp. 63–64, n. 35.
2. Ed. in PDR, 11, pp. 64–65, n. 36.
3. Ed. in PDR, 11, pp. 65–66, n. 37.
4. Ed. in PDR, 11, pp. 66–67, n. 38.
5. Ed. in PDR, 11, pp. 67–68, n. 39.
6. Ed. in PDR, 11, p. 68, n. 40.
7. Ed. in PDR, 11, p. 69, n. 41.
8. Ed. in PDR, 11, pp. 69–70, n. 42.

Chapter Seven: Batavia Again

1. Ed. in SD, p. 152, n. 12. Brother Alphonsus (Antoon Koenen) had come to Surinam in 1869.
2. Ed. in PDR, 11, pp. 70–71, n. 43.
3. Ed. in PDR, 11, p. 72, n. 44.

Chapter Eight: Autobiographical and Other Writings

1. Ed. in PDR, 12, pp. 90–94.
2. "Conscientiae ratio P. Donders, ex obedientia data..." [October 13, 1874], among "Lettere Ven P. Donders tradotte in latino, con il Curriculum vitae," preserved in the Redemptorist General Archives, Rome. Our translation is taken from the copy found in SD, 174–175.

Notes

3. *Positio super Introductione Causae Servi Dei Petri Donders* (Rome: 1913), *Summarium*, pars II, 534–540. Our translation is taken from the copy found in SD, 176–180.
4. Father Frederick de Held was the great developer of Redemptorist presence in Belgium, Holland, England, Ireland, and the United States.
5. Father Bernard Hafkenscheid was one of the most famous Redemptorist preachers and promoters of the Congregation in Europe and the United States.
6. "In partibus infidelium," i.e., "in the lands of unbelievers." This title is given to bishops who are responsible for areas in which a diocese has not been erected or who are in exile from their dioceses.
7. Samuel J. Boland, C.Ss.R., "Peter Donders as His Contemporaries Saw Him," SD, 273–277.

PART III. BLESSED PETER DONDERS: HIS SPIRITUALITY

Chapter One: The Missionary Spirit of Peter Donders

1. J.P. Didier, *Un nuevo apóstol de los negros, indios y leprosos en el continente sudamericano, o sea, biografía del Rdo. P. Pedro Donders, de la Congregación del Smo. Redentor* (Buenos Aires, 1893), 3.
2. I am applying to Donders, words that Jon Sabrino uses to describe Bp. Oscar Romero in his book, *Oscar Romero, profeta y mártir de la liberación; testimonios de Germán Schmitz y Jesús Calderón* (Lima, Perú : Centro de Estudios y Publicaciones, 1981), 7.
3. Second Autobiography, Part II, Chapter Eight, p. 222 above.
4. These faculties allowed the priest to perform some functions generally reserved to bishops or allowed only under conditions that could not be reasonably met in mission territory.
5. First Autobiography, Part II, Chapter Eight, p. 216 above.
6. *Ibid.*
7. Second Autobiography, Part II, Chapter Eight, p. 223 above.
8. First Autobiography, Part II, Chapter Eight, p. 223 above.
9. Letter #2, p. 113 above.
10. Letter #42, p. 196 above.
11. Letter #2, p. 105 above.
12. *Ibid.*, p. 106 above.
13. *Ibid.*, p. 107 above.
14. *Ibid.*
15. *Ibid.*
16. Leonardo Boff, *La fe en la periferia del mundo. El camino de la Iglesia con los oprimidos* (Santander, Spain, 1981), 23–24.
17. Juan Sobrino, 19.
18. Letter #6, p. 132 above.

19. Letters #2, #6, and #10; pp. 109, 112, 130, 142 above; also Second Autobiography, Part II, Chapter Eight, p. 226 above.
20. Letter #6, p. 130 above.
21. Letters #2, p. 105 above.
22. Letter #6, p. 128 above.
23. Letter #50, p. 208 above.
24. Letter #6, p. 129 above.
25. Letter #23, p. 173 above.
26. See Letters #11, #13, and #22; pp. 144, 153, 171 above.
27. Giuseppe Orlandi, "Il Vicariato Apostolico del Suriname e la relazione di mgr. H. Schaap del 18 luglio 1880," SD, 94.
28. *Ibid.*, 75–76.
29. Letter #2, p. 109 above.
30. See Sacra Rituum Congregatio, *Surinamen, seu Buscoducen, Beatificationis et Canonizationis Servi Dei Petri Donders, Sacerdotis professi e CSsR, Positio super Introductione Causae* (Rome, 1913), 64.
31. *Ibid.*
32. *Ibid.*, p. 63.
33. *Ibid.*, pp. 66, 599.
34. *Ibid.*, pp 64–67, 587.
35. Letter #8, p. 136 above.
36. Second Autobiography, Part II, Chapter Eight, p. 225 above.
37. Letters #9 and #14 p. 138 above.
38. Second Autobiography, Part II, Chapter Eight, p. 226 above.
39. Letter #9, p. 138 above.
40. *Ibid.*, p. 139 above.
41. Letter #41, p. 194 above.
42. Letter #43, p. 197 above.
43. Letter #45, p. 201 above.
44. Cited by Orlandi, p. 71.
45. Letter #52, p. 211 above.
46. Letter #53, p. 214 above.
47. J.P. Didier, 112.

Chapter Two: The Spirituality of Father Peter Donders

1. See A. Sampers, "Einige Briefe und andere schriften des seligen Peter Donders," SD, 174.
2. J. Kronenburg, *De Eerbiedwaardige Dienaar Gods Petrus Donders C.Ss.R.* (Tilburg, 1925), 18.
3. *Ibid.*, 39.
4. *Ibid.*, 121–123.
5. *Ibid.*, 123–124.
6. *Ibid.*, 197.
7. *Ibid.*, 194.

8. *Ibid.*, 212.
9. *Ibid.*, 57. Testimony of Norbertus Donders, of Tilburg.
10. *Ibid.*, 95.
11. *Ibid.*, 48.
12. *Ibid.*, 16.
13. First Autobiography, Part II, Chapter Eight, see p. 217 above.
14. *Ibid.*, p. 218.
15. Second Autobiography, see Part II, Chapter Eight, p. 225 above.
16. *Ibid.*
17. Letter #1, p. 103 above.
18. Letter #52, p. 211 above.
19. Kronenburg, 107.
20. *Ibid.*, 315.
21. *Ibid.*, 21.
22. *Ibid.*, 99.
23. *Ibid.*, 303.
24. *Ibid.*, 101.
25. *Ibid.*, 131–132.
26. *Ibid.*, 137.
27. Letter #6, p. 128 above.
28. Kronenburg, 41.
29. *Ibid.*, 49.
30. *Ibid.*, 62.
31. *Ibid.*, 49.
32. *Ibid.*, 81.
33. *Ibid.*, 184.
34. *Ibid.*, 178.
35. Second Autobiography, Part II, Chapter Eight, p. 226 above.
36. Kronenburg, 186–187.
37. *Ibid.*, 187.
38. Letter #49, p. 207 above.